Results-Oriented Financial Management

A Step-by-Step Guide to Law Firm Profitability

SECOND EDITION

JOHN G. IEZZI, CPA

LAW PRACTICE MANAGEMENT SECTION

MARKETING • MANAGEMENT • TECHNOLOGY • FINANCE

Commitment to Quality: The Law Practice Management Section is committed to quality in our publications. Our authors are experienced practitioners in their fields. Prior to publication, the contents of all our books are rigorously reviewed by experts to ensure the highest quality product and presentation. Because we are committed to serving our readers' needs, we welcome your feedback on how we can improve future editions of this book. We invite you to fill out and return the comment card at the back of this book.

Cover design by Jim Colao.

Nothing contained in this book is to be considered as the rendering of legal advice for specific cases, and readers are responsible for obtaining such advice from their own legal counsel. This book and any forms and agreements herein are intended for educational and informational purposes only.

The products and services mentioned in this publication are under or may be under trademark or service mark protection. Product and service names and terms are used throughout only in an editorial fashion, to the benefit of the product manufacturer or service provider, with no intention of infringement. Use of a product or service name or term in this publication should not be regarded as affecting the validity of any trademark or service mark.

The Law Practice Management Section, American Bar Association, offers an educational program for lawyers in practice. Books and other materials are published in furtherance of that program. Authors and editors of publications may express their own legal interpretations and opinions, which are not necessarily those of either the American Bar Association or the Law Practice Management Section unless adopted pursuant to the bylaws of the Association. The opinions expressed do not reflect in any way a position of the Section or the American Bar Association.

© 2003 American Bar Association. All rights reserved.
Printed in the United States of America.

Library of Congress Control Number 2003108784
ISBN 1-59031-238-4

06 05 04 03   5 4 3 2 1

Discounts are available for books ordered in bulk. Special consideration is given to state bars, CLE programs, and other bar-related organizations. Inquire at Book Publishing, American Bar Association, 750 N. Lake Shore Drive, Chicago, Illinois 60611.

Contents

CHAPTER TWO
Financial Management: The Process   21

CHAPTER THREE
The Financial Plan: Determining Gross Income   27

CHAPTER FOUR
The Billing Rate Formula Model   **35**

CHAPTER FIVE
Expenses   **47**

CHAPTER SIX
Calculating Net Income   **61**

Preface

By the time this book is published, I will have spent almost one-half of my life in the legal business, either managing it or consulting to it. It was only proper, therefore, that I memorialize some of my more significant experiences for those who follow me.

I'm not suggesting that everything I've done has been right or in the best of taste. However, my experiences do provide a starting point for the novice—and perhaps even the veteran—manager, if for no other reason than to present a differing viewpoint.

This updated version of my 1993 publication on law firm financial management represents the accumulation of thirty years of knowledge acquired from working in and with the legal profession in a variety of capacities. Most if not all of the analyses and methodologies used in this publication come from actual experiences in my dealings with firms of all sizes and practice disciplines.

There have not been that many changes in the financial management area over the years. The debits are still toward the windows and the credits toward the doors. However, the advances in technology has now enabled managers to more easily and efficiently manipulate the debits and credits so that informed decisions can be made to better utilize the firm's resources and improve firm profitability.

After spending eight years at Price Waterhouse, in both audit and administrative capacities, I came to legal administration with my CPA certificate and very little idea of how a law firm operated. But I was convinced that it couldn't be much different than the accounting profession I had just left.

This was my first mistake. Lawyers have their own style of management, whether dealing with their clients, each other, or the problems they face in administering to the needs of the firm. If you learn nothing else from this book, I hope that you recognize the significance of how law firms are different from other organizations.

In the end, I knew that making money for the firm would be the ultimate test of my success, so I concentrated almost exclusively on financial management issues. While I devoted many hours to personnel, equipment, technology, and general administrative problems, my focus on financial management gave me the most exposure in the firm and the most notoriety outside of it.

My first speech as a legal administrator was in 1974 at the Association of Legal Administrators convention in Florida. I remember about 150 people were there. (Now the convention attracts thousands!) I made a comment at that meeting that has been identified with me ever since. I stated that the successful manager will be the one who knows the numbers. This is still important today, and many of my articles and speeches have assisted administrators in this crucial area.

Many midsized law firms cannot afford a high-powered chief financial officer to handle their financial affairs. I've written this book to provide some "how-tos" that these firms can use to take advantage of more-sophisticated financial management techniques, either with their current personnel or with the help of outside accountants.

I have devoted the majority of this book to financial management in the legal environment, leaving to others such related issues as taxes, audits, pensions, and other heavy accounting problems. I also leave to others the task of imparting views on the best way to interview secretaries or buy the least expensive yellow pads.

The information in this book should benefit managing partners and law firm managers with varying degrees of experience. There are chapters on basic budgeting and financial planning that will assist those new in the field, and chapters on more-sophisticated areas for those who have been in the law firm management field for some time and now wish to advance to new levels of knowledge and understanding on how the financial management process operates within the law firm environment.

The chapters on compensation and equity accumulation will appeal to managing partners who are seeking to find new ideas on how to compensate its owners and to provide for a payout system for those who terminate the firm for whatever reason.

I hope that you will find this new version interesting and informative and that this book will better prepare those who come after me—not necessarily giving them all the answers, but at least a better idea of the questions. You may reach me at:

John G. Iezzi, CPA
Iezzi Management Group
1906 Hamilton St., Suite A
P.O. Box 1711
Richmond, VA 23218-1711

Phone: (804) 775-6805
Fax: (804) 775-6911
E-mail: jgiezzi@iezzigroup.com
Web site: www.iezzigroup.com

The Life Phases
of a Law Firm

1

Regardless of its size, location, or type of practice, every law firm, like most businesses, goes through a series of phases during its existence. In most cases, the beginning and ending of each of these periods are marked with significant changes in a firm's financial condition. Good times bring about a series of decisions and actions that allow a firm to continue its prosperity and generate even more profits for the owners. Bad times create the need for decisions and actions that determine whether a firm can continue to exist under the current circumstances, and what must be done to improve the situation and avoid a complete dissolution.

Unfortunately, in many law firms opportunities are often missed and trouble signs ignored. The result is that a firm is constantly involved in crisis management, without a plan and without a methodology to deal with the normal highs and lows that it will surely experience.

As an introduction to the issues of financial management, this chapter discusses the life phases of a law firm from a management and financial perspective. It discusses how to plan for the future, and be in a better position to recognize when difficult decisions must be made. It offers some suggestions on what these decisions should be, given the situation at the time. Later chapters in the book assist in analyzing and resolving some of the problems that occur throughout a law firm's existence.

The Planning Phase

Somewhere in books you have read or seminars you have attended, you have been exposed to the strategic-planning process. Strategic planning is important for a law firm, because it determines a firm's goals and objectives and establishes a methodology and timetable for implementing policies and procedures that achieve those goals and objectives. While still in its early stages, a firm must focus on certain issues that it will face in the months and years to come. In addition to management structure, marketing considerations, client service needs, technology, and so on, a firm must focus on how it can generate the most profits for the owners. It must do this in conjunction with the expectations of the owners, in line with their individual goals. Obviously, a firm will not last very long if its financial plan cannot support the income goals of its owners.

Preparing the Financial Plan

The financial plan is part of the overall business plan and incorporates a firm's income projections over at least a three-year period. In preparing the revenue portion of this plan, a firm should consider the following:

- *Hourly rate.* If it is a general practice firm, what hourly rate will it charge? The rate must take into account the area of practice, geographical location, types of clients, experience levels of the lawyers and legal assistants, and the competition. There are many different formulas for calculating billing rates, most of which take into account compensation, overhead, and expected profit. Chapter 4 describes in some detail a sophisticated methodology for determining a rate structure that will produce a desired profit level. A firm must also recognize that alternative billing systems will be a reality in the near future, and should be seriously considered in proposals to prospective clients.

- *Lifestyle.* How hard does the firm want its people to work? Since gross revenues are a function of hours worked multiplied by hourly rates, the number of billable hours that are expected from each level of time-keeper becomes a crucial ingredient in the income-projection process. A firm must make a conscious decision to strike the proper balance between work and personal life. Everyone in a firm must buy into the production goals that are set for each timekeeper. Initially at least, compensation is tied to an individual's ability to meet a prescribed number of billable hours.

    There are surveys published in many of the leading law office economic journals that provide guidance on average billable hours at each timekeeper level. This information is arranged by category—years at the bar, area of practice, location, and so on. As a general rule, owner hours are usually set at fourteen hundred to sixteen hundred; associates at seventeen hundred to nineteen hundred, and legal assistants at one thousand to twelve hundred. The expected number of hours depends on a firm's culture and how it views the production of hours among all of the other factors involved in a lawyer's association with the firm.

◆ *Leverage.* Although at the outset most lawyers strive to support themselves on their own time production, at some point a firm needs to understand the concept of leverage. In other words, there must be others in a firm who generate more profits than they consume and thus provide additional income to the owners. Leverage can come from younger owners, associates, and legal assistants. The key is that a firm needs to understand that eventually a structure must exist within the organization whereby each owner can make a reasonable income but not have to provide all of it himself. This must occur in order for the more senior lawyers to spend their time on nonbillable matters, such as generating new business, training associates, or managing the firm.

This issue is particularly important as a firm begins to get some age on it and the more senior lawyers start reducing their hours production. Unless there are younger lawyers or other timekeepers generating revenues, it is difficult for the more senior members of a firm to sustain their earnings expectations. Again, the issue of alternative billing rates may change the leverage concept. There are some who believe that once firms start charging for what they produce rather than how long it takes to produce it, there will be less emphasis on leverage and more emphasis on hiring experienced lawyers who can work efficiently and profitably.

◆ *Staffing levels.* The other side of the net-income equation is expenses, and this is strictly a question of expected level of service. Since a large percentage of expenses is devoted to compensation and benefits, the decision on staffing levels is very crucial. Staffing levels are dictated by the level of service that a firm is willing to accept, given its present situation. The issue of secretarial support, outsourcing of various administrative services, and the extent of day-to-day office administration and management must be addressed very early on as part of the financial planning process. The impact of technology needs to be considered in order to determine whether a firm can indeed live with fewer support people, given a more sophisticated level of automation within the organization. Most general-practice firms operate with a 1:2

or 1:3 staff-to-lawyer ratio. This has not changed much over the years, even though firms have spent considerable amounts on technology. However, since new lawyers generally have a much higher level of computer skills, this ratio should improve substantially.

◆ *Billing and collections.* Finally, in order to convert the billable hours into cash to pay expenses and owners, a firm must have the systems in place to reduce the conversion cycle to a minimum. Ultimately, the success of the firm's ability to generate profits rests in whether it can create a billing and collection philosophy within the firm and with its clients that produces the maximum amount of revenues for the hours worked.

The hours-to-collection cycle varies with the type of practice and clientele, but generally work should be converted into a bill within sixty to seventy-five days after it is performed, and translated into cash sixty to seventy days after the bill is issued. The longer the cycle, the more cash (at least initially) a firm will need to borrow or contribute as capital to keep going. Chapter 8 addresses the timing issue in some detail.

Creating a Budget

Once a firm addresses the financial management issues listed above, it then must create a financial plan or budget that will enable it to make certain that it can meet its net income projections, considering the expected billable hours, rates, expenses, and so on. In its early days, a firm must make assumptions based on the experiences of other firms, or by using surveys or other statistics. As it grows and matures, a firm can use its own historical information to provide the assumptions that will go into the financial planning process.

In addition to hours, rates, and expenses, a firm must also budget for write-downs in the billing process and write-offs in the collection process. The magnitude of these amounts depends on the ability of the firm to get good paying clients, to obtain engagement letters on all assignments, to get retainers wherever possible, and to foster an attitude among the lawyers regarding the necessity to manage their individual files so that reductions from standard rates are minimized.

This is easier said than done, since in its early stages a firm generally takes on certain work just to "pay the light bill" and doesn't worry so much about profits. However, if this mentality becomes pervasive throughout a firm, it is infectious. Soon a firm has an abundance of timekeepers and high billable hours, but no profits. There must be constant vigilance over the types of clients obtained, and a close watch kept over clients who cannot pay the amounts being charged to them. More importantly, there must be vigilance over those lawyers who constantly cut their bills. Originating business is important, but profitability on that business is what really matters and sustains a firm over the long term, even if it means reductions in lawyers and staff.

Financial Reporting

The financial planning process does not end with simply creating a budget. A firm must have a system of financial reporting at both the firm level and the individual lawyer level. These reports should be reviewed monthly, and problems corrected as soon as possible. There should be an individual or a group whose job it is to review new work, billing and collection activity, and write-downs and write-offs. Each lawyer must understand that he is accountable for his performance; generally this is accomplished at compensation-setting time, if financial management of client files is one of the criteria for determining a lawyer's contribution to the firm.

Cash Flow

One cannot discuss financial management issues without addressing the issue of cash flow, a subject that is foreign to most lawyers, even those heavily involved in their firm's management. Chapter 10 addresses cash-flow issues and solutions. Ultimately, however, each partner must have some stake in the game in the form of capital contributions, or a firm must have some alternative plan for providing cash to pay for those items that do not find their way into the income statement.

Financing

Whether a firm is financed with debt or capital generally depends on the philosophy of the owners, who determine how much equity comes from the owners and set the limit on outside borrowing. Some firms believe strongly that a firm should be owned by its owners and not by the bank. Others feel just the opposite. There should be some balance, but currently there are no guideline ratios for equity and debt. In a world where younger owners are buying more expensive goods and paying more for educating their children, chances are that bank borrowing is usually the predominate source of additional funds.

If a firm decides that it must get some of its capital from the owners, then how are the capital contributions allocated? The first rule is to tie the balances to the income percentage. A firm should first set new income percentages and then apply those percentages to the capital balance. For example, if I am a 15 percent income owner, then I should also be a 15 percent capital owner. If my income percentage is *less* than my capital percentage, then I am in essence providing capital financing so that others can make more income than me. If my income percentage is *more* than my capital percentage, the opposite is true. Those owners who take the most out of a firm should be prepared to put the most into it. Once the total capital needed for the year is determined, the amount required from each owner is then reduced by the owner's existing balance, and the new balance due is calculated.

Paying Interest to Owners

There are some firms who pay interest on individual owner capital accounts. The paying of interest on capital only makes sense when the income percentage and the capital percentage are not in proper alignment. If the income percentage and the capital percentage are exactly the same, then to pay interest on capital is a wash. In other words, an owner gets his share of the interest and then pays his income percentage share of the interest to all the other owners, in effect ending up with a zero balance. If a firm does not maintain a direct relationship between income percentages and capital percentages, then paying interest on capital does make sense and in effect gives a benefit to those owners who have put up the most money to run the law firm.

A majority of firms do have income percentages that are disproportionate to capital percentages, and this can justify some type of interest payment. There are actually some tax advantages to the owners for paying interest on capital. First, it is income not subject to the Medicare tax (assuming the owners have already passed the FICA threshold), and second, it may provide investment income that can be offset against personal-investment expenses of the owners.

There is no magical formula or amount that should be charged to newly admitted owners. The amount is based solely on the cash needs of a firm and how a firm wishes to satisfy these needs. Some firms pick an arbitrary number that has no relationship to the real capital requirements of a firm. This is fine, except that if an owner invests more in the firm than another owner, but still receives the same earnings, he is not being compensated fairly. Paying interest can make up the difference.

Paying for Good Will

A question that constantly gets asked is whether or not a new owner should pay for the good will that was created prior to his becoming an owner. This is a difficult question to answer, since in a personal-service environment it is difficult to value good will. However, it is possible to account for it.

There are situations where the founding owners have invested considerable amounts over the years to build a firm's name and reputation. In this situation, there is some justification for new owners paying something for the right to significantly increase their earnings as a result of the founders' effort. One option is to assess each new owner a fixed amount upon admission, determined on a year-by-year basis by the current equity owners. Rather than the new owner making a capital contribution for this amount, it can be deducted from his compensation over a five-year period. For example, if the amount is $40,000, the new owner's compensation is reduced by $8,000 per year, which would then inure to the benefit of the existing owners in accordance with their income percentages. This is one method of having good will paid to the older owners with pretax dollars from a new owner.

Capitalizing Profits

One method used to get owners to ante up some capital is to capitalize undistributed profits. The method that you use to do this will vary, depending on your ownership form. With a partnership or limited liability corporation, the owners are taxed on their distributed share of earnings, regardless of whether they actually receive the earnings in cash. Thus, it is possible for a firm to simply capitalize undistributed profits as the owner's capital contribution for that year. Since an owner never sees the money, in some cases he may not miss it. If necessary, a firm can give each owner enough cash to pay the taxes on the amounts that are not distributed, and then capitalize the rest.

If the firm is a professional corporation (PC), there is a different issue. Owners are treated just like employees. They receive compensation in the form of salaries and bonuses that are reflected on their W-2 forms. This can create a problem. The owner must actually receive the payment in order for it to be taxed as regular income and avoid both the personal service company income tax (currently 35 percent at first dollar) that is imposed at the corporate level, and the tax on dividends paid to owners. This can be a major dilemma, since most PCs, like other law firms, are undercapitalized. Therefore, a firm often does not have the necessary cash to make the distribution and avoid the tax.

The answer to this problem is either to issue notes at a nominal interest rate, or to permanently capitalize the excess earnings (or some combination of these two strategies). This records the compensation on the W-2 form for tax purposes, but retains cash in the firm without it being taxed at the corporate level.

Taxes

Unfortunately, many professional corporations are still paying taxes at the end of the year. This happens for several reasons.

◆ A firm does not have the systems in place so that the books can be closed in sufficient time to distribute all the cash-basis income as of December 31. Some firms complain that the year-end closing is delayed because of year-end entries, like depreciation, that are not known until late in January. The way to deal with this is to have a rule in the firm whereby no fixed assets are purchased after December 10. On that date, a firm sends the list of new assets to the accountants, and they prepare the depreciation entry by December 31 so it can be recorded in the December entries. In addition, a firm should start correcting any major accounting problems that could affect year-end closing in November, so that year-end closing can occur on time. Also, there is no accounting rule that I know of that prevents month-end closing entries from being made prior to the month's end.

◆ Some firms pay taxes because they do not have a compensation system that permits all the income to be allocated to the owners. Some firms have a small draw but a large bonus pool, and the bonus pool generally is estimated. This problem can be solved by assigning a percentage interest in the firm to each owner, thus permitting all of the income to be allocated at the end of the year.

◆ Firms generally do not have enough cash to pay the net income that was earned. As noted earlier, this problem can be resolved by processing the net income through the compensation amounts of the owners, paying the taxes, and recording the balance as owner notes. These notes can then either be paid the following year, or better yet, capitalized.

The Growth Phase

Assuming a firm is somewhat successful, it begins to undergo significant changes brought about simply by the addition of more work and more people to service the work. This growing-up stage is very important, and if it is not handled correctly, there may be future problems when the situation begins turning downward.

Unfortunately, smaller firms, of which there are thousands, prepare to get bigger without really knowing what it means. The following discussion may be helpful in determining what happens as growth occurs, and learning how to deal with the inevitable changes.

The Institution Emerges

The first thing that happens in the larger organization is the emergence of the firm as an institution, as opposed to a group of lawyers sharing space and expenses while operating as sole proprietors. Decisions are made with the entity in mind, rather than to satisfy individual desires. This group focus becomes the overriding factor for many of the other changes that begin to take effect.

More Emphasis on the Planning Process

The increased number of people and the magnitude of the revenues to be generated places special emphasis on the planning process. A firm begins to question many issues that it took for granted or paid no attention to in the past, such as

- ◆ How large do we want to be?
- ◆ How many offices do we want, and where should they be located?
- ◆ What kind of associates do we want to hire?
- ◆ How do we handle recruiting and compensation issues?
- ◆ Which services should we expand, and which should we eliminate?
- ◆ How do we want to be owned, governed, and managed?
- ◆ What are our overall objectives?

Suddenly a firm realizes that it is a large business with several employees who depend on it for their livelihood and the welfare of their families. Questions of how to deal with lateral hires, merger opportunities, and branch offices are now being raised. The owner retreat now takes on more significance than just being an event where the prior-year financial results are discussed.

Governance and Management

The planning process may reveal that a firm, operating as a loose confederation, cannot make the right decisions at the right time without more structure. This structure may take the form of a policy committee, headed by a strong managing owner, which guides the firm through the growth process. A firm may struggle with selecting the persons involved in this new governance mechanism. The result of this struggle can create certain problems among the owners, particularly those who believe their book of business justifies a major role in the decision-making process. Compromises must be made to keep a firm together as the management structure unfolds.

Expanded Client Services

The expansion of client services to a larger group of clients may create certain management problems, primarily in selecting work to be performed and scheduling people to perform it. A firm must decide on a practice-management structure that allows for the work to be performed at the most economical level without sacrificing quality. This means creating department managers or coordinators to assist the policy committee in managing the work and the people. A firm must also initiate a system for examining new work and making certain that it fits the service and profitability criteria established by the firm.

Nonlawyer Management

As part of its examination of governance and structure, a firm may find that the owners can no longer devote the necessary time to many of the management and administrative tasks required by a larger organization. To compensate for this, the owners may consider employing a nonlawyer professional manager, either full- or part-time, who can assist in handling these activities as well as help the firm realize its longer-term objectives. The person hired for this position needs a strong financial background, and must be able to deal with the many personnel problems that now confront the firm on a routine basis. Chances are that if the firm has never had such a person, it will take two or three tries before the right person is hired. The main problem is likely to be the firm's reluctance to turn over many of the responsibilities that were previously the province of the owners.

Capital Needs

With the increase in size of staff, space, and equipment, a firm may find itself with a major capitalization problem for the first time in its history. Before, certain items were often simply purchased out of current earnings. But with a larger organization, the magnitude of purchases makes that option no longer feasible. A firm needs to consider debt financing more than ever before, and determine how that debt is to be divided among the owners. As the firm's capital needs increase, it must wrestle with a more formalized capitalization system where after-tax dollars are contributed by the owners not only upon admission, but for each year as well. Some owners may be opposed to debt financing, particularly if they are required to be guarantors on the loans.

Ownership Issues

Reviewing capitalization needs may ultimately raise the question, "what is an owner?" For perhaps the first time, a firm wrestles with the problem of having too many owners, which may dilute profits. There are several options to consider, including multitier ownership with nonequity owners, or permanent associates. The firm may have to develop more stringent criteria for ownership admission and may have to turn away some associates, even if it means losing good people who cannot pass the new criteria.

Retirement Planning

When owners reach their late forties or early fifties, some begin to think about retirement. A firm needs to address how retirement is funded—from current earnings, future earnings, or not funded at all. Questions may be raised about how to deal with the accumulation of work-in-process (WIP), accounts receivable, and unsettled cases, and whether any of these amounts actually belong to the owners and are earned by them over their lifetimes as owners. A firm must also decide how retirement amounts are determined, and whether owners are "forced" to retire at a certain age to make room for new owners to come in at the bottom and ensure continued growth and success. This issue is addressed more fully in Chapters 18 and 19.

Strategic Automation Planning

The growth in a firm's size and complexity creates a need for new types of information. For this reason, a firm needs both an overall strategic plan and a strategic automation plan, so the overall plan can be measured against expectations. With all the changes taking place in a firm's practice and administrative sectors, technology plays a key role in providing management with the efficiencies and economies required to practice in a different competitive environment. An increased number of computer-literate lawyers will put added pressure on a firm to provide terminals at everyone's desk as well as portable laptops for travel and home use. Some lawyers may want to work out of their homes for part of their workweek. This creates a constant problem of finding a way to recapture the huge capital investment required by more creative billing practices. The much greater level of technology will also require additional time and personnel. This issue is discussed more fully in Chapter 13.

Strategic Marketing Planning

To reach its objectives, a firm needs to develop a marketing plan that is in line with its desired clients and services. More emphasis is placed on individual lawyers marketing the firm to potential clients. The firm also will change the way it views marketing as one of the contributions made by partners and associates to the overall goods and objectives of the firm.

Compensation Policy Adjustments

Ultimately, all the changes that take place in a growing firm alter a firm's reward systems at all levels, but particularly for owners. With the emphasis on the institution as opposed to individual production, the compensation policy needs to be reviewed and perhaps changed to a system that evaluates total contribution to the firm, measured in more than just billable hours or collections. The increased need for management, marketing, associate training, and recruiting results in establishing criteria to which all owners must agree and understand as their basis for compensation. It is likely that reviewing compensation will create the need to establish policies for those owners who, for whatever reason, are not making a contribution commensurate with their compensation levels. A firm may realize the necessity of having a formal annual review program for owners, just as it does for associates and staff. The owner compensation issue is addressed in Chapter 17.

Looking into a crystal ball is not easy. However, as small firms become medium-sized firms, small problems become very large ones. The firm must begin at an early stage to identify those issues that will result from growth, and begin addressing them so that it can realize its strategic objectives while retaining an atmosphere that promotes the proper quality of work style and lifestyle.

The Trouble Phase

Unfortunately, despite all the warnings and despite all the advice regarding the need to constantly keep one's finger on the pulse of a firm, at some point even the most successful firm begins to get into trouble. You would think that with all that has been said and written over the past several years, that major problems in law firms simply could not develop without warning. Perhaps the signs are not obvious that adversity is right around the corner. Perhaps the firm leadership is not able to recognize the underlying problem areas that have the greatest potential for harm

Following is a discussion of the "danger areas." These may be of use to those firms who have been successful and want to continue that way. Some of these situations may not seem like problems, since they may be the very things that allowed a firm to prosper in the past. But each firm needs to examine itself and decide if warning signs are apparent and, if so, whether corrective action should be taken. Having only a few of these problems, in most instances, may not be significant.

Relying on One Client

A firm should perform an annual analysis and ascertain the extent to which each client is generating revenue. A firm should be aware of the problems that can develop if one or more major clients disappear. In addition, this analysis reveals whether the firm is case-oriented or client-oriented, and the problems that develop if the firm cannot build a client base that supplies a steady stream of revenue over a long period of time. This analysis also reveals whether major clients are more aligned with specific lawyers rather than with the firm, which could be a financial disaster should those lawyers leave or retire, jeopardizing continuing work for those clients.

Democratic Management

Unfortunately, democracy does not work in a law firm. A firm needs to select from its ranks of owners and associates those people who are the best managers, put them on the significant committees, and let them run the firm. It's generally unproductive to include more than a few people in the management process. Obviously, there are decisions such as mergers, borrowings, lateral hires, expansion, office relocations, and owner admissions that require a consensus; however, these decisions should be based on recommendations by those entrusted with the management of the firm.

Lobster Taste and Hamburger Rates

As some firms try desperately to keep up with the Joneses, with respect to both associate compensation and office location and decor, their hourly rates are unable to keep pace. The result is that they can't produce the necessary income per owner even though they may have significant billable hours.

Firms need to look within themselves and decide who they are and what they want to be. It doesn't make sense to move into an office building with a significant square-foot decoration allowance and space per lawyer yet only be able to charge nominal rates. A firm should make certain that its lifestyle coincides with its client base and its revenue-producing capacity.

Information Blackout

In some firms it is believed that the less people know about what's going on, the better off they are, or that the more information they have, the more they have to gripe about. In addition, some firms feel that information, if not interpreted correctly, creates divisiveness within a firm. Experience shows that the opposite is usually true, particularly at the associate level, where blackouts appear to be the most prevalent. Why not articulate associate expectations, or tell associates how much the firm makes? Why not divulge what the criteria is to be an owner, and what it means in capital investment and compensation to be elevated to that position? Why not spell out how the owners' retirement plan works or how the compensation system is administered? Generally, dissemination of information creates more positive than negative results. In a law firm that's already a frail entity and struggling with owners, associates, and staff retention, these kinds of factual disclosures become even more important.

Formula-Based Compensation System

Listing this as a problem always raises eyebrows, since there are many firms with formula-based compensation systems that are indeed very successful. In the long run, however, formula-based compensation may not work. A firm should develop criteria for compensation that take into account not only objective factors such as billings, collections, and billable hours, but also many subjective factors such as firm management, practice development, *pro bono* activities, community and civic activities, and so on. Most pure formula-based systems seem to short-change these latter factors. Nothing can be more divisive and destructive than a compensation plan that's perceived as basically inequitable. A balance needs to be struck between a subjective system based on objective data and an incentive-based system that rewards those with exceptional performance.

High Owner Billable Hours

If owner billable hours are higher than associate billable hours, it can be a problem. This is related somewhat to formula-based compensation. In a system that rewards billable hours more than any other criteria, there's less incentive for owners to pass work down to younger associates, and less incentive to pass the work to others who can do it better and perhaps more efficiently. Generally, in firms where owner billable hours are higher than associate hours, it's a result of a compensation system that places excessive emphasis on hours production.

If one believes in the concept of leverage, then it makes sense that associates have more hours than owners. Owners should devote a significant amount of time to activities outside of client billable hours. Having owner billable hours exceed those at the associate level, while perhaps a short-term benefit, can indeed be a long-term problem.

Low Owner-to-Associate Ratio

Relating again to the question of leverage, firms need to seriously examine their current owner-admission policy and decide whether or not relatively unrestricted advancement to owner should be changed in favor of some other method. This could either be lengthening the time to achieve ownership, or creating a multitier ownership system. Statistics show that firms with the highest net income per owner are usually those that are highly leveraged with associates and legal assistants.

Undercapitalization

The question of capitalization is probably one of the more significant issues facing most firms, regardless of size. As firms continue to spend substantial amounts of money on new space, technology, and other inflation-driven expenses at the same time that owners want more take-home cash, they are often caught in a cash bind.

There's no right or wrong proportion of debt to equity in a law firm, except that the more successful firms seem to be those that have taken the position that a firm should be owned primarily by the owners and not by the bank. In these firms, each owner must make a capital contribution on some basis every year. It's bad enough that the firm must use the bank for operating capital to take care of slow months or receivable stretch-outs, let alone borrow heavily for capital asset additions, or even worse, to make scheduled payments to the owners.

No Ownership Agreements

You would think that most law firms would have a formal and appropriately detailed owner agreement. It's interesting to note that many do not. A firm may have an agreement, but often it's far from sufficiently detailed. As a result, when problems occur and owners start leaving, there's no clear, structured way for a firm to deal with issues such as paying out an owner, transferring clients, dealing with governance questions, practice-management issues, and so on. The ownership agreement should be updated on a periodic basis.

No Formal Retirement Program

Most small and medium-sized firms haven't even begun to address the question of how to deal with owner retirements. The problem becomes significant when owners reach their mid-fifties, and no plan has been put in place. There are enough pension vehicles available that firms should be able to provide adequate retirement for all owners and employees. Such programs tend to stabilize a firm, engender more firm loyalty, and create a cohesive team.

A retirement plan should be structured so that it fulfills two major goals: to provide adequate compensation so that owners are able to retire at a reasonable age (whether it is age 60, 65, or 70), and to serve as a funding mechanism so that young owners will have minimal or no liability in the future.

No Formal Plan of Governance

A firm should have a plan that allows for an orderly transition of management at all levels. A mechanism encouraging the best people to move into substantive management roles is critical. A firm should address the types of committees it wishes to have (recognizing that a too-elaborate committee system can be as troublesome as an excessively democratic process), how these committees are structured, how people are rotated on and off, whether specific constituencies are represented, and how the committees perpetuate themselves through the lifetimes of many owners. The system should be designed so that people are motivated to participate in management, and the firm should be in a position to select those who are the best managers (and not necessarily the best lawyers or biggest rainmakers).

Expense Orientation

Regardless of how many times it's been refuted, many lawyers still believe that the key to making more money in their firm is cutting overhead. But that just isn't true, as confirmed by practically every study that's been made on the economics of a law practice. *The key to more net income is more gross income.* A firm should develop procedures and programs that allow it to increase its gross revenues as much as possible.

There's no question that expense control (as opposed to expense reduction) is necessary, and management must be constantly aware of those areas of costs that can be controlled. In many instances, however, expense control is affected more by lifestyle and level of service than by objective economic considerations. Everyone wants to reduce expenses unless it affects him or her personally.

Inadequate Budget Reviews

A large percentage of law firms still don't follow through on periodic comparisons of actual-to-budget amounts to determine whether or not targets are being reached and, if not, what can be done to prevent an income shortfall. In addition, firms generally budget on an annual basis without further dividing the year into months or into seasonalized billings, collections, and hours so historical income trends can be projected. Making midcourse corrections during the year helps ensure that December 15 doesn't arrive to find the firm 20 or 30 percent below expectations.

No Institutional Focus

I've purposely left this issue for the end because it's the most important. A firm must do everything possible to create an environment in which all lawyers and staff have an institutional focus. As a partner once said to me, "If it is not good for the firm, then it is not good, regardless of how it affects individual partners." This is the ultimate institutional philosophy.

One cannot help but notice that the issues that a firm confronts as it grows are the very issues that will give it the most problems unless it can forecast what lies ahead and plan for the eventual results. While it may be difficult to predict the future, there are certain fundamental steps that a firm can take to avoid the full impact of potential problems caused by growth, by loss of significant clients, by loss of significant lawyers, or by a downturn in the overall economy.

Ownership

As a firm grows, it faces the question of who are the owners, and when and on what basis new owners are admitted. This brings up the question of whether the firm needs to consider a multitier structure to include nonequity, salaried owners. If not handled properly, a multitier ownership system can create a certain level of strife and low morale among both owners and associates.

In most cases, the issue of ownership can be dealt with effectively through the compensation process. However, if that is not possible, then you need to examine creating a different ownership level.

Although many firms believe that some type of second-tier owner is required, there usually is no general consensus on what it represents and more importantly, on the time and criteria for moving into the equity class. This issue is covered in Chapter 18.

Terminating Owners

Equally as important as the issue of promoting owners is the issue of terminating them in the event that a downsizing of the firm is required. This is not easy to do; however, it is the eventual result of making bad decisions in the hiring or promotion process, or of bringing in new laterals or owners in a merger situation.

Dealing with nonproductive owners is difficult and controversial, and each firm needs to develop its own individual, specific way to handle the problem. The discussion here is very general; the goal is to present the issues that a firm confronts when dealing with a nonproductive owner, and to suggest a variety of ways to resolve the situation. Of all the issues that a firm must face, this is perhaps the most private and personal, and the solution must be tailored for each individual firm.

Definition of a Nonproductive Owner

The nonproductive owner usually has some or all of the following characteristics:

♦ Doesn't work as hard as other owners
♦ Doesn't generate new business
♦ Is a trouble-maker
♦ Doesn't train associates or younger owners
♦ Doesn't participate in management
♦ Doesn't participate in outside activities that enhance the status of a firm
♦ Doesn't keep current in his field of legal expertise
♦ Was nonproductive as an associate

What Makes an Owner Become Nonproductive?

There are many reasons why an owner falls into this category. Unfortunately, most people either do not recognize or refuse to recognize the symptoms, and do not work to correct the situation. Here are some reasons why an owner may be nonproductive:

♦ Burnout
♦ Illness

- Substance abuse
- Personal tragedy
- Outside interests interfere with work
- Loss of interest in practicing law
- Legal specialty becomes obsolete, and won't or can't retrain
- Loss of major client
- Perception of unfair treatment by other owners
- Compensation too high
- Compensation too low
- Firm has not provided rules to follow

How to Deal with a Nonproductive Owner

Once you have identified individuals in the firm that may fit into this category, then the firm must work diligently and quickly to rectify the situation. Here are some suggestions:

- Cut compensation, or place on separate system geared to both originations and working credits
- Create a plan with expected milestones of achievement, where failure to achieve milestones results in dismissal
- Place in of-counsel relationship, with incentive-based compensation system
- Retrain
- Determine strengths, and offer assignments that utilize them
- Out-place to client or in other position
- Offer early retirement
- Terminate

Deciding Whether to Take Action

There are both downsides and upsides to effectively dealing with a nonproductive owner. Each situation must be examined separately to determine how best to deal with a particular one. They are all different, and there are no cookie-cutter solutions.

What Happens if You Do Nothing?

- Negatively affects the morale of the owners
- Provides bad example for rest of firm
- Hurts future business
- Drains cash through payout
- Reduced loyalty from others may cause split
- May affect future recruiting, lateral hires, or merger opportunities

What Happens if You Do Something?

- ◆ Improves morale
- ◆ Gives message that firm is serious about problem
- ◆ Increases income share for other owners
- ◆ Makes firm feel good to be helping fellow owner
- ◆ Reduces number of future nonproductive owners

Preventing an Owner from Becoming Nonproductive

Obviously, the best solution of all is to prevent the situation from occurring in the first place. Here are some suggestions on how this can be accomplished:

- ◆ Set standards that everyone understands, adhere to them, and enforce them
- ◆ Have a formal evaluation program for all owners
- ◆ Anticipate client loses
- ◆ Anticipate major changes in specialty areas
- ◆ Cross-train owners where possible
- ◆ Have a mentor program at the owner level
- ◆ Develop a formal retirement program with early-retirement options
- ◆ Provide an out-placement service
- ◆ Offer a professional counseling program
- ◆ Have a serious attitude about dealing with the problem
- ◆ Set strict owner admission policies along with a formal associate evaluation program
- ◆ Set compensation fairly and equitably

The subject of dealing with nonproductive owners is a difficult one and must be addressed individually in each firm rather than on a broad scale of what everyone else is doing. Each firm needs to examine its group of owners, evaluate them against some type of criteria or standard, and determine which are not producing in comparison to the standard.

Obviously, the first thing that needs to be done is to develop criteria or standards, which is missing from most firms. Generally, people respond well to rules if they know what the rules are and know that they are applied universally to everyone. Without standards, it is difficult not only to prevent a problem from occurring, but also to deal with it in an organized, meaningful, and effective way.

Payout of Terminated Owners

Eventually a firm will have the responsibility for paying out those owners who leave the firm, either voluntarily or involuntarily. Unfortunately, most firms address this issue only when the problem presents itself. This is the worst time to do so, since the departing owner may now be in an adversarial position with the owners who are staying, and who want to protect the long-term financial viability of the firm.

There is a popular view that payouts should be different, based on the nature of the termination. For example, an owner who retires or who terminates to become a judge should be treated differently from one who leaves to join a firm across the street, creating a competitive situation. I do not subscribe to this view, since I believe that during the lifetime of ownership, an owner of a law firm accrues certain benefits. The circumstances of his termination do not necessarily alter the value of those benefits, even though they may alter the provisions under which the payment is made. However, the amount may, in fact, be altered if certain conditions regarding the termination are not met in accordance with the firm's standing agreements.

Rather than provide examples of types of payouts and how they should be funded and recorded, in this discussion I instead have presented several aspects of termination that a firm needs to consider. In many cases, a firm's history and philosophy in dealing with departing owners determine the methodology that it selects to ascertain the payment that is to be made. It is important to emphasize that there are many legal, funding, and tax ramifications of paying terminated owners that must be examined very closely. Chapter 19 addresses this fairly complicated and important issue.

Summary

During its lifetime, a dynamic law firm will evolve through a series of events and conditions, both external and internal, which will materially affect its existence. The firm needs to be able to keep focused on its mission and to make certain that it has the management awareness to foresee problems and make plans to correct them. The planning process must be accomplished on an annual basis and updated periodically in order that the impact of current situations that affect the profession in general and the firm in particular can be evaluated. I hope that this chapter has set the stage for the remainder of this publication, which will address some of the issues noted in more detail.

Financial Management: The Process

2

Financial management is a process, not a function performed by someone who simply knows the difference between debits and credits. The process starts with the initial preparation of a financial plan or budget, follows through with a system of analysis, review, and interpretation for the year, and then stretches out even further to become part of a firm's long-term strategic plan. No law firm can adequately plan for the future without an internal financial management system that allows it to examine the impact of its long-range decisions.

I realize that everybody does things differently, and that every firm has its own personality, culture, and history. What works for one firm may not necessarily work for another. I certainly don't want to give the impression that my way is the only way. However, I will say that my way worked for a firm that grew from fifty-three to three hundred lawyers during a fifteen-year period. Most, if not all, of my ideas and philosophies work equally as well for the fifteen-lawyer firm; it's just a question of the magnitude of the numbers.

For starters, let's examine the entire area of financial management on the basis of some arbitrary categories that I envision make up the process. Each category leads to the next one, until the entire process is completed. If your firm is deficient or void in any of the categories listed below, then it's not fully maximizing the benefits of a complete financial management program.

Historical Data

Without the benefit of what has happened in the past, it's difficult, if not impossible, to project the future accurately. For this reason, a minimum of three or, better yet, five years of your firm's historical data must be available for comparison. The fluctuations that take place in a firm's operations, particularly a firm involved in large litigation, preclude the use of fewer than three years of data. The key elements to be maintained are as follows:

- *Personnel data.* This includes the number of partners, associates, legal assistants, and staff personnel, perhaps further weighted by month so that annual averages can be accurately computed on a full-time equivalent basis.
- *Billable hours.* This statistic should be total hours for the firm, office, or department, further subdivided into each of the "producing groups"—partners, associates, and legal assistants. If possible, these averages should be weighted using the personnel data discussed above. In today's legal environment, there may also be categories for contract lawyers or a variety of other paraprofessionals.
- *Billing rates.* Trends in rate adjustments should be developed and compared to regularly published data on the economy as a whole. This helps to ascertain whether or not these adjustments are in line with corresponding changes of other service industries. The rates should also bear some relationship to the changes that take place in the cost of living or inflation. If possible, comparable rates should be obtained from other firms in the same geographical area that provide similar services.
- *Net income.* This should be kept in actual dollars as a percentage of gross fees and on a per-partner basis.
- *Expenses.* This information should also be kept in actual dollars and as a percentage of gross fees and should be segregated by major expense categories (compensation, occupancy, benefits, and so on). If possible, expenses should be kept on the basis of "lawyer equivalents." This information helps develop long-term profitability data. Note: Lawyer equivalents represent the number of full-time lawyers and is calculated in order to give some weight to the use of nonlawyer timekeepers. For example, legal assistants may be given a weight of .60. Thus, a firm with 10 lawyers and 4 legal assistants would have 12.4 lawyer equivalents (10 + (.60 x 4)).
- *Realization.* Records should be maintained as to how a firm has fared in billing and collecting against the standard value, measured by the hourly rate structure. This element is key in setting rates and the overall budget; thus it's important that your firm be aware, on a historical

basis, of its ability to bill clients at the standard hourly charge. This should also include historical information on accounts receivable write-offs.

The Budget Process

The budget process is relatively straightforward, and most firms follow it in one way or another. There are, however, some very basic concepts that you should apply properly, or the whole exercise could be counterproductive and you won't get the anticipated and necessary results. Remember, the budget forms the basis for all current and subsequent analyses of financial results; thus its preparation is very important to the overall financial management process.

- ◆ *Accrual basis versus cash basis.* Every firm needs to budget on both the accrual and cash basis. (Accrual basis as used in this book refers to the value of the billable time for all timekeepers at their standard hourly rates. It is also referred to as input.) To simply budget cash collections without examining the input or fluctuations that take place in work-in-process and accounts receivable balances may be a useless undertaking. There should always be the constant reminder that expenses are being incurred *not* to produce cash collections but to support a given level of billable hour activity. Accrual-basis budgeting permits you to examine the extent to which billable hours are not finding their way to the bottom line and whether or not anticipated billings and collections goals are proper and achievable. Oftentimes, firms get a false sense of security when cash collections are very good. In some cases, this is a short-lived windfall that could turn completely around if there is not enough time in the pipeline for future billing and collection.
- ◆ *Seasonal fluctuations.* To simply divide the annual amounts by twelve doesn't provide management with accurate information for the purpose of examining monthly activity with respect to gross, billings, expenses, and net. Therefore, some seasonalization of the data relevant to the budget should be performed. By relating monthly activity to historical trends, management can compare a month's performance with the same period in prior years and ascertain whether problems are developing. A poor September from a net income standpoint is of little concern if historically September has always been a poor net income month.
- ◆ *Cash flow.* Since everything in a firm revolves around its ability to pay its bills and its partners (or shareholders) and since short-term borrowing may be a viable alternative to cash shortages, the budget

process must include an examination of cash flow on an annual and monthly basis. By coordinating seasonal fluctuations in collections with average payments of expenses and other items affecting cash, the firm can project on a monthly time frame your firm's requirements for major cash outlays, particularly the timing of partner distributions and purchases of major capital assets.

Analysis, Evaluation, and Interpretation

Unfortunately, most financial managers don't advance beyond the actual mechanics of the budget preparation. Many times they fall short of the most critical aspects of analysis, evaluation, and interpretation of the results. Preparing the budget is not a fully worthwhile experience unless the results can be evaluated—comparisons made to projections—and interpreted so that significant deviations from projections can be determined and rectified. In addition, during the budget process itself, you must make certain analyses or "what-ifs" that enhance the results and provide guideposts, offering you a certain degree of comfort with the final results.

Some of the more important items in this area are as follows:

◆ *Inventory turnover.* The firm's ability to convert a dollar's worth of time into a dollar's worth of cash is probably the most critical element in the financial management process. The turnover statistic, expressed in terms of months, should be evaluated monthly and prepared not only for the firm as a whole but, if appropriate, by office, department, or even individual lawyer. As will be explained later, turnover is used not only as an evaluation tool but also as a budgeting tool. The firm's turnover rate actually drives the budget and is a critical element in helping to realize a firm's greatest profit.

◆ *Effects of volume and price.* A firm must compare its budgeted amounts with the actual from the prior year to determine the extent to which the increases in gross income (on the accrual basis) are resulting from increases in volume (billable hours) or increases in price (hourly rates). You must be aware of the problem that could develop if the majority of the firm's increases in any given year is coming from raising prices rather than increasing volume through more billable hours. There must be a balance of the two with more weight given to volume.

◆ *Inflation impact.* The firm must produce inflation-adjusted amounts so that the partners can readily determine the increases in net income represented in real dollars. This same analysis should be made with expenses, which have an impact on whether or not a firm is becoming more efficient through productivity increases, which offset actual dollar increases. Although this has not been a problem in recent years, it still should be considered to the extent it has materially impacted the financial results.

♦ *Cost per billable hour.* This key calculation determines the cost for a firm to produce its basic product, the billable hour. Since the amount is not affected by cash-basis or accrual-basis accounting or by many of the other factors in the budget, the statistic is very important. It reflects a firm's ability to produce its product at the lowest possible cost. Achieving the highest level of profit is accomplished by taking the same amount of overhead dollars and spreading them over more gross income dollars. Thus, a firm realizes a greater net profit at perhaps the same net cost to the client. The cost-per-billable-hour computation provides this analysis. By coupling this with the comparison of the effects of inflation, you can obtain additional information on a firm's efficiency and increases in productivity.

This book attempts to cover many of the above items in a fairly complete way, with the goal of providing you with a broader perspective of financial management in the environment in which we currently operate.

Since becoming involved in this profession, and throughout most of my articles and speeches, I have emphasized that, regardless of all the duties performed for a firm, all roads lead to the same place—the financial statements.

I don't want to downgrade the other functions that are accomplished, because obviously they are important. However, a manager's success may ultimately be measured not by the ability to hire secretaries or install technology but rather by the ability to function financially at an advanced level and find ways to make a firm more profitable.

We've been forced by many factors to turn our attention to ways to control expenses and, more importantly, to increase income. Until financial management is accepted as a major part of the overall management responsibilities, legal managers will not, in my opinion, reach the levels of economic rewards or creditability to which we all aspire.

There are some who say that the budgeting process needs to be tied to the strategic plan of a firm. This might be true when looking out three to five years and making *pro-forma* projections. However, on a year-to-year basis, the factors listed above must be considered, regardless of the overall long-term plan that a firm has set for itself. The current financial plan focuses on the current resources available to achieve income commensurate with the expectations of the owners. While in theory this process should be tied to some plan, the fact is that for yearly planning purposes, the strategic plan serves no real purpose except as a guide to what the future may hold.

The Financial Plan: Determining Gross Income

3

Financial management begins with the preparation of a budget or financial plan. Once the budget is understood, the remainder of the process falls into place. However, beginning with a budget isn't all that easy if you've never done it before. Therefore, this chapter illustrates budget preparation in some detail, hoping not to offend the more experienced financial managers.

The Key to More Net Income

A point of emphasis here—and one that will be stressed many times—is that no firm should be overly preoccupied with expenses. The key to making more net income is generating more gross income. This doesn't mean that expenses shouldn't be controlled; it simply means that more time and emphasis should be placed on increasing the revenue side of the income statement.

On other occasions when I've made that remark, I've been accused of advocating increasing net by simply raising billing rates to generate more gross. Obviously, this is one method, but there are others. Increasing gross doesn't necessarily mean increasing rates, but rather setting competitive rates. It means developing a realistic financial plan of income and expenses on a short- and long-term basis so that decisions can be made on the prospect of future owner or shareholder earning levels. It means having a financial management system that allows for timely and accurate time accumulation that permits prompt reporting and billing to clients. It means billing clients currently and establishing procedures for prompt collection to reduce write-offs. It means letting the work flow to the lowest level within the firm that can perform it satisfactorily and economically, so that a $150-per-hour shareholder isn't doing a $75-per-hour project. It means better and more effective use of legal assistants and other nonlawyer personnel to free lawyers to perform more important and perhaps more profitable work, including many other functions required for a successful firm, such as marketing and management.

Obviously, increasing gross income is more than simply increasing rates. It's establishing a management system so the work-flow produces the most profitable result. The process must have the flexibility to make the necessary adjustments as conditions change during the year.

Steps in the Plan

The financial plan can be prepared in a variety of ways—some very simple, others more sophisticated. Two major approaches are the "tops-down" and "bottoms-up." In the tops-down approach, you calculate the value of the time by multiplying the expected billable hours by the standard rate of each time-keeper. Then, by factoring in realization, billing and collection cycles, and expenses, the net income is determined. In the bottoms-up approach, the firm's shareholders first decide how much they want to make and, using that amount, then work back to the value of time that must be obtained to achieve the desired income levels.

In either method, the key ingredient remains the value of billable hours. The example presented here uses the tops-down approach.

1. Calculate gross income by multiplying the total hours for all time-keepers by their standard average rates. This includes shareholders, associates, and legal assistants.
2. Estimate total expenses for the year.
3. Determine historical realization rates, both rate and billing, and accounts receivable write-offs.
4. Determine other cash-basis income items such as interest income, directors' fees, and so on.
5. Determine the average time it takes to render a bill once the work has been performed, and the average time it takes to collect a bill once it has been issued.
6. Place the information in a budget model and calculate net income.

Throughout this book, I use as an example the firm of Able, Baker, Charles & Dogg, PC, who for the budgeted year ending 12/31/YY was projecting 8 shareholders, 8.5 associates and 5 legal assistants (see Figure A). Pertinent information about the firm is provided as appropriate.

The Hours Budget

The number of people is based on an analysis of expected changes in levels of shareholders, associates, and legal assistants during the twelve-month period. In most cases, this information can be readily estimated, since certain information is known, such as new shareholders, shareholder retirements, and perhaps withdrawals. You may know which associates are leaving and how many new recruits are scheduled to start and their expected starting date. Armed with this information, a firm can now calculate the weighted average number of people scheduled for the year.

The billable hours budget is usually based on a five-year, historical moving average. The firm should keep this information, and each year decide whether to use the averages for that year's budget or some other hours expectation level. Another method is to obtain the expected billable hours on a per-timekeeper basis and compute the average for the group.

As noted in Figure B, the five-year averages for the shareholders, associates, and legal assistants at Able, Baker were 1,589, 1,737, and 1,175, respectively. Based on these averages, the firm set budgeted billable hours at 1,600 for shareholders, 1,750 for associates, and 1,200 for legal assistants. The increases have little impact on the individual lawyers and shouldn't be a problem to achieve.

In an effort to enhance billable hour production, beginning January 1 the firm instituted a new policy where all regular timekeepers must account for an eight-hour day. This policy isn't intended to provide a "big brother" approach to the practice, but rather to force everyone to examine each day's activity

	12/31/YY Budget Number of People	
	12/31/XX	*12/31/YY*
Shareholders	7.0	8.0
Associates	6.7	8.5
Legal Assistants	4.8	5.0

Figure A

12/31/YY Budget Billable Hours			
	Shareholder	Associates	Legal Assistants
12/31/XX	1,580	1,735	1,198
12/31/DD	1,605	1,740	1,150
12/31/CC	1,579	1,705	1,091
12/31/BB	1,612	1,765	1,186
12/31/AA	<u>1,571</u>	<u>1,742</u>	<u>1,250</u>
Total	7,947	8,687	5,875
Average	1,589	1,737	1,175
12/31/YY	1,600	1,750	1,200

Figure B

more closely and capture time that previously wasn't properly accounted for. The firm is also going to improve its tracking of nonbillable time in an effort to channel that time to those projects and activities that produce the greatest benefit to the firm. This includes setting budgets, by lawyer, for activities such as marketing, continuing legal education, outside activities, firm administration, and so on.

For comparison purposes, the average number of billable hours for law firms can be obtained from a variety of sources. Several national surveys provide this information according to firm size, geographical location, and even for legal specialties within firms. These statistics can then be compared with your firm's averages to ascertain whether your timekeepers are working hard enough in keeping with the firm's overall income expectations (see Chapter 15 for more information on using surveys).

Able, Baker is working with billable hours on an average basis for each timekeeper group based on expected levels for each person. However, certain individual variations must be taken into account. For example, the shareholder who has significant administrative or management responsibilities or those individuals heavily involved in bar, recruiting, or other activities may be budgeted with a lower billable-hour commitment. For the larger firms, the use of averages takes many of these items into account, and exceptions are explained at a later date, usually at the time of the annual evaluation. The five-year averaging method prevents a particularly high or low year from affecting the overall firm averages.

Budgeting hours in a law firm isn't easy, particularly for those involved in large litigation matters that appear or disappear on short notice. However, if a firm is a successful, ongoing operation, the hours in any given twelve-month period are generally equal to the average, with the assumption that there is enough work in the office to keep everyone busy, including new associates.

There is no right or wrong number of hours. Each firm has its own culture that determines how hard its members wish to work while still maintaining some sanity and personal life. But once the firm decides what that level should be, everyone should buy into it. There's nothing wrong with shareholders working only 1,400 billable hours per year, if all the shareholders have agreed to that level, and they each recognize the effect it has on the bottom line. One of the problems with low hours at the owner level, however, is that associates will generally work only as hard as the shareholders. Thus, low hours at the senior-lawyer level will usually translate to low hours at all levels. Again, as long as everyone understands the effect of this lifestyle, there is no problem. Trouble develops when expectations among the shareholders are different, with some working much harder than others but receiving less for it. At that point, the firm must reexamine its direction and change course, if necessary.

Billing Rates

Although much attention has been paid to the concept of alternate billing methods—a subject discussed later in this book—everyone recognizes that billing rates continue to play a significant role in the financial management process. It remains probably the easiest and perhaps the most understandable method of establishing a value for the services rendered. Most clients are accustomed to this method, and firms must live with it, at least for now.

Establishing an actual billing rate on a year-to-year basis can sometimes be an agonizing experience for a firm. Various formulas are used to set rates, most of which have no relation to the components in the rate. In very few cases do firms understand the actual method by which the rates are established. Most set their rates on whatever the market will bear (a definite consideration) or whatever other firms in the area are charging (also a consideration). But having done that, they have no scientific way of determining whether these rates are good or bad and what effect they have on earnings.

This book includes a computer model, along with appropriate explanations, that can be used to create rates that produce the expected levels of profit. Further explanation can be found in Chapter 4.

Able, Baker went through the exercise of reviewing the rates of all timekeepers using the billing rate model. The firm decided that an adjustment in rates was in order, given its client base, the type of work, and desired profit levels. It arrived at an average shareholder rate of $210, an average associate rate of $180, and an average legal assistant rate of $75. Keep in mind that these are averages for each of the timekeeper groups—simply a matter of adding the rates for each timekeeper and dividing by the number of time-keepers.

In this example, the firm set its rates with the market and client base in mind, probably meeting with each shareholder to make certain that the rate was realistic. Many firms do this, although as the firm gets larger, this type of individual input may not be practical.

Rate Differentials

Rates must take into account hours production. The group that only produces 1,500 hours and makes the same salary as the group that produces 1,800 hours should not have the same billing rate, unless a firm is assuming that it will lose money on the person producing 1,500 hours and make that up with the person producing 1,800. As a general rule, associates at different experience levels have different hours-production goals. This could be a compelling reason for establishing rates on a class-year basis for the associate group, if it is large enough to warrant this level of detail.

The question of establishing different billable-hour levels and billing rates for associates in the same law school class is difficult for some firms to answer. At one end of the scale are those who say that two associates from the same class should have the same number of billable hours. If they don't, then one should be paid more than the other but still have the same billing rate. Another school of thought says that in many cases the nature of the work dictates the number of hours an associate can charge, and, therefore, some billing-rate adjustments must be taken into account, and the billable-hour differences should not be adjusted for in compensation.

The best example for this is an associate who is on a large litigation matter versus a tax associate who spends the majority of time in the office working on a variety of matters. It is easy for the litigation associate to log 2,000 or 2,100 billable hours a year. This is particularly true on out-of-town assignments. On the other hand, the tax associate frequently works just as hard but has a difficult time coming up with 1,600 or 1,700 billable hours. In addition, the tax associate may spend more time keeping up with his or her practice than does the litigator. Therefore, the justification for a higher rate for the tax associate may be that the work is more specialized and requires more non-billable time in reading and studying to keep up with the specialty.

Each firm needs to come to grips with this issue. If, in fact, a firm has the same rates for everyone in the class, then it runs into the situation of making money (or more money) from the associate who charges 2,000 hours and losing money (or making less money) on the associate who has 1,600 to 1,700 hours.

There is no right or wrong answer to this question. A firm must examine its associates and make the decision as to whether or not differentials in rates should exist among those associates within the same law school class, particularly if compensation is the same. Using the billing rate model will greatly assist in this determination.

Standard Hourly Rates

While working with different firms, I find that many of them do not have a standard hourly rate against which to measure actual results against projections. The reason is usually that there are certain clients, such as insurance companies, that dictate the rates (usually low), and that to have a standard rate might make the lawyers who work for those clients look bad. This situation should not drive the decision to have a standard rate structure. A firm needs to constantly examine whether or not certain clients or types of practice are producing at expected profitability levels, and it can't do this if there isn't a standard rate to use for comparison.

Rates should be set using some type of formula, so that decisions regarding the type of practice or clients can be made properly. To not operate this way hides the facts and produces false information from which important decisions are made. A firm's time-accounting system should produce each of the variances from the standard rate, which is addressed later.

Once the average rate for the average associate is determined, a firm then reviews the other timekeeper groups and its areas of practice, makes a comparison with prior years' rates and the geographical marketplace, and decides on a rate structure for the firm as a whole.

Gross Income Calculation

Able, Baker now has all the ingredients necessary to calculate the accrual-basis gross revenue side of the budget. The actual budget model is discussed later. For now, it is important only to recognize that the model makes many of the calculations and allows for various "what-if" scenarios. In Figure C, the input numbers include the number of people, the rates, and the hours. Note

	1993 Budget Gross Income	
Shareholders	8.0	
Average Rate	$210.00	
Average Hours	1,600	$2,688,000
Associates	8.5	
Average Rate	$180.00	
Average Hours	1,750	2,677,500
Legal Assistants	5.0	
Average Rate	$75.00	
Average Hours	1,200	450,000
Other		55,000
Total		**$5,870,500**

Figure C

the "Other" category that will generate $55,000 of gross. These are people other than normal timekeepers who have billable time, including perhaps the librarian, law clerks, and certain administrative personnel. This may also include time charged for legal research on databases such as Lexis and Westlaw. Generally, this amount is estimated based on the prior year.

The model then calculates the total hours and gross income for each timekeeper group and for the year as a whole. Able, Baker has projected its gross revenues on the accrual basis for the year at $5,870,500.

THE BILLING RATE FORMULA MODEL

4

The Billing Rate Formula Model calculates billing rates for the various timekeepers in a law firm given a set of assumptions. The model is included as a Microsoft Excel file called **billrate formula.xls** on the CD-ROM that is included with this book. Appendix A in this chapter contains a sample printout of the model. The instructions that follow lead you through the model and allow you to use your firm's information to calculate your own billing rates.

BILLING RATE FORMULA MODEL

Prepared by:
John G. Iezzi, CPA
Iezzi Management Group
1906 Hamilton St., Suite A
P.O. Box 1711
Richmond, VA 23218-1711
Phone: (804) 775-6805
Fax: (804) 775-6911
Email: jgiezzi@iezzigroup.com
www.iezzigroup.com

BILLING RATE FORMULA MODEL

TABLE OF CONTENTS

Introduction

This billing rate formula model, **billrate formula.xls,** assists in determining the billing rates for individual timekeepers in order to provide a law firm with its expected level of profit. These rates are then used to prepare the firm's annual financial plan. The model makes two separate calculations:

1. Required billing rate, assuming a given level of profit, hours, compensation, overhead, and realization factor
2. Required hours, assuming given level of profit, compensation, overhead, billing rate, and realization factor

Each section of the model is divided into worksheets, with sections within the worksheets themselves. The section names are located in the upper left-hand corner of each worksheet, underneath the name of the model. The section designations identify the print ranges that can be invoked at any time using normal Excel printing techniques.

If you have any questions or comments, you may contact me using the information below. For further information on the Iezzi Management Group, you are invited to visit my Web site at **www.iezzigroup.com**. Good luck!

John G. Iezzi
P.O. Box 1711
Richmond, VA 23218-1711
Voice: 804-775-6805
Fax: 804-775-6911
E-mail: jgiezzi@iezzigroup.com

Description of Model

The following definitions apply throughout this model:

- *Billable Hours.* The hours a timekeeper expects to charge during the year
- *Compensation.* Base salary, excluding bonuses or benefits
- *Overhead.* The amount of expenses, other than compensation, attributable to a timekeeper which would have been calculated in other analyses prepared by the firm, such as a profitability study at the practice area or billing attorney level. The amount derived from this calculation is converted into a percentage of compensation for purposes of the formulas.

◆ *Profit Margin.* Expected level of profit computed on a cash basis

◆ *Realization Factor.* Represents all of the various deductions that normally are subtracted from accrual-basis gross to get to cash-basis gross. Includes rate realization, billing realization, accounts receivable write-offs, and billing and collection timing differences.

Formula for Billing Rate Computation

The Billing Rate Computation is prepared from the assumptions noted on the schedule located in the worksheet named **RATE** (see page 42).

Based on these assumptions, the formula produces a billing rate of $193.18, which when combined with each of the other assumptions, produces a profit margin of 30 percent.

Any change in the assumptions produces a different billing rate and different profit percentage.

Formula for Billable Hours Computation

This part of the formula, shown in the worksheet **HOURS** (see page 43), calculates the level of billable hours necessary to achieve a given level of profit based on an already established, or presumed, billing rate. Again, any change in the assumptions such as desired profit, billing rate, and so on, produces a different required level of billable hours.

Examples

Some examples are provided in the worksheet **EXAMPLES** (see page 44). These can be expanded to include your own lawyers, and the information calculated by copying the various cells to the respective locations. Note that by using a profit percentage of 0.0, breakeven points can be calculated both as to hourly rate and billable hours.

Formulas

For those who are interested in how the algebraic formulas actually work, I refer you to the worksheet **FORMULAS** (see page 45) that details how the formulas are constructed and how the various assumptions relate to each other.

Appendix A
BILLING RATE FORMULA MODEL

BILLRATE FORMULA
RATE

FORMULA FOR BILLABLE RATE COMPUTATION

ASSUMPTIONS:

COMPENSATION		85,000 COPIES TO FORMULA
OVERHEAD	1.25	106,250 COPIES TO FORMULA
ESTIMATED NUMBER OF BILLABLE HOURS		1,800 COPIES TO FORMULA
DESIRED PROFIT MARGIN		30.0 COPIES TO FORMULA
REALIZATION FACTOR		0.15 COPIES TO FORMULA
BILLING RATE		?

Rate Computation

				ANALYSIS
Profit Percentage	30.0	Gross Income		347,727
Realization Factor	15	Less Compensation		(85,000)
(Calculation)	55	Less Overhead		(106,250)
Expenses	106,250	Less: Realization factor		(52,159)
Overhead (x.xx)	1.25			
(Calculation)	2.25	Net Income		104,318
(Calculation)	24.44			
		Profit Percentage		30.00
Value of Factor	4.1			
Annual Compensation	85,000			
Billable Hours	1800			
Rate	**193.18**			

BILLRATE FORMULA
HOURS

FORMULA FOR BILLABLE HOURS COMPUTATION

ASSUMPTIONS:

COMPENSATION		85,000 COPIES TO FORMULA
OVERHEAD	1.25	106,250 COPIES TO FORMULA
ESTIMATED NUMBER OF BILLABLE HOURS	?	
DESIRED PROFIT MARGIN		30.0 COPIES TO FORMULA
REALIZATION FACTOR		0.15 COPIES TO FORMULA
BILLING RATE		193.18 COPIES TO FORMULA

Hours Computation ****Profit Calculation****

Annual Salary	85,000	Annual Salary	85,000
Profit Percentage	30.0	Realization Factor	15
Overhead Factor (x.xx)	1.25	Billable Hours	1,800
(Calculation)	2.25	Overhead (xxx)	1.25
Realization Factor	15	Billing Rate	193.18
Calculation	55	Overhead Amt	106,250
Billing Rate	193.18		
(Calculation)	24.44		
(Calculation)	4.1		**ANALYSIS**
(Calculation)	347,727	Gross Income	347,727
		Less Salary	(85,000)
Hours Required	**1,800**	Less Overhead	(106,250)
		Less: Realization factor	(52,159)
		Net Income	104,318
		Profit Percentage	30.00

BILLRATE FORMULA
EXAMPLES

EXAMPLES OF BILLING RATE CALCULATIONS

ATTORNEY	COMPENSATION	OVERHEAD PERCENT 1.25	OVERHEAD AMOUNT	PROFIT PERCENT	REALIZATION PERCENT	BILLABLE HOURS	CALC	FACTOR	CHECK	CHECK	COMP RATE	BILLING RATE
1	60,000	1.25	75,000	30	4	1,500	29.33	3.4	100	340.9	40.00	**136.36**
2	75,000	1.25	93,750	30	4	1,800	29.33	3.4	100	340.9	41.67	**142.05**
3	85,000	1.25	106,250	30	4	1,900	29.33	3.4	100	340.9	44.74	**152.51**
4	65,000	1.25	81,250	30	4	1,700	29.33	3.4	100	340.9	38.24	**130.35**
5	70,000	1.25	87,500	30	4	2,000	29.33	3.4	100	340.9	35.00	**119.32**

ATTORNEY	BILLING RATE	BILLABLE HOURS	GROSS REVENUES	COMP	OVERHEAD	REALIZATION	NET PROFIT	PROFIT PERCENT
1	136.36	1,500	204,545	-60,000	-75,000	-8,182	61,364	30
2	142.05	1,800	255,682	-75,000	-93,750	-10,227	76,705	30
3	152.51	1,900	289,773	-85,000	-106,250	-11,591	86,932	30
4	130.35	1,700	221,591	-65,000	-81,250	-8,864	66,477	30
5	119.32	2,000	238,636	-70,000	-87,500	-9,545	71,591	30

NOTE: This is only a portion of the worksheet

BILLRATE FORMULA
FORMULAS

FACTORS FOR BILLING RATE CALCULATION

COMPENSATION	85,000
OVERHEAD AS PERCENTAGE OF COMPENSATION	1.25
AVERAGE NUMBER OF BILLABLE HOURS	1,800
DESIRED PROFIT MARGIN	30.0
REALIZATION FACTOR	15.0

	AS PERCENT OF SALARIES	**AS PERCENT BILLING VALUE**
SALARY	1.00	
OVERHEAD	1.25	
PROFIT		30.0
REAL		15.0

FIRST:

FIND PERCENTAGES THAT SALARY AND OVERHEAD BEAR TO TOTAL
BILLING VALUE:

SALARY + 1.25 OF SALARY = 100 - 30 - 15

SALARY AS % OF BILLING VALUE =		24.4
OVERHEAD AT	1.25	30.6

THE PERCENTAGES OF BILLING VALUE ARE THUS:

SALARY	24.4
OVERHEAD	30.6
PROFIT	30.0
REALIZATION	15.0
TOTALS	100.0

SECOND:

CONVERT PROFIT MARGIN AND REALIZATION AS PERCENT OF SALARIES.

SALARY	24.4	1.00	4.1
OVERHEAD		1.25	
PROFIT		1.23	
REALIZATION		0.61	
TOTALS		4.1	

FACTORS FOR BILLING RATE CALCULATION—*(Continued)*

SALARY	85,000
HOURLY COMP RATE	47.22
BILLING RATE FACTOR APPLIED AGAINST COMP RATE	4.1
TOTALS	347,727
HOURS	1,800
RATE	193.18

TEST:

HOURS		1,800
RATE		193.18
BILLABLE VALUE		347,727
SALARY		85,000
OVERHEAD		106,250
REALIZATION	0.15	52,159
PROFIT		104,318
PROFIT MARGIN		0.30

EXPENSES

5

The next step in financial management (actually, this process is ongoing during the budget preparation) is to determine the expenses for the year. There are various methods of doing this, from zero-based budgeting (accounting for every dollar spent) to the "Kentucky Windage" system (adding x percent to last year). Most firms operate somewhere between these two extremes. Fortunately, the zero-based system can be used effectively for those expenses that make up the largest percentage of the total.

Is Expense Reduction Possible?

There is no question that expense control (as opposed to expense reduction) is an important subject, and one that will be discussed. However, firms have shown—on many occasions—that the time devoted to saving a few dollars on expenses is rarely, if ever, commensurate with the amount of money saved, particularly when the time could have been spent increasing revenues.

A firm can do many things to keep expenses to a minimum. Different types of copying equipment can be considered, saving a few cents per copy; or a cheaper vendor can be found for the firm's letterhead and file folders. I knew of one firm years ago that issued #3 pencils instead of #2 pencils because they lasted longer. However, when all the expense savings are taken into consideration, the effect on a firm's overall financial picture isn't significant.

Expense Dollar: Leading Law Firms	
Payroll and Benefits	67.6
Occupancy	11.8
Other	11.4
License Fees, Professional Dues, Insurance, Library	09.2

Figure D

The main problem with expense reduction in a service-oriented business is that there are only two major items of expense: payroll and occupancy. Any significant reductions must come from these two areas. The relationship of these two items to overall expenses can be seen in Figure D, which shows the expense dollar of some of the leading law firms in the country. Note that payroll (with related benefits) and occupancy make up 79.4 percent of the operating expense dollar. These are the only two areas where an impact on the expense levels can be made.

Even more of a firm's expenses, besides occupancy and compensation, are fixed. To prove this, take all your firm's expenses and separate them into fixed costs and variable costs. Look at each expense carefully and determine where substantial cuts can be made. You will quickly realize that there is a higher percentage of fixed costs in a law firm than you might initially suspect. I'm talking about many of the expenses that affect the level of service within the organization such as continuing legal education (CLE), practice development, insurance, telephone service, messenger service, accounting department services, firm meetings, bar meetings, recruiting, and so on. Most of these expenses are fixed unless a firm is willing to change its lifestyle and, more importantly, change the level of service it provides for its clients.

So the question is not whether expenses can be reduced, but whether current expenses can be better utilized to more fully realize a firm's gross income potential. In other words, how can a firm take the same amount of overhead dollars and spread them over more gross income dollars to realize a greater profit at perhaps the same net cost to the clients?

Functional Expense Categories

It's a good idea to place the expenses into functional categories, which makes them easier to analyze and include in periodic reports. The major expense categories, the manner in which the budget is usually determined, and some thoughts about controlling these costs are discussed below.

Compensation

As noted, compensation, along with benefits, represents your firm's largest expenditure. Thus, when cuts need to be made, this is where you look first. An examination of various surveys over the past several years shows that the ratio of staff to lawyers has not changed much and is 1.2:1 to 1.4:1. This comes after firms have invested millions of dollars in technology that was supposed to reduce the number of people and pay for itself over a short time. This hasn't happened. What has happened, in many cases, is that low-paid, low-skilled employees have been replaced with much higher-paid, higher-skilled employees who manage this new technology.

I'm convinced—although I may not fully see it in my lifetime, it is beginning to occur—that the position of legal secretary as we know it today will disappear. Replacing it, probably on a 1:4–1:5 basis, will be an administrative assistant working for several lawyers and managing the technology available to them. This will be a highly skilled and highly paid position, but will cost less than the legal secretary positions it replaces. This is already happening at many firms as the new crop of computer-literate lawyers begins their careers. It is no longer taboo for lawyers to create their own work product.

It's difficult to convince a firm to spend $100,000 today for a payback that may take several years to realize. There needs to be a constant educational process so that a firm's lawyers can be kept abreast of how technology can affect their work style and translate into savings that ultimately will be converted into higher profits. This isn't always easy to do.

If this does occur, eventually the administrative staff will reduce accordingly. In the meantime, these steps can be taken to keep the nonlawyer group to a minimum:

1. Maintain training of your staff so they perform at maximum levels.
2. Pay competitive salaries and provide competitive benefits to reduce turnover.
3. Don't tolerate marginal employees. Have an evaluation system that permits the firm to sort out the nonperformers, and a system for handling their departure as quickly as possible.
4. Let the work flow to the person who can do it the best for the least amount of money. Don't use highly paid secretaries or administrative personnel to copy documents or deliver mail.
5. Use temporary agencies to handle peak loads. Find an agency you like, make sure it understands your requirements, and then give it all your business. You may be surprised at the quality of people you get under those circumstances. Once you hire permanent people, Murphy's Law comes into play—work expands to fill available time.

6. Seriously consider using outside sources for many administrative tasks, such as the copy center, mail, messenger services, and managing the firm's technology. This is less expensive in the long run, and head count will reduce, along with the corresponding benefits.
7. Make use of controlled overtime, or it will get out of hand. Make certain there is a formal approval process and be wary of employees who constantly incur excessive overtime.

Payroll Taxes

Payroll taxes change in direct proportion to the number of people hired or terminated. There's not much that can be done about them, since the amounts are out of a firm's control. Using outside sources for some administrative tasks reduces the payroll-tax expense, although obviously it is built into the facility manager's charge structure. There are also benefit plans that permit a firm to reduce gross earnings and thus payroll taxes, if the amounts are paid in connection with a qualified benefit plan, such as a Section 125 plan.

Other Personnel Costs

Other personnel costs include all the benefit costs such as medical insurance, life insurance, disability insurance, pension plan, and so on. This area has been under attack recently, not only in law firms but in other businesses as well. Medical costs are the most significant, and everyone is trying to invent the new mousetrap that provides quality benefits at the best price. A firm must remain competitive with other firms in the geographic area. You don't want to lose highly trained, highly motivated employees to the firm across the street because your medical plan calls for a disproportionate share of the cost to be paid by your employees.

Additionally, look seriously at some type of cafeteria plan that allows employees to pick benefits. I remember years ago when we had to cover employees who were also covered by their spouses' policies. This was an unnecessary expense on our part, and gave employees a benefit that they didn't need or want. Likewise, today, not everyone wants or needs the same benefits, and offering employees the opportunity to pick and choose for themselves may reduce your costs while meeting their needs more directly.

Depreciation and Amortization

There isn't much that can be said about depreciation and amortization, since this is more of a tax issue than an accounting issue. Ultimately, each partner or shareholder in your firm ends up preparing a 1040 form just like you do. If you can legally reduce the gross earnings of the owners from a tax standpoint, as opposed to a book or cash standpoint, then you've accomplished just as much as reducing expenses on the firm's books. This is particularly important if the firm can shift certain after-tax expenses such as automobiles, parking, club dues, and entertainment to pretax expenses by having the firm pay for them. This way a partner can make less money but have more personal disposable income available. The firm needs to constantly review these rules with its accountants to make certain that the owners are receiving all of the latest tax benefits.

Occupancy Costs

Occupancy costs are the second-largest expense after compensation and benefits. These include rent, maintenance of the premises, alterations to the space that are not capitalized, and moving costs. Rent costs are generally controlled in the lease-negotiation process. Certain issues need to be reviewed carefully, particularly those that relate to rent-escalation provisions for operating expenses. In most cases, the lease provides two rent figures: base rent, which is subject to the escalators and usually tied to the consumer price index, and operating expenses, which is the landlord's expenses for operating the building.

Many leases combine these into one amount. Thus, a firm could end up paying the percentage escalation on the total rent, including operating expenses, in addition to the operating-expense increase over the prior year. This is equivalent to a tax on a tax. Unfortunately, although most firms pay close attention to the rent, they don't pay enough attention to the operating expenses. Over a long lease, these could actually be more than the base rent on the premises.

Another major unnecessary cost is using air conditioning services during off hours. Make certain that the lease calls for extended hours of operation and that the lawyers and staff understand the costs involved in turning on the air conditioning on Sunday, simply because some partner wants to come in for thirty minutes to organize his office.

Another suggestion is to hire a local contractor to perform maintenance tasks such as painting, electrical work, carpentry, and so on, if the building management doesn't provide that service. Even if it does, the building management can be kept honest by the threat of using an outside contractor to do the work.

Professional Expenses

Professional expenses include lawyer-associated costs such as bar dues, CLE, and attendance at bar-sponsored and other social, educational, and professional functions. This category isn't significant, and the current year's expenses are usually based on a percentage increase over the prior year, or on a per-lawyer amount. A consideration here is whether a firm wants to have some type of allowance system. Experience has shown that there are often so many exceptions to the allowance that the system doesn't work. If a firm can strictly enforce a system like this, then it may reduce expenses somewhat; but in the overall scheme of things, this isn't a big number. One of the issues that a firm faces frequently is expenses for spouses at various social functions. This isn't usually a lot of money, but it can become a very irritating issue if some people get their spouse's expenses paid and others don't.

Firms in states with mandatory CLE have also seen this expense increase over the past several years.

Practice Development Activities

Firms spend considerable sums on practice development or marketing activities and much of it is spent foolishly, without any plan or direction for helping a firm get business. This category includes client entertainment, trade association activities, client seminars sponsored by the firm, professional marketing consultants, and firm publications.

My advice is to make sure that a firm has a marketing plan in place, with a budget that is examined monthly, and that somebody is held accountable for the dollars spent. This area has seen significant abuse as lawyers attempt to justify various expenses as marketing costs. The fact is that marketing is a skill that very few lawyers have. The dollars should be channeled to those who can do the best job and get the biggest bang for the buck. Unfortunately, in the interest of peace and harmony, many firms allocate the money to all the lawyers, many of whom have no idea how to use it in ways that bring in more clients.

This accountability also extends to justifying expenses for firm brochures, outings, and parties that are planned under the guise of marketing. In today's marketing world, firms have concluded that expensive brochures are a waste of money and instead have devoted a significant amount of marketing money to enhancing their Web sites. This is where firms are found and reviewed for potential work either by clients or by other lawyers for referrals. In my opinion, the two most effective marketing tools are newsletters and seminars. These appear to give the most exposure to a firm's expertise and usually are very cost-effective.

Recruiting

Depending on your firm's size, recruiting may or may not be a separate functional expense category. This category includes all expenses related to the recruiting of professional staff personnel, excluding the actual time that lawyers and staff spend on recruiting activities. Included are travel expenses of recruiters and candidates, entertainment expenses for candidates, and perhaps the law clerk summer program. My general experience has shown that more money is spent here than needs to be, particularly with a summer clerkship program. The issue is not so much the actual dollars as it is the perception. Nothing makes people angrier than to have firm members complain about expenses, then the next day take the law clerks out on a fishing trip.

Most law firms do a lousy job of controlling recruiting expenses. They continue to believe in the idea that if somehow they cut back, it hurts their image at the various law schools or in the community. That may be true, but in all my years I've never seen it. The fact is, most clerks don't want to be wined and dined. They just want interesting work and enough exposure to a firm to make an employment decision. This has been confirmed in interviews with young clerks over the years. Regardless, these expenses need to be budgeted, and someone must be held accountable.

General Staff Expenses

This usually minor category of expenses includes many of the staff-related costs such as firm outings, partnership meetings, educational expense reimbursements, ads and agency fees associated with nonlawyer recruiting, messenger service, and firm meetings. The biggest expense is probably partner meetings, particularly if a firm has an annual retreat. However, this can be money well spent, provided the retreat has a theme, and something is actually accomplished besides complaining about the messenger service.

Firm activities bind a firm together, improve morale, and can be justified easily, particularly if the entire family is included in the event.

Library

Although it doesn't involve a lot of money, there are abuses in the payment of items for a firm's library. Most of it comes from lack of a control system to make certain that duplicate payments are not made to publishers. Most firms can't afford a full-time librarian, so the job of reviewing invoices falls on a bookkeeping clerk with no idea what the item is, who got it, or whether the invoice should be paid. Often it's paid, sometimes once, sometimes twice, sometimes three times.

This category also includes charges for legal research, which can be controlled through a system of charging clients where appropriate. The suggestion here is that for billing purposes, a firm treat automated research tools such as Lexis and Westlaw as lawyer expenses for billing purposes rather than as out-of-pocket expenses. Using this type of system permits faster billing for this service, higher and faster cost-recovery, and allows a firm to obtain reports on usage the same way it receives reports on lawyer performance.

One more item of note is to be careful regarding expenditures for library materials that are for a specific lawyer. Lawyers love to build up their own libraries in their offices, or worse yet, in their homes. This creates all kinds of problems in controlling books and periodicals, particularly with respect to keeping up with loose-leaf services. There are now companies that provide out-sourced loose-leaf filing services. This is more cost effective than having someone at the firm perform this service.

Office Supplies

Generally, a firm administrator has more control over office supplies and services than any other expense. It is interesting that almost all of the résumés I've received from administrators looking for work mention how much money they've saved their firms in office supplies.

Many of these expenses can be seen as image enhancers, including how your stationery looks, how good your copies are, the type of dining services in a firm, and so on. Each firm has a different image, and costs are affected accordingly. The costs should be in line with the image a firm wishes to project.

One of the more recent cost-saving ideas in the area of office supplies is to replace the firm's custom-printed letterhead with one produced using the in-house technology systems, and printed when the letter is printed. This saves literally thousands of dollars each year and makes changing the letterhead very easy and inexpensive. The raised lettering effect disappears; however, do you know anyone who rubs a finger over the letterhead when reading a letter? Envelopes can be printed in the same manner.

Telecommunications

Telecommunications includes the costs for the telephone system (including maintenance), fax, and postage. Probably no area is more confusing than trying to interpret telephone rates. Everybody wants your business, and you will go either with the company that makes your belly feel the best or, in many cases, with a company your firm represents.

Other Operating Expenses

This is a catchall category that includes expenses such as contributions; professional liability and other insurance; state and local taxes; professional fees to accountants, other lawyers, or consultants; interest expenses; and miscellaneous items not included elsewhere. The major expense is malpractice insurance, and it fluctuates from year to year, sometimes rather drastically. A firm can generally save some money by increasing the deductible and taking the chance that nothing is going to happen. Each firm has to weigh its risk based on the types of legal services that it provides. It's one thing if all your firm does is residential house closings; it's another if it does a large amount of Securities and Exchange Commission work. This expense was seriously impacted by the events of 9/11/01.

Contributions should be geared to a firm's marketing effort, so that these costs correlate with how a firm wants to be regarded in the community and the extent to which support of charitable activities translates into business. Keep in mind that as of this writing, contributions are not tax deductible.

Interest expense is guided by a firm's philosophy on partner capital. If a firm is owned by the partners, the interest expense is much lower than if a firm is owned by the bank. Each firm has a different view on this matter. In addition, at those firms where the partner capital accounts are disproportionate to income percentages, there should also be a budgeted expense to pay interest on partners' capital. In those firms where the percentages are the same, there is no such expense.

Technology

Technology charges include supplies and maintenance associated with a firm's various automated systems such as individual workstations, laptops, accounting systems, database management tools, and so on. This expense has grown over the past several years, and, in many larger firms, has gotten out of control. In many cases, because the firm administrator is busy with other issues, someone else takes over technology and builds a huge empire. Make certain that this doesn't happen in your firm. The most significant item in this list is usually maintenance, which should be reviewed annually. If possible, competing vendors should be considered, if for no other reason than to keep the current contractor honest.

As noted earlier and discussed more fully later, there are various surveys that permit firms to examine their expenses in relation to other firms of the same size and geographical area. This comparison doesn't necessarily mean that the expenses need to change, but it gives you some way of determining how your firm's expenses deviate from the norm. Again, the level-of-service consideration generally establishes the level of expenses.

Monthly Accruals

In order to spread the cost of major expenses throughout the twelve-month period and avoid significant fluctuations in net income, a firm may decide to record certain expenses on a monthly basis by setting up accrued expense accounts. For example, this means that a major expense paid for in September is prorated on a monthly basis. When eventually paid, the charge is made to the accrual account rather than to the expense account. In the twelfth month, the accrual account would be adjusted to zero.

Expenses that are candidates for this treatment include:

- Malpractice and other insurance
- Associate and staff bonuses

- ◆ Staff pension-plan expense
- ◆ Partner pension-plan contributions charged to draw accounts
- ◆ Significant professional fees to lawyers, accountants, and consultants, if known at budget time
- ◆ Other major expenditures deemed appropriate for the twelve-month prorating process

Expense Ratios

Before leaving the subject of expenses, I want to address briefly the subject of expense ratios, a subject that many lawyers think they know a lot about but actually understand very little.

The expense ratio is simply a function of gross revenues; it attempts to depict the amount of expenses required to support a given level of gross income. Each firm needs to determine an acceptable level and work towards achieving it or improving upon it. Over a long period, the expense ratio fluctuates significantly as a firm grows. Starting from day one, the overhead in relation to gross decreases as the gross catches up with the available capacity. As growth occurs, more space, more people, and more peripheral administrative support are acquired—more than is actually needed at that time. This tends to have the effect of increasing the ratio. Gross then begins catching up with the capacity, and the cycle starts all over again. As a practical matter, if the expense ratio is not acting this way, then a firm is simply putting out fires and not planning for the future.

Perhaps equally or more important than developing the ratio on a cash basis is examining it on an accrual basis. An expense ratio on a cash basis is materially affected not only by the timing of collections but also by the improper matching of current-year expenditures against prior-year revenues. As a financial manager, the question you want answered is "what does it cost the firm to produce its basic product—the billable hour?" Therefore, this expense ratio is more indicative of how a firm is performing *vis-a-vis* expenses in relation to gross income dollars, represented by the value of time worked. As emphasized earlier, expenses are being incurred to support billable hour production and not cash collections.

Many lawyers ask why one firm's expense ratio is different from that of another firm. Don't get hung up on this issue. First of all, it's important to compare apples to apples; that is, determine whether the other firm's ratio includes or excludes associate salaries and benefits, partners' compensation, and the like. Different firms have different ways of computing the ratio, and before making any comparison it's important to know if everyone is playing by the same set of rules.

Your ultimate concern is to review the expense ratio on the accrual basis. You need to know how your firm is doing in spreading the same amount of overhead dollars over more income dollars and thus making a greater profit at perhaps the same net cost to clients.

As a practical matter, as noted earlier in this chapter, once a firm matures beyond a certain point there is very little that can be done to reduce expenses unless a firm is willing and prepared to reduce its level of service. It cannot reduce expenses and retain the same level of service unless it is already overstaffed, which is not the case in most mature firms.

Contribution to Owner Compensation

In a professional services firm, much of the work is performed by the owners, who are essentially paid the net income of the organization. Therefore expense ratios can better be analyzed on the basis of contribution to owner compensation. This is done by looking at expenses in relation to accrual-basis gross revenues, as noted earlier. What is left essentially represents net income, or the owner's share of the excess of revenues over expenses. A firm looks for a 40 to 45 percent contribution to the bottom line, which is the remaining portion of this excess after deductions for all expenses except owner compensation.

Client Cost Recoveries

This chapter has not addressed the issue of cost-recovery devices for what are generally referred to as "soft costs," such as copying, phone, fax, and so on. This is because the trend around the country is for firms to get out of the copying business, phone business, and postage business and simply practice law. Clients hate to be charged for what they perceive as nickel-and-dime amounts, particularly when lawyers are already charging what may look like exorbitant rates. A firm should make the decision to discontinue this policy and in fact, use it as a marketing tool against those who continue the archaic practice of charge-backs. In addition, oftentimes the cost of people and equipment resources is greater than the amount of the recovery itself.

Evaluating Accounts Payable

Since most law firms use cash-basis accounting, and record expenses only when bills are paid rather than when the item was received or services performed, the issue of accounts payable is foreign to many law firm managers. However, these balances need to be monitored on a daily basis to make certain that bills are being paid on time so that a firm does not get a deadbeat reputation in the community in which it practices or have its credit rating adversely affected.

What should the accounts payable balance be, and how can it be properly monitored? One method of ascertaining the reasonableness of accounts payable is by applying a concept called "days expenses in accounts payable" or DEAP. It is a similar analysis to "days billings in accounts receivable," which is used to monitor collections and utilized in the budget process to more accurately predict cash receipts.

The concept of DEAP is to correlate outstanding payables with expenses, exclusive of those related to payroll (which includes all compensation paid along with the applicable payroll taxes and depreciation). Most companies strive to have a DEAP of thirty days, meaning that they are paying their current bills on time, recognizing that some payables could still exist in the older aging categories.

Let's assume that a firm's budgeted expenses for the year amount to $1,500,000, or $4,110 per day. At 30 DEAP, this means that the payables balance should be approximately $123,300. At 45 DEAP, the balance would be about $185,000.

By examining accounts payable on at least a monthly basis using the DEAP concept, a firm can make certain that its payables are not getting out of control, and that owners are not being paid at the expense of increasing payables beyond what should be considered a reasonable balance.

Evaluating Support Costs

Law firms have done a good job at developing various techniques for evaluating performance at the firm and lawyer level. From revenues-per-lawyer to billable hours, managers are able to review performance at the professional level and take corrective action to insure that profit objectives are met.

But this has not been the case in the support area, even though support costs are the majority of expenses the firm spends to support its revenue base. This discussion addresses how to evaluate support costs so that some control can be placed on these very significant expenses.

When you think about how revenues are generated in a service-related business, you soon realize that it is a team effort. Not only are the lawyers involved in the delivery of client services, but also the support staff, whether they are legal assistants, secretaries, or the timekeeper clerks who send out the monthly bills. Since this is the case, then it is possible to use some of the same valuation techniques for reviewing support staff costs that are used for the professional staff.

There are two major statistical criteria that can be used to determine whether support costs are in line. Be aware that since very few law firms keep these statistics, there is no published survey data for comparing your firm with others. Thus, you need to keep the information on some periodic basis within the firm, and then compare it from period to period to determine whether performance is improving or getting worse. As an alternative, you can get several firms to share this information, assuming you can do this without disseminating proprietary financial data about your firm.

The first analysis is to relate support costs to billable hour production. This is a take-off on the popular cost-per-billable-hour analysis that is usually performed at the firm level. To make this analysis, you need to know the total compensation of all support staff, and divide that into the total billable hours produced by the normal timekeepers for the same period. The net result is a cost-per-billable-hour for the support staff.

The support staff includes all nonlawyers, including legal assistants, secretaries, administrative personnel, and so on. Make certain that you subtract from the support costs any collections of time that the firm may have received. These are normally referred to as "handling" dollars; the information about these comes from a firm's timekeeping system.

As stated earlier, information on similar firms is probably not available. Thus, you will need to compare results within the firm for different time periods rather than compare your results with another firm's. If the data is available, you can start by going back to prior years and looking at your firm's trends.

The second analysis, equally as important, is to look at revenues in relation to support-cost dollars. In this analysis, you divide the total revenues of a firm by the support costs to obtain revenues-per-dollar-spent by a firm to support the level of revenue production.

These analyses are particularly important in evaluating practice-support costs at the practice group or department level. The results permit you to identify those groups in a firm that are using (or over-using) support staff to produce lower billable hours or a lower revenue stream.

CALCULATING NET INCOME

6

In the previous chapter I discussed the problem of trying to reduce expenses, concluding that the better approach is controlling expenses. Yet, the question still remains of how you can take the same amount of expenses or overhead and prorate it over more gross income to realize a greater net profit. Examining various realization analyses and expense write-offs aids in this process. In addition, a firm needs to consider its turnover rate and sources of other cash income in determining its final net income.

Realization

Realization rates determine how your firm has fared against standard values, both historically by comparing present rate structures to past ones, and in terms of cash flow by comparing cash collections against the corresponding value of billable hours. There are various realization analyses that must be examined.

Rate Realization

This is the realization percentage that results from comparing the actual rate charged to a client against a timekeeper's standard rate. In the case of Able, Baker, the rate realization has been budgeted at 98 percent. This means that on the average, the firm's lawyers reduce their standard rate by 2 percent on all client matters. This produces a rate variance of –$117,400.

Billing Realization

This amount is obtained by comparing the rate actually billed to the client against the rate charged to the client, after any rate discounts have been taken into account. The historical realization rate (applied at the time the bill is prepared) should be used for the current year's budget, unless you anticipate something unusual occurring during the year that precludes its use. For example, a firm may have cleaned out its work-in-process in the prior year and anticipates a higher billing realization rate as a result. Or it could have set higher-than-normal billing rates and, as a result, forecasts higher-than-normal net write-downs. Since this amount is significant to the overall budget, care should be exercised to use the most realistic percentage. If circumstances are not unusual, as described above, then the five-year historical average rate should be used.

At Able, Baker, a billing realization rate for the year of 95 percent is being used. This means that on the average, this firm will have write-downs of 5 percent on all bills sent to clients. The effect of this is to incur a billing variance of –$264,563.

It is important that these variances are understood and that they are not confused with each other. The rate variance is a client-intake issue, making certain that the firm has the client base to support its billing rate structure. The billing variance is a file-management issue, making certain that the work is performed efficiently and in accordance with a pre-arranged fee schedule with the client.

Write-Offs

Write-offs of accounts receivable can be calculated from a review of the aged trial balance of billed fees, which provides an estimate of the amount expected to be written off during the year. Some firms automatically write off outstanding bills after a certain period. This information, if known, is then used as the estimate for the year. Another method is to calculate a historical percentage of write-offs; the numerator is the historical write-offs for a period of time and the denominator is the value of the beginning accounts receivable and bills rendered. This percentage is then applied against the like amounts for the budgeted year. Generally, the percentage will be low. Most write-offs of fees take place in the billing process. Write-offs of accounts receivable generally occur when the bill is disputed or something happens to the client, such as a bankruptcy, that prevents the bill from being collected at its full amount. Able, Baker reviewed its accounts receivable trial balance and arrived at an estimated fee write-off of $125,000.

In the case of both realization and accounts receivable write-offs, a conservative but realistic approach is suggested.

Overall Cash Realization

The overall cash realization percentage represents the percentage of actual collections against the firm's standard value of billable time.

This rate is not used in the budget process but can be used to make estimates when your firm needs a "quick-and-dirty" analysis of its ability to turn billable dollars into cash. It is also a good barometer for ascertaining whether the financial management system is being properly managed. In Able, Baker, the cash realization rate is 81.7 percent, derived by dividing the total net collections of $4,799,094 by the standard billable value of time of $5,870,500. This is below average, since the more successful firms seek a cash realization percentage of around 90 percent.

Expense Write-Offs

Write-offs of billed and unbilled expenses are usually treated separately from fees since they have a direct effect on income, having been recorded as assets when added to the client's file. Generally, these write-offs involve the same clients included in the fee realization or fee accounts receivable calculated earlier.

In some firms, expenses are sometimes written off without affecting the fee amounts. While this may not be the rule, it does happen and should be accounted for. Without specific identification of client write-offs, an estimate can be used. A firm's accounting system should be able to age both billed and unbilled expenses and thus help form the basis for the estimate.

Some firms account for disbursements on the expense method rather than on the asset method. Under the expense method, all reimbursable cost recoveries such as copying, telephone, and postage remain expenses until they are collected from the client. Proponents of this system say it's better than the asset method because partners don't take into income those items that have not been collected in cash. My problem with this system is that there is a tendency for items to get lost in the system. Keeping track of what is being collected and what is being written off sometimes becomes a problem. As far as paying taxes prematurely, once the first year has passed, the only additional taxes paid are for those items that have increased from the year before. The benefits of using the asset system, in my opinion, far outweigh the disadvantages. As noted elsewhere, the recovery of these soft costs will soon disappear and this will no longer be an issue. On the other hand, hard costs, or those represented by actual check disbursements on behalf of clients, are recorded as assets and written off against income if deemed uncollectible.

Turnover

The next and probably most important ingredient in the budget process is turnover—predicting the time it will take a firm to convert billable time into bills and bills into cash. It's very significant in helping to achieve the desired level of profit.

Unfortunately, most law firm balance sheets are missing two of the most significant assets the law firm has: work-in-process and accounts receivable. Since most law firms are on a cash basis, *neither* of these items appears on periodic financial statements so that management can deal with them properly.

Everyone usually understands the income cycle: first, the time is worked; second, it is billed currently; and third, it is collected as quickly as possible. The evaluation of this process—converting a dollar's worth of time into a dollar's worth of cash—is the concept of turnover. Any retailer will tell you that turning over inventory is the only way to survive without extensive borrowing. Law firms are no different. Their inventory is their time, whether reflected as unbilled in work-in-process, or billed and not collected, resting in accounts receivable.

The turnover evaluation can be stated in a combined way as the number of months from time to cash, or in two separate statistics as time to bill and time to collect. The overall turnover calculation states the relationship of the amount of input to work-in-process during a period (hours multiplied by rates) to the total amount in work-in-process and accounts receivable at a point in time.

In Figure E, Able, Baker has calculated its ending work-in-process balance of $1,342,388 and its ending accounts receivable balance of $895,166, or a total investment in client services (ICS) of $2,237,553. Dividing the firm's total input for the year (gross income on the accrual basis) of $5,753,090 (after the rate

Work-in-Process (WIP) Turnover	
WIP at Beginning of Year	$880,560
Value Added	5,753,090
Billings	(5,026,699)
Net write-downs (Billing variance)	(264,563)
WIP at End of Year	1,342,388
Accounts Receivable at End of Year	895,166
Investment in Client Services = A	$2,237,553
Monthly Input ($5,753,090 divided by 12) = B	$479,424
Turnover Rate: A divided by B	4.7 months

Figure E

adjustment) by twelve months provides an average monthly input of $479,424. Dividing that into the total ICS balance gives the firm an overall turnover rate of 4.7 months. This means that on the average, it takes this firm 4.7 months to convert a dollar's worth of time into a dollar's worth of cash.

This overall rate can be further subdivided into a time-to-bill and a time-to-collect amount. Figure F reflects this analysis. Note that on the time-to-bill side, the relationship between the average monthly input of time to the work-in-process balance is determined. This yields a time to bill of 2.8 months. The collection counterpart relates the average day's billings to the accounts receivable balance. In this case, the average billings per day are $13,772; dividing that into the accounts receivable balance produces the days billings in receivables of 65.0 days. This means that on the average, it takes sixty-five days to collect a bill once it is issued.

In the budgeting process, you need to estimate the time to bill and time to collect. These numbers then go into the model and help to "force" out billings and collections amounts. As noted above, at Able, Baker, those numbers are 2.8 months for the time to bill and 65 days for the time to collect. This produces $5,066,699 as the firm's projected net bills to be rendered after application of the 95 percent realization factor. By applying the days billings number and taking into consideration the accounts receivable write-offs of $125,000, the collections for the year are projected at $4,799,094.

Figure G demonstrates the effect of a change in the time-to-bill amount. Note that, at 2.8 months, the bills-rendered amount is as originally budgeted. If the firm does a better job of billing and reduces that rate to 2.3 months, the net billings will increase approximately $228,000, to $5,254,426. Conversely, if the time-to-bill rate deteriorates to 3.5 months, the net billings are reduced by approximately $319,000, to $4,707,882.

Time to Bill	
Total Annual Input	$5,753,090
Monthly Input	$479,424
Ending Work-in-Process	$1,342,388
Time to Bill	2.8 months
Time to Collect	
Total Annual Billings	$5,026,699
Daily Billings	$13,772
Ending Accounts Receivable	$895,166
Time to Collect	65.0 days

Figure F

Effect of Time to Bill on Billings	
Beginning Work-in-Process	$880,560
Amount Added	5,753,090
Net Bills Rendered	(5,026,090)
Net Write-downs	(264,563)
Ending Work-in-Process at 2.8 months	$1,342,388
At 2.8 Months	
Net Bills Rendered	$5,026,699
At 2.3 Months	
Net Bills Rendered	$5,254,426
At 3.5 Months	
Net Bills Rendered	$4,707,882

Figure G

Effect of Days Billings on Collections	
Beginning Accounts Receivable	$792,560
Net Bills Rendered	5,026,699
Collections	(4,799,094)
Write-Offs	(125,000)
Ending Balance at 65.0 Days	$895,166
At 60 Days	$4,867,952
At 75 Days	$4,702,691

Figure H

The collection period also can have a dramatic effect on cash collections. In Figure H, note that at the sixty-five-day rate this firm produces $4,799,094 in collections.

If it does a better job of collecting and reduces its days billings to sixty days, its collections will likewise improve by $69,000. If it does poorly, and the days billings deteriorates to seventy-two days, the firm will lose approximately $96,000 in collections, which will directly affect the bottom-line average income for each shareholder.

Turnover drives the budget. In many cases, after all other avenues have been exhausted, improving turnover may be a firm's only choice for improving net income. However, recognize that improving the turnover rate has a one-time effect of increasing net income in the year in which the improvement takes place. From that point forward, the firm must maintain that rate or suffer a one-time deterioration in net.

Other Cash Income

The only item left in completing the assumptions for the budget model is other cash income. This primarily represents cash receipts other than for legal services, such as interest, sale of fixed assets, and so on. In some cases, this amount reflects the recovery of certain reimbursable expenses, principally associated with the copying department, which this firm does not capture. At Able, Baker, the other cash income amounts to $15,000. The model is now complete, and an estimated net income (as noted in Figure I) of $1,142,414 is now determined.

Income Statement	
Gross Income	$5,879,500
Rate Variance	(117,410)
Billing Variance	(264,563)
Accounts Receivable Write-Offs	(125,000)
Other Income (Deductions)	15,000
Expenses	(3,671,680)
Net Income—Accrual Basis	$1,706,847
Minus Increase in Work-in-Process	(461,828)
Minus Increase in Accounts Receivable	(102,605)
Net Income—Cash Basis	$1,142,414

Figure I

THE FINANCIAL PLANNING MODEL

7

Once all the assumptions are made, you can use a program to compute the budgeted amounts through to net income. This brings us to the use of the Financial Planning Model. The actual model is included as a Microsoft Excel file called **ABCDPC.xls** on the CD-ROM included with this book. Appendix A in this chapter contains a sample printout of the model. The instructions that follow lead you through the model and allow you to use your firm's information to create your own financial analysis.

Also included on the CD-ROM is the file **budsimple.xls,** which creates a budget for a firm using the bottoms-up approach. In this method, a firm decides what net income it wants to achieve, and the model determines whether that income level is possible, using the firm's financial information (see Appendix B in this chapter).

FINANCIAL PLANNING MODEL

Prepared by:
John G. Iezzi, CPA
Iezzi Management Group
1906 Hamilton St., Suite A
P. O. Box 1711
Richmond, VA 23218-1711
Phone: (804) 775-6805
Fax: (804) 775-6911
Email: jgiezzi@iezzigroup.com
www.iezzigroup.com

ABLE, BAKER, CHARLES & DOGG, PC
Financial Planning Model

TABLE OF CONTENTS

Overall Description of Model

This financial planning model, **ABCDPC.xls,** shows the calculations for the fictitious law firm of Able, Baker, Charles & Dogg, PC that are used to prepare the firm's annual budget, using certain assumed data. The example is for a one-office firm, but the model can be adapted to fit any situation, including firms with multiple offices where budgets are established for each office. When used in its entirety, the model prepares the following:

1. Budgeted net income on a cash basis to include the changes in work-in-process and accounts receivable that occur during a twelve-month period
2. A budget summary which emanates from the model to create a workable and easy-to-understand schedule for review by firm management
3. Using historical data, a monthly budget for billings, collections, and gross income (that is, the value of hours for all timekeepers during the year)
4. Using the monthly budget, the monthly net income budget after factoring in other income items and expenses
5. A volume/price analysis that isolates the extent to which the increase in gross income results from volume, (increased hours), or from higher prices (increased rates). This analysis enables the firm to make certain that its pricing structure is in line with the environment in which it operates, and that its utilization of that timekeepers are at a satisfactory level.
6. An annual cash flow analysis, taking into consideration acquisition of fixed assets, capital contributions, changes in various asset and liability accounts, debt changes, and partner distributions
7. Utilizing the budgeted billable hour information and the historic percentages, the monthly budgeted billable hours for shareholders, associates, and legal assistants

Each section of the model is divided into worksheets, with sections within the worksheets themselves. The section names are located in the upper left-hand corner of each schedule, underneath the name of the full model. The section designations identify the print ranges that can be invoked at any time using normal Excel printing techniques.

On the following pages are explanations of the various schedules that are produced, and the information that is required for their completion.

If you have any questions or comments, you may contact me using the information below. For further information on the Iezzi Management Group, you are invited to visit my Web site at **www.iezzigroup.com**. Good luck!

John G. Iezzi
P.O. Box 1711
Richmond, VA 23218-1711
Voice: 804-775-6805
Fax: 804-775-6911
E-mail: jgiezzi@iezzigroup.com

Information Required

The net income budget requires the following information, which can be found in the **INFO** section of the **HOWTO** worksheet, and is included here as Exhibit A. This information is required for the current year and should also include the prior year so that comparisons can be made, and the volume-price analysis can be prepared.

1. The full-time equivalent number of shareholders, associates, and legal assistants
2. The average billing rate for shareholders, associates, and legal assistants
3. The average billable hours for shareholders, associates, and legal assistants
4. The amount of other accrual income to be generated by those who are timekeepers but not partners, associates, or legal assistants. This includes litigation clerks, law clerks, librarians, litigation support personnel, and so on. This is generally an estimate based on historical information.
5. The work-in-process and accounts receivable balances at the beginning of the year
6. The billing realization percentage anticipated on bills rendered during the year. This represents the projected level of write-downs for the year.
7. The rate realization percentage, which is the amount by which clients will be charged (not billed) for an amount less than the standard hourly rates of the timekeepers
8. The average amount of time, represented in months, that the firm believes it will take to convert a dollar's worth of time into a bill. This number drives the billings for the period.
9. Write-offs of accounts receivable, which should come from an analysis of the aged trial balance prepared as of the end of the prior year

ABCDPC
INFO
The following information is required in order to complete
this financial model. Each of these amounts, titles, dates,
etc., copy over to the appropriate sections of the model
itself. It is suggested that a copy of this spreadsheet be
saved prior to performing any "what-if" calculations in
order to preserve the original budget estimates. The first
section is for the budget itself. The second section is for
completion of the Cash Flow Analysis.

NAME OF SPREADSHEET:	ABCDPC
NAME OF FIRM:	ABLE, BAKER, CHARLES & DOGG, P. C.
YEAR ENDING:	12/31/YY

	SHAREHOLDERS	ASSOCIATES	LEG ASSISTANTS
PRIOR YR. ACTUAL:			
AVERAGE NUMBER	7.0	6.7	4.8
AVERAGE HOURS	1610	1751	1250
AVERAGE RATE	200.25	175.68	62.58
CURRENT YEAR ESTIMATES:			
AVERAGE NUMBER	8.0	8.5	5.0
AVERAGE HOURS	1600	1750	1200
AVERAGE RATE	210.00	180.00	75.00

	PRIOR	CURRENT
OTHER ACCRUAL GROSS	52,850	55,000
BEG OF YR WIP	875,690	880,560
RATE REALIZATION %	0.975	0.980
BILLING REALIZATION %	0.936	0.950
BEG OF YR A/R	752,650	792,560
A/R WRITEOFFS	120,000	125,000
TIME TO BILL	3.0	2.8
TIME TO COLLECT	68.5	65.0
EXPENSES	2,976,889	3,671,680
OTHER CASH INCOME	10,250	15,000
PTR SHARE OF INCOME	900,000	1,087,500

CASH FLOW:	
BEGINNING CASH BALANCE	15,250
EXPECTED ENDING CASH BALANCE	45,000
EXPECTED PRINCIPAL PAYMENTS ON DEBT DURING THE YEAR	80,000
ANNUAL DEPRECIATION	35,000
EXPECTED CAPITAL CONTRIBUTIONS	75,000
BALANCE UNBILLED ADVANCES BEG OF YEAR	126,580
BALANCE UNBILLED ADVANCES END OF YEAR	115,265
(-INCREASE) DECREASE IN UNBILLED ADVANCES	11,315
FIXED ASSET ADDITIONS	10,000
BALANCE BILLED ADVANCES BEG OF YEAR	86,592
BALANCE BILLED ADVANCES END OF YEAR	100,520
(-INCREASE) DECREASE IN BILLED ADVANCES	(13,928)
NET CHANGE IN OTHER ASSETS/LIABILITIES	(5,000)
PERCENTAGE OF SHAREHOLDER DISTRIBUTIONS BY YEAR-END	100

Exhibit A

10. Days billings in receivables, or the estimated amount of time it will take to collect a bill once it is rendered to a client. This number is expressed in days, and drives the anticipated collections for the year.
11. Total expenses for the year. This estimate will generally be done at the same time that the overall budget is being prepared.
12. Other cash income items, which represents cash receipts that are not generated from client fees
13. Anticipated partner share of income based on amounts established for each partner at the beginning of the year. This in effect becomes the "partner salary" amount, which when compared against the actual budgeted net income, creates the anticipated bonus pool.
14. Anticipated cash information, which includes:
    a. Cash balance at the beginning of the year
    b. Debt increases or decreases during the year
    c. Depreciation for the year
    d. Changes in unbilled client advances
    e. Changes in billed client advances
    f. Additions to fixed assets
    g. Changes in other assets and liabilities
    h. Anticipated partner capital contribution for the year
    i. Estimated percentage of profits to be distributed by the end of the year
    j. Payment of prior year undistributed profits (if partnership form)

Once these amounts are keyed into the model, all calculations are performed automatically through to net income.

As indicated above, the number of months required to convert a dollar's worth of time into a bill, and the number of days necessary to collect a bill once it is rendered, are the driving forces that produce the most significant effect on net income once the rates and hours production are established. Performing "what-if" calculations on these numbers produces varying net income scenarios.

Annual Budget

The annual budget, located in the worksheet **BUDGET**, is prepared from the information provided above, identified as **BUDGET1** and **BUDGET2,** and included as Exhibits B and C.

Note that for this firm, the net income for the year is projected to be $1,142,414, compared to $970,697 for the prior year. Any changes in the assumptions located in the **INFO** section in the **HOWTO** worksheet affect the net income amounts.

```
ABCDPC
BUDGET1
                    ABLE, BAKER, CHARLES & DOGG, P. C.
                    BUDGET FOR YR ENDING                        12/31/YY
```

	12/31/YY	12/31/XX
SHAREHOLDERS		
NUMBER	8.0	7.0
HOURS	1600.0	1610.0
RATE	210.00	200.25
TOTAL	**2688000**	**2256818**
ASSOCIATES:		
NUMBER	8.5	6.7
HOURS	1750	1751.0
RATE	180.00	175.68
TOTAL	**2677500**	**2061025**
L/ASSTS:		
NUMBER	5.0	4.8
HOURS	1200.0	1250
RATE	75.00	62.58
TOTAL	**450000**	**375480**
OTHER	55000	52850
TOTAL ACCRUAL GROSS	**5870500**	**4746173**
ASSUMPTIONS:		
WORK IN PROCESS		
BEG OF YEAR	880560	875690
RATE REALIZATION	0.980	0.975
BILLING REALIZATION	0.950	0.936
NET GROSS	5753090	4627518
WIP TURNS	2.8	3.0
ACCOUNTS RECEIVABLE:		
BEGINNING OF YEAR	792560	752650
WRITE OFFS	125000	120000
DAYS BILLINGS	65.0	68.5
EXPENSES	3671680	2976889
OTHER CASH INCOME	15000	10250
PTR SHARE OF INCOME	1087500	900000
GROSS BILLS RENDERED	5291262	4346329

Exhibit B

```
ABCDPC
BUDGET2                                   12/31/YY          12/31/XX

WIP REPORT:
    BEG BALANCE                            880560            875690
    NET ADDED                             5753090           4627518
    NET BILLS RENDERED                   -5026699          -4068164
    NET WRITE DOWNS                       -264563           -278165

    ENDING BALANCE                        1342388           1156880

ACCTS RECEIVABLE:
    BEG BALANCE                            792560            752650
    NET BILLS RENDERED                    5026699           4068164
    COLLECTIONS                          -4799094          -3937336
    WRITE OFFS                            -125000           -120000

    ENDING BALANCE                         895166            763477

CALCULATION CHECK:
    ICS                                   2237553           1920357
    AVG INPUT                              479424            385627
    WIP BALANCE                           1342388           1156880
    TURNOVER                                  4.7               5.0
    WIP TURNS                                 2.8               3.0

    DAILY BILLS RENDERED                    13772             11146
    ACCOUNTS RECEIVABLE                    895166            763477
    DAYS BILLINGS                            65.0              68.5

GROSS INCOME SUMMARY:
    GROSS INCOME                          5870500           4746173
    RATE VARIANCE                         -117410           -118654
    BILLING VARIANCE                      -264563           -278165
    ACCTS REC WRITEOFFS                   -125000           -120000
    CHANGE IN ICS                         -564433           -292017

    NET COLLECTIONS                       4799094           3937336

    OTHER CASH INCOME                       15000             10250
    EXPENSES                             -3671680          -2976889

    NET INCOME                            1142414            970697
    S/H SHARE OF INCOME                  -1087500           -900000

    EXCESS (-DEFICIT)                       54914             70697

    NET INCOME PER SHAREHOLDER             142802            138671
```

Exhibit C

Summary Budget Information

The purpose of this schedule called **SUMBUD,** located in the worksheet **BUD-GET** and included here as Exhibit D, is to provide an easy-to-understand analysis of the budget for presentation and explanation to members of management. This enables management to take an overall look at key elements of the budget and make whatever changes they believe are required. All of the information for this schedule copies from other schedules; nothing has to be keyed in to produce this information.

Comparison of Budget versus Actual

This schedule, located in the worksheet **BUDGET,** compares the current year's budgeted information to the prior year's actual amounts, again so that management is able to reflect on the changes that will occur in the upcoming year. This schedule is identified as **SUPP1** and included here as Exhibit E.

All of the information for this schedule copies from other schedules; nothing has to be keyed in to produce this information.

Cash Flow Analysis

Using budgeted net income, and taking into account the various assumptions that were included in the **INFO** data, including depreciation, capital contributions, asset additions, changes in other asset and liability accounts, and so on, the model prepares the annual cash flow analysis, included in the worksheet **BUDGET**, identified as **CSHFLW,** and included here as Exhibit F.

The analysis already reflects an estimated capital contribution from the shareholders of $75,000. Many firms do have the ability to determine beforehand what this amount should be. If this was not included in the analysis, then this firm would not be able to make the level of distributions budgeted, or other changes would have to occur such as reducing debt payments, reducing fixed asset additions, and so on.

Using other more detailed information, the firm could also prepare a monthly cash flow statement that provides even more ability to manage the cash resources of the firm based on monthly cash needs that usually occur unevenly throughout the course of the year.

Included as Exhibit G, and identified as **CASHSUP,** is another version of the cash flow analysis that may be easier for nonaccountants to understand. It begins with fee revenues and ends with the estimated cash balance at the end of the year.

```
ABCDPC
SUMBUD
            ABLE, BAKER, CHARLES & DOGG, P. C.
            SUMMARY BUDGET INFORMATION
            FOR THE YEAR ENDING                    12/31/YY
```

	12/31/YY	12/31/XX
AVERAGE HOURS:		
SHAREHOLDERS	1600	1610
ASSOCIATES	1750	1751
LEGAL ASSISTANTS	1200	1250
AVERAGE RATE:		
SHAREHOLDERS	210.00	200.25
ASSOCIATES	180.00	175.68
LEGAL ASSISTANTS	75.00	62.58
TURNOVER:		
TIME TO BILL	2.8	3.0
TIME TO COLLECT	65.0	68.5
OVERALL TURNOVER	4.7	5.0
RATE REALIZATION:		
PERCENTAGE	0.980	0.975
AMOUNT	-117410	-118654
BILLING REALIZATION:		
PERCENTAGE	0.950	0.936
AMOUNT	-264563	-278165
INC (-DEC) IN WORK IN PROCESS	461828	281190
INC (-DEC) IN ACCOUNTS RECEIVABLE	102606	10827
INC (-DEC) CLIENT INVESTMENT	564433	292017
SUMMARY BUDGET:		
TOTAL GROSS INCOME	5870500	4746173
BILLS RENDERED	5026699	4068164
COLLECTIONS	4799094	3937336
EXPENSES	-3671680	-2976889
NET INCOME	**1142414**	**970697**
SHAREHOLDER DRAWS	-1087500	-900000
EXCESS (-DEFICIT)	**54914**	**70697**
NET INCOME PER SHAREHOLDER	**142802**	**138671**

Exhibit D

ABCDPC
SUPP1

ABLE, BAKER, CHARLES & DOGG, P. C.
COMPARISON OF BUDGET VS. ACTUAL
FOR THE YEARS ENDING　　　12/31/YY　AND　12/31/XX

	CURR YR BUDGET	PRIOR YR ACTUAL	VARIANCE AMOUNT Inc (-Dec)	VARIANCE PERCENT Inc (-Dec)
CASH GROSS (INC OTHER INCOME)	4814094	3947586	866507	22.0
EXPENSES (W/O SHAREHOLDERS)	-3671680	-2976889	-694791	23.3
NET INCOME	1142414	970697	171716	17.7
BILLABLE HOURS (TOTAL)				
SHAREHOLDERS	12800	11270	1530	13.6
ASSOCIATES	14875	11731.7	3143	26.8
LEGAL ASSISTANTS	6000	6000	0	0.0
BILLABLE HOURS (AVERAGES)				
SHAREHOLDERS	1600	1610	-10	-0.6
ASSOCIATES	1750	1751	-1	-0.1
LEGAL ASSISTANTS	1200	1250	-50	-4.0
BILLABLE VALUE OF HOURS:				
STANDARD VALUE	5870500	4746173	1124328	23.7
ACTUAL VALUE	5753090	4627518	1125572	24.3
RATE VARIANCE–AMT	-117410	-118654	1244	-1.0
RATE VARIANCE–%	0.020	0.025	0.005	
BILLS RENDERED	5026699	4068164	958536	23.6
BILLING VARIANCE–AMOUNT	-264563	-278165	13602	-4.9
BILLING VARIANCE–%	0.050	0.064	0.014	
ACCTS REC WRITEOFFS	-125000	-120000	-5000	4.2
TIME TO BILL–MONTHS	2.8	3.0	0.2	
TIME TO COLLECT–DAYS	65.0	68.5	3.5	
OVERALL TURNOVER–MONTHS	4.7	5.0	0.3	
SHAREHOLDER SHARE OF INCOME	1142414	970697	171716	17.7
SHAREHOLDER DISTRIBUTIONS	0	-970697	-970697	-100.0
UNDISTRIBUTED PROFITS	1142414	0	1142414	

Exhibit E

ABCDPC
CSHFLW

	ABLE, BAKER, CHARLES & DOGG, P. C.	
	CASH FLOW ANALYSIS FOR THE YEAR ENDED	12/31/YY

CASH FROM OPERATIONS:

NET INCOME (-LOSS)	1,142,414

ADD EXPENSES NOT REQUIRING OUTLAY OF CASH:

DEPRECIATION AND AMORTIZATION	35,000

CHANGES IN OPERATING ASSETS & LIABILITIES:

(-INC) DEC IN UNBILLED CLIENT ADVANCES	11,315
(-INC) DEC IN BILLED CLIENT ADVANCES	(13,928)
(-INC) DEC IN OTHER ASSETS/LIABILITIES	(5,000)

NET CASH PROVIDED BY OPERATING ACTIVITIES	**1,169,801**

INVESTING ACTIVITIES:
NET PURCHASES (-DISPOSALS) OF FIXED ASSETS	(10,000)

FINANCING ACTIVITIES:
NET INC (-DEC) IN DEBT	(80,000)

OTHER CHANGES:
INC (-DEC) IN SHAREHOLDER EQUITY	75,000

TOTAL OTHER CHANGES	**75,000**

NET INCREASE (-DECREASE) IN CASH	1,154,801

CASH BALANCE BEGINNING OF PERIOD	15,250

TOTAL AVAILABLE FOR DISTRIBUTION	**1,170,051**

CASH BALANCE END OF YEAR	(45,000)

AVAILABLE FOR DISTRIBUTION	**1,125,051**

NET INCOME FOR THE YEAR	1,142,414
AVAILABLE FOR DISTRIBUTION	(1,125,051)

UNDISTRIBUTED PROFITS END OF YEAR	**17,363**

Exhibit F

```
ABCDPC
CASHSUP          ABLE, BAKER, CHARLES & DOGG, P. C.
                 SUPPLEMENTAL CASH FLOW ANALYSIS
                 FOR THE YEAR ENDED                          12/31/YY

    RECEIVED IN FEE REVENUES                                 4,799,094
    RECEIVED IN OTHER INCOME                                    15,000
    BALANCE BEGINNING OF YEAR                                   15,250

    OTHER NET CASH RECEIVED (-PAID)                            (5,000)

    TOTAL GROSS CASH AVAILABLE                               4,824,344

    TOTAL EXPENSES EXCLUDING DEPRECIATION                  (3,636,680)

    TOTAL CASH AVAILABLE TO SHAREHOLDERS                     1,187,664

    CASH WAS ALSO USED FOR:
        NET CHANGE IN UNBILLED ADVANCES                         11,315
        NET CHANGE IN BILLED ADVANCES                         (13,928)
        PURCHASE OF FIXED ASSETS                              (10,000)
        NET CHANGE IN DEBT BALANCES                           (80,000)

    BALANCE LEFT TO PAY SHAREHOLDERS                         1,095,051

    PAYMENTS MADE TO SHAREHOLDERS                          (1,125,051)

    CASH OVER (-SHORT)                                       (30,000)

    ESTIMATED CAPITAL CONTRIBUTIONS                            75,000

    CASH BALANCE END OF YEAR                                  45,000
```

Exhibit G

Historical Monthly Information

The five-year history of firm activity, identified as **DATA** in the worksheet **DATA** and included here as Exhibit H, takes the prior five years' data for collections, billings and input (gross income), and calculates the relative amounts for each of the individual months based on the five-year average. Each year, as this is recalculated, one year is dropped off and the current year is added, so that the rolling five-year average is always maintained. Once the percentages are calculated, the system produces the monthly budgets for the items produced from the budget created earlier.

ABCDPC

DATA ABLE, BAKER, CHARLES & DOGG, P. C.
FIVE YEAR HISTORY OF ACTIVITY
AS OF 12/31/XX

THOUSANDS

	19AA	19BB	19CC	19DD	19XX	TOTAL	PERCENT	CUM %	BUDGET 12/31/YY
COLLECTIONS:									**4799094**
JANUARY	189454	200326	213018	226526	249843	1079167	6.3	6.3	304526
FEBRUARY	212227	224405	238622	253755	279874	1208882	7.1	13.5	341129
MARCH	250062	264411	281163	298993	329769	1424398	8.4	21.8	401945
APRIL	225117	238035	253116	269168	296873	1282309	7.5	29.4	361849
MAY	236300	249860	265690	282539	311621	1346010	7.9	37.3	379825
JUNE	296270	313271	333118	354243	390705	1687607	9.9	47.2	476218
JULY	241214	255056	271215	288414	318101	1374001	8.1	55.3	387723
AUGUST	254613	269223	286280	304435	335771	1450322	8.5	63.8	409260
SEPTEMBER	281873	298048	316931	337030	371720	1605603	9.4	73.3	453078
OCTOBER	258698	273543	290873	309319	341158	1473591	8.7	81.9	415826
NOVEMBER	199744	211205	224586	238829	263412	1137776	6.7	88.6	321064
DECEMBER	340087	359602	382385	406634	448490	1937199	11.4	100.0	546650
	2985660	**3156985**	**3356998**	**3569885**	**3937336**	**17006864**	**100.0**	**100.0**	**4799094**
BILLINGS:									**5026699**
JANUARY	200995	214598	233413	248832	267306	1165144	6.6	6.6	330289
FEBRUARY	249662	266559	289929	309081	332029	1447260	8.2	14.7	410262
MARCH	239851	256084	278536	296935	318982	1390387	7.8	22.6	394140
APRIL	278235	297065	323111	344454	370029	1612894	9.1	31.7	457214
MAY	275974	294652	320486	341656	367023	1599790	9.0	40.7	453500
JUNE	265444	283409	308257	328620	353019	1538750	8.7	49.4	436197
JULY	247110	263834	286966	305922	328636	1432467	8.1	57.4	406068
AUGUST	263145	280954	305587	325774	349961	1525422	8.6	66.0	432418
SEPTEMBER	258167	275639	299806	319610	343340	1496561	8.4	74.5	424237
OCTOBER	221899	236917	257689	274711	295107	1286322	7.3	81.7	364640
NOVEMBER	268843	287038	312204	332828	357539	1558451	8.8	90.5	441781
DECEMBER	289638	309240	336353	358572	385194	1678997	9.5	100.0	475953
	3058962	**3265988**	**3552336**	**3786995**	**4068164**	**17732445**	**100.0**	**100.0**	**5026699**
GROSS VALUE OF BILLABLE TIME:									**5870500**
JANUARY	304470	313656	323843	345008	375095	1662071	8.1	8.1	475848
FEBRUARY	313874	323343	333845	355663	386680	1713404	8.4	16.5	490544
MARCH	335300	345417	356635	379943	413077	1830371	8.9	25.4	524032
APRIL	336895	347060	358331	381750	415042	1839078	9.0	34.4	526525
MAY	326138	335978	346890	369561	401789	1780356	8.7	43.0	509712
JUNE	318529	328139	338796	360938	392414	1738816	8.5	51.5	497819
JULY	301029	310111	320182	341108	370855	1643285	8.0	59.5	470469
AUGUST	296486	305431	315351	335961	365259	1618487	7.9	67.4	463370
SEPTEMBER	285519	294133	303686	323534	351748	1558620	7.6	75.0	446230
OCTOBER	321289	330982	341731	364065	395815	1753882	8.6	83.6	502133
NOVEMBER	313819	323287	333787	355601	386612	1713107	8.4	91.9	490459
DECEMBER	302878	312016	322149	343203	373133	1653380	8.1	100.0	473359
	3756225	**3869553**	**3995226**	**4256335**	**4627518**	**20504857**	**100.0**	**100.0**	**5870500**

Exhibit H

It is necessary to gather this information to the extent it is available.

There is no magic to the five years, except that this period of time avoids the problem of one particularly good or bad month significantly affecting the averages. The amounts are keyed in thousands of dollars.

Monthly Budgeted Income

Based on the monthly collections calculated in **DATA**, and taking into consideration other income and expense items and total expenses as assumed elsewhere, the model prepares the monthly net income budget for the overall firm. It is identified as **MONBUD** in the worksheet **BUDGET** and included here as Exhibit I. No additional keying of data is required to prepare this part of the budget as it is automatically calculated from items included elsewhere. It will change as amounts in the budget model change.

It is assumed that other income and expense items and total overall expenses occur ratably throughout the year. This may not be the case. If not, then the individual months need to be keyed in separately.

Monthly Billable Hours Budgets

By applying the historical percentages used in determining the monthly budgets for gross income, the model produces the billable hour budgets on a monthly basis for the shareholders, associates, and legal assistants. It is identified as **MONBUD** and included here as Exhibit I.

Volume-Price Analysis

The volume-price analysis uses prior-year actual numbers and current-year budgeted numbers to calculate the extent to which the increase in gross income on the accrual basis (the value of all hours) is resulting from increasing volume (hours production) or increasing prices (billing rates). It is identified as **VOLPCE** in the worksheet **BUDGET**, and included here as Exhibit J. This analysis is essential in order to achieve a competitive pricing structure and to make certain that hours utilization is at expected levels.

No inputting of data is required for this schedule as all information comes from previous calculations. This may be one of the most important, if not the most important, schedule in the model.

Monthly Financial Report Summary

This monthly financial report represents a summary of the financial data for the month and for the year to date. While not part of the model, it is presented

ABCDPC
MONBUD   ABLE, BAKER, CHARLES & DOGG, P. C.
                MONTHLY BUDGETS
                FOR THE YEAR ENDED   12/31/YY

	COLLECTIONS	OTHER INCOME	EXPENSES	NET INCOME	ACCUM NET	BILLINGS	CUM BILLINGS	GROSS INPUT	CUM GROSS	CUM COLLECTS
		15000	-3671680							
JANUARY	304526	1250	-305973	-198	-198	330289	330289	475848	475848	304526
FEBRUARY	341129	1250	-305973	36406	36208	410262	740550	490544	966392	645655
MARCH	401945	1250	-305973	97221	133429	394140	1134690	524032	1490424	1047599
APRIL	361849	1250	-305973	57126	190555	457214	1591905	526525	2016948	1409449
MAY	379825	1250	-305973	75101	265657	453500	2045405	509712	2526660	1789273
JUNE	476218	1250	-305973	171495	437152	436197	2481601	497819	3024480	2265492
JULY	387723	1250	-305973	83000	520152	406068	2887669	470469	3494949	2653215
AUGUST	409260	1250	-305973	104537	624689	432418	3320088	463370	3958319	3062475
SEPTEMBER	453078	1250	-305973	148355	773043	424237	3744325	446230	4404549	3515553
OCTOBER	415826	1250	-305973	111103	884147	364640	4108965	502133	4906682	3931380
NOVEMBER	321064	1250	-305973	16341	900487	441781	4550746	490459	5397141	4252444
DECEMBER	546650	1250	-305973	241926	1142414	475953	5026699	473359	5870500	4799094
TOTALS	4799094	15000	-3671680	1142414	1142414	5026699	5026699	5870500	5870500	4799094

MONTHLY BILLABLE HOURS BUDGETS

MONTH

	INPUT %	MONTH	YTD	MONTH	YTD	MONTH	YTD
			12800		14875		6000
JANUARY	8.1	1038	1038	1206	1206	486	486
FEBRUARY	8.4	1070	2107	1243	2449	501	988
MARCH	8.9	1143	3250	1328	3777	536	1523
APRIL	9.0	1148	4398	1334	5111	538	2061
MAY	8.7	1111	5509	1292	6402	521	2582
JUNE	8.5	1085	6595	1261	7664	509	3091
JULY	8.0	1026	7620	1192	8856	481	3572
AUGUST	7.9	1010	8631	1174	10030	474	4046
SEPTEMBER	7.6	973	9604	1131	11160	456	4502
OCTOBER	8.6	1095	10698	1272	12433	513	5015
NOVEMBER	8.4	1069	11768	1243	13676	501	5516
DECEMBER	8.1	1032	12800	1199	14875	484	6000

Exhibit I

here to provide a complete summary of financial activity for the month and year-to-date that permits management to view all of the major items of concern on one convenient schedule. This form is entitled **SUMMARY** and can be adapted for your firm's process of presenting monthly and year-to-date financial information. It is included here as Exhibit K.

ABCDPC
VOLPCE

ABLE, BAKER, CHARLES & DOGG, P. C.
VOLUME/PRICE COMPARISON
FOR THE YEARS ENDING 12/31/YY AND 12/31/XX

	BUDGET HOURS 12/31/YY	ACTUAL HOURS 12/31/XX	BUDGET AMOUNT 12/31/YY	ACTUAL AMOUNT 12/31/XX	CURRENT YEAR RATE
SHAREHOLDERS	12800	11270	2688000	2256818	210.00
ASSOCIATES	14875	11732	2677500	2061025	180.00
LEGAL ASSISTANTS	6000	6000	450000	375480	75.00
OTHER	1833	1976	55000	52850	30.00
TOTAL	**35508**	**30977**	**5870500**	**4746173**	**165.33**

INC/DEC
SHAREHOLDERS

HOURS	1530	HOURS	306383
AMOUNT	431183	RATE	124800
CYRATE	210.00		
PYRATE	200.25		
DIFF	9.75	TOT CHANGE	**431183**

ASSOCIATES

HOURS	3143.3	HOURS	552215
AMOUNT	616475	RATE	64260
CYRATE	180.00		
PYRATE	175.68		
DIFF	4.32	TOT CHANGE	**616475**

LEGAL ASSTS:

HOURS	0	HOURS	0
AMOUNT	74520	RATE	74520
CYRATE	75.00		
PYRATE	62.58		
DIFF	12.42	TOT CHANGE	**74520**

OVERALL CHANGE:

HOURS	4531	HOURS	694202
AMOUNT	1124328	RATE	430125
CYRATE	165.33		
PYRATE	153.21		
DIFF	12.11	TOT CHANGE	**1124328**

Exhibit J

ABCDPC
FIRMCARD

ABC LAW FIRM, PC
FIRM REPORT CARD
FOR THE PERIOD ENDING   XX/XX/XX

GRADING SYSTEM: POINTS
          EQUAL TO 95 PERCENT OR HIGHER   A   3
          85-94   B   2
          76-84   C   1
          70-75   D   0
          LESS THAN 70   F   -1

		ACTUAL	BUDGET	VARIANCE FAV (-UNFAV)	PERFORMANCE PERCENT	GRADE
BILLABLE HOURS	PARTNERS	6,348.5	6,592.0	-243.5	96.3	A
	ASSOCIATES	7,305.6	7,660.6	-355.0	95.4	A
	LEG ASSTS	2,896.5	3,090.0	-193.5	93.7	B
	TOTAL	16,550.6	17,342.6	-792.0	95.4	A
STANDARD VALUE OF BILLABLE TIME		2,886,354	3,024,480	(138,126)	95.4	A
ACTUAL VALUE OF BILLABLE TIME		2,799,764	2,963,990	(164,227)	94.5	B
RATE VARIANCE	AMOUNT	(86,591)	(57,727)	(28,864)	66.7	F
BILLINGS		2,265,954	2,481,601	(215,647)	91.3	B
BILLING REALIZATION	AMOUNT	(95,170)	(113,298)	18,128	119.0	A
ACCOUNTS RECEIVABLE WRITE-OFFS		(45,260)	(62,500)	17,240	138.1	A
TIME TO BILL (MONTHS)		2.8	2.5	-0.3	89.3	B
TIME TO COLLECT (DAYS)		68.0	65.0	-3.0	95.6	A
CASH RECEIPTS		$2,096,558	$2,265,492	-$168,934	92.5	B
EXPENSES		1,796,552	1,835,840	39,288	102.2	A
NET INCOME		300,006	437,152	(137,146)	68.6	F
OVERALL AVERAGE						B

Exhibit K

MODEL CHART OF ACCOUNTS

FOR A LAW FIRM

Appendix A
MODEL CHART OF ACCOUNTS

ABCDPC

> **ABCD LAW FIRM, P. C.**
> **CHART OF ACCOUNTS**

ASSETS

1000	CASH OPERATING
1010	CASH PAYROLL
1100	CASH SAVINGS
1150	PETTY CASH
1160	TRUST ACCOUNT #1
1165	TRUST ACCOUNT #2
1200	ACCOUNTS RECEIVABLE
1220	WIP
1240	CLIENT ADVANCES UNBILLED
1250	CLIENT ADVANCES BILLED
1400	FURNITURE & EQUIP
1410	COMPUTER EQUIPMENT
1420	COMPUTER SOFTWARE
1430	TELEPHONE EQUIPMENT
1440	AUTOMOBILES
1450	LEASEHOLDS IMPROVEMENTS
1500	A/D FURNITURE & EQUIPMENT
1510	A/D COMPUTER EQUIPMENT
1520	A/D COMPUTER SOFTWARE
1530	A/D TELEPHONE EQUIPMENT
1540	A/D AUTOMOBILES
1550	A/D LEASEHOLD IMPROVEMENTS
1590	A/DEPREC CURRENT
1600	ADVANCES TO EMPLOYEES
1620	ADVANCES TO SHAREHOLDERS
1700	PREPAID EXPENSES
1750	OTHER ASSETS

LIABILITIES AND OWNER EQUITY ACCOUNTS

2000	ACCOUNTS PAYABLE
2010	UNALLOCATED PAYMENTS
2015	GARNISHMENTS
2020	CLIENT ADVANCE DEPOSITS
2030	CLIENT TRUST ACCOUNTS
2100	FICA/MED WITHHELD
2120	FITW WITHHELD
2130	SITW WITHHELD
2140	FICA/MED PAYABLE
2150	ACCRUED PAYROLL TAXES
2200	LOANS FROM SHAREHOLDERS
2210	LINE OF CREDIT
2220	NOTES PAYABLE—SHORT TERM
2230	OTHER CURRENT LIABILITIES
2240	NOTES PAYABLE—LONG TERM
3000	MEMBER CAPITAL ACCOUNT

INCOME AND EXPENSES

4000	FEE INCOME
4050	FEES REFUNDED
4060	INTEREST INCOME
4070	MISC INCOME
5000	COMPENSATION—BASE—SHAREHOLDERS
5010	COMPENSATION—BONUSES—SHAREHOLDERS
5020	COMPENSATION—BASE—ASSOCIATES
5030	COMPENSATION—BONUSES—ASSOCIATES
5100	OUTSIDE LABOR
5120	COMPENSATION—SECRETARIES
5130	COMPENSATION—SECRETARIES—OT
5200	COMPENSATION—ADMINISTRATION
5250	COMPENSATION—ADMINISTRATION—OT
5300	COMPENSATION—PARALEGALS
5350	COMPENSATION—PARALEGALS—OT
5400	COMPENSATION—INTERNS

5450	COMPENSATION—PART TIME
5900	COMPENSATION—MISCELLANEOUS

PAYROLL TAXES

6010	FICA/MED TAXES
6020	OTHER PAYROLL TAXES

OTHER PERSONNEL COSTS

6100	GROUP LIFE INS
6110	GROUP DISABILITY INS
6120	GROUP HEALTH INS
6130	WORKERS COMP INS
6140	PENSION PLAN
6150	MEDICAL REIMBURSEMENT
6160	TEMPORARY OFFICE SERVICES
6170	PAYROLL PROCESSING

DEPRECIATION AND AMORTIZATION

6290	DEPRECIATION AND AMORTIZATION

OCCUPANCY COSTS

6300	RENT EXPENSE
6310	OUTSIDE FILES STORAGE
6320	MOVING EXPENSE—OFFICE
6340	M & R—OFFICE FACILITIES
6350	MINOR ITEMS OF FURNITURE AND EQUIPMENT
6360	EMPLOYEE PARKING
6370	UTILITIES
6390	OTHER OCCUPANCY COSTS

PROFESSIONAL ACTIVITIES

6400	MEETINGS PROFESSIONAL ORGANIZATIONS
6410	CLE—GENERAL
6420	MEETINGS—BAR ASSOCIATIONS
6430	MEETINGS—OTHER
6440	DUES & FEES—BAR ASSOCIATIONS

| 6450 | DUES & FEES—OTHER PROFESSIONAL ORGANIZATIONS |
| 6490 | OTHER PROFESSIONAL ACTIVITIES EXPENSE |

PRACTICE DEVELOPMENT ACTIVITIES

6500	ADVERTISEMENTS/LISTINGS
6510	CLIENT ENTERTAINMENT
6520	CLIENT DEVELOPMENT
6530	FIRM PUBLICATIONS
6540	FIRM SPONSORTED SEMINARS
6550	WEBSITE
6590	OTHER PRACTICE DEVELOPMENT ACTIVITIES

GENERAL STAFF EXPENSES

6600	FIRM MEETINGS
6610	ADMINISTRATIVE TRAVEL
6620	OUTINGS AND PARTIES
6630	EDUCATIONAL EXPENSES—EMPLOYEES
6635	ADS AND AGENCY FEES
6640	PROFESSIONAL RECRUITING EXPENSES
6650	AUTO LEASE
6655	OTHER AUTO LEASE EXPENSE
6660	EMPLOYEE GIFTS
6690	OTHER GENERAL STAFF EXPENSES

LIBRARY SERVICES

6700	GENERAL LIBRARY REFERENCE MATERIALS
6710	LIBRARY SUPPLIES
6720	AUTOMATED RESEARCH
6730	SUBSCRIPTIONS
6790	OTHER REFERENCE MATERIALS

OFFICE SUPPLIES AND SERVICES

6800	OFFICE SUPPLIES
6810	OUTSIDE PRINTING COSTS
6830	OUTSIDE COPYING EXPENSE
6840	COPYING EQUIPMENT
6845	COPYING CREDITS

6850	LEASED EQUIPMENT
6860	OFFICE CANTEEN SERVICES
6870	M & R EQUIPMENT
6880	OUTSIDE DELIVERY EXPENSE
6890	MISC OFFICE EXPENSE

TELECOMMUNICATIONS & POSTAGE

6900	TELEPHONE—FIXED COSTS
6910	TELEPHONE—TOLL COSTS
6920	CELLULAR SERVICE
6930	TELEPHONE—CREDITS
6940	FEDERAL EXPRESS
6950	POSTAGE
6990	OTHER TELECOMMUNICATIONS & POSTAGE EXPENSE

OTHER OPERATING EXPENSES

7000	PROFESSIONAL LIABILITY INSURANCE
7010	INSURANCE—OTHER
7020	PERSONAL PROPERTY TAX
7030	BUSINESS LICENSE TAX
7100	PROFESSIONAL FEES—ATTORNEYS
7120	PROFESSIONAL FEES—ACCOUNTANTS
7130	PROFESSIONAL FEES—OTHER
7200	FILING FEES
7300	INTEREST EXPENSE
7350	BANK CHARGES
7400	COSTS WRITTEN OFF
7500	CREDIT CARD EXPENSES
7690	OTHER OPERATING EXPENSES

TECHNOLOGY SERVICES

7700	COMPUTER MAINTENANCE
7710	SOFTWARE SUPPORT—GENERAL
7720	SOFTWARE SUPPORT—TIMEKEEPING SYSTEM
7730	COMPUTER SUPPLIES
7790	OTHER TECHNOLOGY EXPENSE

SIMPLE BUDGET MODEL

Appendix B
SIMPLE BUDGET MODEL

BUDSIMPLE
REPORTS
INCSTMT

ABLE, BAKER, CHARLES & DOGG, P. C.	
FOR THE YEAR ENDED	12/31/YY

INCOME STATEMENT

	REQUIRED	ACTUAL CAPACITY	DIFF
VALUE OF BILLABLE TIME	$5,776,896	$5,870,500	$93,604
RATE VARIANCE	-115,538	-117,410	-1,872
BILLING VARIANCE	-261,047	-264,563	-3,516
WRITTEN OFF AT TIME OF COLLECTION	-125,000	-125,000	0
NET (-INCREASE) DECREASE IN WIP BALANCES	-440,424	-461,828	-21,404
NET (-INCREASE) DECREASE IN A/REC BALANCES	-90,708	-102,606	-11,898
NET COLLECTIONS (AS ABOVE)	$4,744,180	$4,799,094	$54,914
OTHER CASH INCOME	15,000	15,000	0
LESS: EXPENSES	-3,671,680	-3,671,680	0
NET INCOME	$1,087,500	$1,142,414	54,914

BUDSIMPLE
WHATIFS

ABLE, BAKER, CHARLES & DOGG, P. C.	
FOR THE YEAR ENDED	12/31/YY

LEVEL OF INCOME REQUIRED	1,087,500
BILLABLE VALUE REQUIRED	$5,776,896
BILLABLE VALUE CAPABLE OF PRODUCTION	5,870,500
EXCESS (-DEFICIT)	93,604

ACTUAL CAPACITY BASED ON ACTUAL ASSUMPTIONS

PARTNERS:
NUMBER	8.0
HOURS	1600
RATE	210.00
TOTAL	2688000

ASSOCIATES:
NUMBER	8.5
HOURS	1750
RATE	180.00
TOTAL	2677500

L/ASSTS:
NUMBER	5.0
HOURS	1200
RATE	75.00
TOTAL	450000

OTHER	55000
TOTAL ACCRUAL GROSS	5870500

ASSUMPTIONS:
WORK IN PROCESS
BEG OF YEAR	880560
RATE REALIZATION	0.98
BILLING REALIZATION	0.95

NET GROSS	5753090
WIP TURNS	2.8

ACCOUNTS RECEIVABLE:
BEGINNING OF YEAR	792560
WRITE OFFS	125000
DAYS BILLINGS	65.0

EXPENSES	3671680
OTHER CASH INCOME	15000
PTR SHARE OF INCOME	1087500
GROSS BILLS RENDERED	5291262

```
WIP REPORT:
    BEG BALANCE                       880560
    NET ADDED                        5753090
    NET BILLS RENDERED              -5026699
    NET WRITE DOWNS                  -264563

    ENDING BALANCE                   1342388

ACCTS RECEIVABLE:
    BEG BALANCE                       792560
    NET BILLS RENDERED               5026699
    COLLECTIONS                     -4799094
    WRITE OFFS                       -125000

    ENDING BALANCE                    895166

CALCULATION CHECK:
    ICS                              2237553
    AVG INPUT                         479424
    WIP BALANCE                      1342388
    TURNOVER                             4.7
    WIP TURNS                            2.8

    DAILY BILLS RENDERED               13772
    ACCOUNTS RECEIVABLE               895166
    DAYS BILLINGS                       65.0

GROSS INCOME SUMMARY:
    GROSS INCOME                     5870500
    RATE VARIANCE                    -117410
    BILLING VARIANCE                 -264563
    ACCTS REC WRITEOFFS              -125000
    CHANGE IN ICS                    -564433

    NET COLLECTIONS                  4799094

    OTHER CASH INCOME                  15000
    EXPENSES                        -3671680

    NET INCOME                       1142414
    SCHEDULED S/H DISTRIBUTIONS     -1087500

    EXCESS (-DEFICIT)                  54914

    NET INCOME PER PARTNER            142802
```

BUDSIMPLE
HOWTO

INSTRUCTIONS FOR USING THE FINANCIAL MODEL BUDSIMPLE

THIS MODEL IS DESIGNED TO PERFORM BUDGETING USING THE "BOTTOMS UP APPROACH." THE FIRM DECIDES THE NET INCOME THAT HE WANTS TO OBTAIN AND THEN USING THE VARIOUS ASSUMPTIONS, THIS MODEL DETERMINES WHETHER OR NOT THAT INCOME NUMBER CAN IN FACT BE ACHIEVED.

THE DATA FOR THIS MODEL IS INPUTTED IN THE **"DATA"** SECTION OF THE MODEL. FROM THIS INFORMATION, THE MODEL CALCULATES. ALL CELLS COLORED YELLOW REQUIRE INPUTTING OF DATA.

1. COLLECTIONS—(PRINT AREA **COLLECTIONS**)
2. BILLINGS—(PRINT AREA **BILLINGS**)
3. REQUIRED GROSS VALUE OF BILLABLE TIME
4. INCOME STATEMENT—(PRINT AREA **INCSTMT**)

A SUMMARY OF THE RESULTS IS INCLUDED IN THE PRINT AREA **SUMMARY**.

WHAT IF SCENARIOS CAN BE PERFORMED IN THE SECTION **WHATIFS**. BY ALTERING NET INCOME, THE FIRM CAN DETERMINE THE NET INCOME IT CAN PRODUCE BASED ON ITS CAPACITY TO GENERATE GROSS VALUE OF BILLABLE TIME.

UNDER THE WORKSHEET NAME **"ACTUAL"** THERE IS A MODEL WHICH CREATES THE ACTUAL NET INCOME RESULTS BASED ON THE DATA PROVIDED. THIS IN ESSENCE IS THE FIRM'S CAPACITY TO GENERATE GROSS BILLABLE VALUE. THE SUMMARY OF THIS INFORMATION IS INCLUDED WITH THE INCOME STATEMENT DATA IN THE PRINT AREA **"INCSTMT"** REFLECTING THE DIFFERENCES.

REVIEWING THE RESULTS

8

Now that the individual components of the financial management process have been presented, it may be worthwhile to look at how it all comes together once the year has started. This chapter discusses the review process.

The date is July 14, and Able, Baker has just completed six months of its new year. The financial statements for the month of June and year-to-date through June 30 have been prepared and the firm's manager must report on the results to the executive committee.

The Firm Report Card

The manager's first task is to prepare a report similar to that in Figure J. This can be called the Firm Report Card. It monitors the health of the firm as it progresses through the year—it provides information on key elements of the financial plan, compares them against the budget, and indicates whether the firm is in a favorable or unfavorable position at the end of any particular period. It also gives a grade from *A* to *F* in each category, which helps identify areas that require immediate attention. When the manager studies this report, he or she can ascertain where problems exist and how to solve them.

Earlier we discussed seasonalizing the budget with respect to input, billings, and collections, so that a firm can determine whether or not it is on target, based on historical amounts at the

Able, Baker, Charles & Dogg, PC
Firm Report Card
For the Period Ending MM/DD/YY

Grading System			Points
95% or Higher		A	3
85-94%		B	2
76-84%		C	1
70-75%		D	0
Less than 70%		F	−1

		Actual	Budget	Variance Favorable (Unfavorable)	Performance Percent	Grade
Billable Hours	Partners	6,348.5	6,592.0	(243.5)	96.3	A
	Associates	7,305.6	7,660.6	(355.0)	95.4	A
	Legal Assistants	2,896.5	3,090.0	(193.5)	93.7	B
	Total	16,550.6	17,342.6	(792.0)	95.4	A
Standard Value of Billable Time		2,866,354	3,024,480	(138,126)	95.4	A
Actual Value of Billable Time		2,799,764	2,963,990	(164,227)	94.5	B
Rate Variance Amount		(86,591)	(57,727)	(28,864)	66.7	F
Billings		2,265,954	2,481,601	(215,647)	91.3	B
Billing Realization Amount		(95,170)	(113,298)	18,128	119.0	A
Accounts Receivable Write-offs		(45,260)	(62,500)	17,240	138.1	A
Time to Bill (Months)		2.8	2.5	0.3	89.5	B
Time to Collect (Days)		73.6	69.4	4.2	94.2	A
Cash Receipts		$2,096,558	$2,265,492	($168,934)	92.5	B
Expenses		1,796,552	1,835,840	39,288	102.2	A
Net Income		300,006	437,152	(137,146)	68.6	F
Overall Average						B

Figure J

end of a given month. Figure J shows seasonally adjusted budgeted amounts as of June 30, based on the firm's historical percentages.

After reviewing the report, Able, Baker's manager is concerned about some of the unfavorable variances—not the net income variance or the expense variance (which is actually favorable)—but rather the $138,126 shortfall in the standard value of billable time. As noted elsewhere, unless time is going in at the top of the funnel, very shortly there will be no time left to come out the bottom in the form of cash. Billings and collections will eventually dry up, and the firm won't meet its net income expectations. Therefore, the first problem to deal with is the gross income issue.

Correcting a Shortfall

The manager must perform two functions to further pinpoint the problem and to provide a solution that will reduce the projected deficits in net income. The first is to calculate the amount of the projected shortfall at year-end if the current trend in gross income production continues, and the second is to determine what must be done in order to still reach the targeted net income and reduce the shortfall, given the accrual gross deficit.

Figure K reflects the manager's analysis. Assuming the trend continues, how can the same billings budget be achieved given the projected level of gross income? The first column, Annual Budget, reflects the reconciliation of the work-in-process amounts as established at the beginning of the year. This analysis shows a time-to-bill of 2.8 months.

Through June, on an historical basis, Able, Baker produces 51.5 percent of its gross income for the year. Thus, by dividing the actual time value through June by 51.5 percent, the amount for the entire year can be projected. This is included in the column called Projected Actual Enhanced. This analysis shows that the firm will have a gross value of time equal to $5,436,434, a

---

Able, Baker, Charles & Dogg, PC
Financial Information
Budget vs. Actual
January 1–December 31, YY

	Annual Budget	Projected Actual Enhanced	Projected Actual Best Case	Projected Shortfall
Beginning Work-in-Process	$880,560	$880,560	$880,560	
Amounts Added	5,753,090	5,436,434	5,436,434	(316,656)
Billings	(5,026,699)	(5,026,699)	(4,796,068)	(230,631)
Net Write-downs	(264,563)	(264,563)	(252,425)	
Ending Work-in-Process	$1,342,388	$1,025,732	$1,268,501	
Beginning Accounts Receivable	$792,560		$792,560	
Billings	5,026,699		4,796,068	(230,631)
Collections	(4,799,094)		(4,609,534)	(189,560)
Write-offs	(125,000)		(125,000)	
Ending Accounts Receivable	$895,166		$854,094	
Turnover:				
Time-to-Bill (Months)	2.8	2.3	2.8	
Time-to-Collect (Days)	65.0		65.0	
Overall (Months)	4.7		4.7	

Figure K

shortfall of $316,656. If this projected amount is correct, and the billings remain as budgeted at $5,026,699, the turnover would need to be reduced to 2.3 months.

Since the firm had enough trouble getting its turnover to the 2.8-month level, there is general agreement that there is no way it can be reduced to 2.3, and that 2.8 is probably the best it can do. So, what is the effect of this? The third column on the schedule, identified as Projected Actual Best Case, shows what will happen, assuming that there is the anticipated shortfall in gross income and that the turnover rate stays at the 2.8 budgeted level. The resulting reduction in gross income of $316,656 translates into a reduction in billings of $230,631 from a budget of $5,026,699. The new estimated actual billings amount is $4,796,068.

Analyzing Billings and Collections

The next analysis shows the changes that will occur in the accounts receivable reconciliation portion of the budget. Note that the collections were budgeted at $4,799,094. As a result of the reduction in billings, assuming the 65-day time-to-collect period can be maintained, receipts will be reduced by $189,560, making the new projection $4,609,534. On a per-shareholder basis, this amounts to a shortfall of $23,695, as shown in Figure L.

This budget review can be done at any time throughout the year to provide the manager with the tools he needs to take action to improve the situation. Note that the analysis incorporates many of the processes and procedures discussed in previous chapters.

Now that Able, Baker has a better idea of the problem, it must work toward lowering the anticipated reduction in billings and collections. This must be done on a firm-wide basis, all the way down to the individual billing-lawyer

---

Able, Baker, Charles & Dogg, PC
Financial Information
Budget vs. Actual
January 1–December 31, YY

Budget Collections	$4,799,094
Actual at Budgeted Turnover	4,609,534
Shortfall	189,560
Per Partner	23,695

Figure L

level, to find out who is controlling the dollars and what must be done to improve the results.

A long-held theory in law firms is that the most important person is the one who bills the most and collects the most. This is not necessarily true. While managing many clients and many dollars is certainly impressive, I believe the most important person is the one who bills and collects the highest portion of the money available to him. A lawyer who bills and collects $50,000 of an available amount of $100,000 is performing poorly compared to a lawyer who has $20,000 available, and bills and collects $20,000. Since most firms operate on a billing lawyer basis, it's possible to pinpoint the billing and collection problem by reviewing how lawyers are doing against the amounts available at any point in time. Figure M illustrates a system that assists in this effort.

The theory behind this reporting system is to first calculate the percentage of collections required as compared to the total amounts available for collection. These amounts are represented in Figure M in the columns titled Beginning Work-in-Process, Beginning Accounts Receivable, and Amounts Added for the Period. This is first done at the firm level and then at the billing lawyer level.

For example, in Figure M, note that through June 30 Able, Baker had $4,472,884 available to collect. This resulted from a beginning work-in-process balance of $880,560, beginning accounts receivable of $792,560, and amounts added of $2,799,764. Since its budgeted collections were $2,265,492, the required percentage of collections in order for the firm to reach its budget at June 30 is 50.6 percent, versus a budgeted percentage of 48.2 percent. Thus, the firm needs to improve its turnover rate of time to cash receipts if it expects to achieve the same level of receipts with a reduced value of billable time. After looking at the figures for the firm, Able, Baker can then examine the numbers for each billing lawyer to determine his or her individual performance.

Figure M includes the individual information for lawyer Mary Smith. Note that her amount available to collect, using the same process as done for the firm, is $508,956. By applying the percentage for the firm of 50.6 percent, we see that Mary's receipts budget is $257,784. Her actual is $206,884, leaving her a deficit of $50,900.

The ultimate goal is for everyone in the firm to meet their targets so that the firm reaches its target. Obviously, not everyone is able to do so. Some lawyers are over and some are under. The objective is for as many lawyers as possible to meet or exceed their budgeted receipts. Those lawyers who accomplish this goal make the "honor roll," which is announced monthly to everyone in the firm. The number of times an individual lawyer makes the honor roll is one of the criteria used in determining compensation.

Able, Baker, Charles & Dogg, PC
Receipts against Amount Available
For the Year Ending 12/31/YY
As of June 30, YY

	Actual for Period	Budget for Period
Beginning Work-in-Process	$880,560	$880,560
Beginning Accounts Receivable	792,560	792,560
Amounts Added for the Period	2,799,764	3,024,480
Total Available	$4,472,884	$4,697,600
Receipts Budget	$2,265,492	$2,265,492
Required Percentage	50.6	48.2

Able, Baker, Charles & Dogg, PC
Receipts against Amount Available
For the Year Ending 12/31/YY
As of June 30, YY

Lawyer: Mary Smith

Beginning Work-in-Process	$157,500
Beginning Accounts Receivable	135,600
Amounts Added	215,856
Total Available	$508,956
Budgeted Receipts Percentage	50.6
Budgeted Receipts	$257,784
Actual Receipts	–206,884
Excess (Deficit)	($50,900)

Figure M

Firms have been very inventive in establishing bonus programs for partners who exceed their budgets for billable hours, origination, working receipts, and so on. However, these figures do not matter if the time value is not converted into a high percentage of the available cash receipts. A partner must bill and collect quickly, with a minimum of write-downs and write-offs. This is the test each partner must pass if a firm is to meet its overall budget and meet or exceed its projected cash realization percentage.

FINANCIAL REPORTING

9

As the discussion in the previous chapter illustrates, all the information and analyses presented in this book can be used effectively to better manage your firm's finances and assist in increasing profitability. The size of your firm doesn't matter. The numbers are simply smaller or larger.

But producing all this information is of very little value if you don't have a meaningful way to present it to the firm's management or partners.

Over the years, I've found very few partners who really wanted to get involved in the details of financial management. As long as they get their checks on time and the amounts are what they expected, that's really all they care about. Therefore, the information they receive should be clear and to the point. You should include a brief memorandum highlighting any unusual items, particularly significant variations from budget.

Information Tracked by Law Firms

Generally, the following information is tracked by law firms and is at three levels:

Firm Level
At the firm level, the firm tracks:

1. Billable hours
2. Rate realization
3. Billing realization

4. Accounts receivable write-offs
5. Gross value of billable time
6. Time to bill
7. Time to collect
8. Billings
9. Cash receipts
10. Expenses
11. Net income
12. Distributions to owners

Billing (Primary) Lawyer Level

At this level, the firm tracks:

1. Billing realization
2. Rate realization
3. Accounts receivable write-offs
4. Cash receipts against amounts available to collect

Working Lawyer Level

The only items tracked at this level are billable hours and cash receipts, since most lawyers who work for others have little or no control over their own cash receipts.

Whenever this information is eventually reported to your partners, it should have two basic characteristics:

- It should give the activity for the month, as well as for the year to date
- It should be compared with the budget for the same period, and variances should be computed in both dollar amounts and percentages

The information should also include some, if not all, of the following:

- Gross income on the cash basis
- Expenses
- Net income on the cash basis
- Gross income on the accrual basis (total hours multiplied by the standard rate)
- Billings
- Realization, in dollar amount and percentage
- Billable hours for all timekeepers (month and year to date, including each group's weighted averages)
- Inventory turnover and days billings in receivables
- Income per partner to date
- Comparison of partner earnings against amounts distributed

Other reports can be prepared, and their content depends upon who is receiving them. The firm's executive, operating, or finance committees may require more detail in order to determine the financial health of the firm. The job of the financial manager, whomever that might be, is to make certain the reports are accurate and concise and that they contain explanations for any unusual items.

There are certain operating ratios and statistics that are common to the analysis of law firm financial operations. If these are made at various times during the year and at year's end, over a period of time the firm will have a good history to use for comparisons. Some of this information is also included in the surveys discussed in Chapter 15.

The key comparison is to the budget, assuming the budget is realistic and in line with partner income expectations and the prior year. If it is in line, then a firm should feel it is making some progress. As noted, these analyses, discussed briefly below, become more meaningful over the years as the firm continues to mature and accumulates historical data of performance. The ease in which charts and graphs can now be prepared enhances the presentation of the data and the knowledge to be gained by the management group.

Accrual-Basis and Cash-Basis Expense Ratios

These ratios are calculated by comparing total expenses, which excludes partners' compensation and benefits, to gross income on the accrual basis and cash basis. Among other factors, these numbers are affected by a higher-than-normal associate-to-partner ratio, which would generally benefit a firm . Whether or not a firm capitalizes on this leverage is evident through other analyses of the financial results. The accrual expense number is the most significant, in that it matches current costs with current revenues.

Accrual and Cash Overhead Expense Ratios

These calculations help determine the extent to which overhead expenses, other than compensation and benefits of the timekeepers, are being utilized to generate billable hours and cash receipts. These ratios are affected in the same way as the accrual-basis and cash-basis expense ratios described above. They are calculated by comparing all overhead, exclusive of the compensation of the timekeepers, to accrual-basis and cash-basis gross income.

Overhead per Timekeeper Equivalent

This statistic looks at the cost to support a timekeeper, or timekeeper equivalent in the case of legal assistants. This statistic isn't for comparison purposes but is kept by the firm for historical analysis.

Cost per Billable Hour

This statistic relates to the cost to produce a firm's basic product, a billable hour. It is commonly referred to as "practice support costs." This is a key statistic that should be watched closely over the years. It can reflect efficiencies, or lack thereof, in a firm's ability to deliver client services in the most effective manner, or it can simply reflect a reduction in hours production affected by business conditions.

Work-in-Process and Accounts Receivable Aging

These should both be provided in amounts as well as percentages, comparing the aged amounts at various periods. At certain times during the year, and certainly at the end of the year, a firm needs to review its outstanding accounts and make some hard decisions as to whether those accounts need to be written off or down. In addition, it's important that the "aging buckets" extend out past 120 days, so that a more meaningful analysis can be made of old, unbilled, or uncollected time. Keep in mind that at some point, a firm needs to bite the bullet and write off accounts that won't ever be translated into cash.

Work-in-Process and Accounts Receivable per Timekeeper

The purpose of this statistic is to relate work-in-process and accounts receivable balances to the number of timekeepers. The fact that these balances change in total amount is not significant if, in fact, the number of timekeepers changes also.

Working Lawyer Billable Hours

Law firms have been fixated on billable hours for longer than most of us can remember. We use them as a guide to billing, as a measure of productivity, as a means to predict future revenues, and as a guide to compensation and bonuses. Unfortunately, reviewing the raw numbers may not reveal the requisite information necessary to make decisions that are based on billable hour production. There is one issue that must be taken into account in examining billable hours production at the individual lawyer level: the standard rate.

While there are many different methods of valuing billable hours that are used by firms, one of the valuations not frequently used relates to the comparison of standard rate hours to actual hours.

In the budgeting process discussed in other chapters, most firms use standard rates assigned to each timekeeper as a starting point in determining the amount of billable value that is available for billing and collection. This value is then affected by various adjustments, such as rate discounting, referred to elsewhere as rate realization. A firm's budget is affected by its ability to charge its clients an amount as close as possible to the individual timekeeper's standard rate.

Thus, if a lawyer has a standard rate of $150, but agrees initially to charge $125, he has discounted the rate by $25 and has achieved a rate realization of 83.3 percent ($125 divided by $150).

The reasons for rate discounting are numerous and include new-client discounts, performing certain types of work which by their nature command lower rates (such as insurance defense), and sometimes the age-old reason that 50 percent of something is better than 100 percent of nothing.

The importance of this analysis relates to how billable hour production is evaluated. Two lawyers who have the same number of billable hours may not be equal if in fact one has reduced his rate so that his actual hours are significantly below his standard rate hours.

For example, if a lawyer's rate is $150 and he has 1,600 billable hours, his standard value should be $240,000. If it is, then his standard rate hours are 1,600 ($240,000 divided by $150). However, if the value of his hours is only $210,00 because of a rate discount, then his standard rate hours are only 1,400 ($210,000 divided by $150).

If there is some correlation between standard billing rates and compensation, then two lawyers with the same compensation and same rate should be reviewed on the basis of more than just the *number* of billable hours. It is necessary to also examine the *value* of those hours as they were recorded in the timekeeping system. This examination allows the firm to more accurately evaluate a lawyer's contribution, rather than just simply looking at raw information, which may not tell the whole story.

As firms begin to examine whether alternative types of billing are appropriate in certain situations, the issue of determining the value of billable hours will take on added importance.

What Does All this Information Mean?

New technology has brought law firms an abundance of financial information. Sometimes it seems as if there is too much information. But the important issue is whether there is enough explanation accompanying the data so that it is usable and understandable, and helps a firm make the major and sometimes painful decisions that allow it to meet its goal and objectives.

In preparing information for law firm owners over the years, I have attempted to follow the following guidelines for each analysis I have completed:

1. Be as comprehensive and accurate as possible in providing the information.
2. Outline what the information means in the context of what you are trying to relate.
3. Provide conclusions and recommendations that will alter the behavior or processes so that the condition that precipitated the analysis can be improved, if improvement is the ultimate objective.

I have found that most people do a good job following the first guideline, are less successful with the second, and fail completely with the third.

Common Problem Areas

The following discussion offers some guidance in determining the reasons for some of the problem areas identified as a result of analyzing a firm's financial information, and includes some recommended actions.

Low Billable Hours

The reasons for this may be obvious to some, but not to others. Possibilities are:

1. Not enough work to go around
2. Poor timekeeping practices
3. Poor supervision of those performing the work
4. Work is being done more efficiently
5. Sheer laziness

Recommendations:

1. Consider terminating some lawyers and staff.
2. See if the marketing program can be turned up a notch to bring in more business.
3. Take a close look at the backlog of work that has not been given proper attention.
4. Make certain there is a correlation between hours charged by timekeepers, and the hours they are physically in the office or working on client assignments.

5. Examine whether some partners are not allowing all hours to be charged on files, in order to avoid excessive write-downs or write-offs. This is particularly true with hours worked by younger associates and legal assistants.
6. Consider not permitting certain partners to manage files that are heavy with associate and legal assistant time.
7. Determine whether a bonus system should be paid for hours above a certain level.
8. Have all timekeepers account for a specific number of hours each day.

Low Billable Value

Possible reasons:

1. Low billable hours, as noted above
2. Excessive rate discounting. This is caused by clients who refuse to be charged (not billed) at the timekeeper's standard hourly rate, creating a rate below standard, or a discounted rate. If not built into the budget, the results could be detrimental to reaching the annual net income goals.
3. Distribution of hours is weighted towards those timekeepers with the lower hourly rates
4. Efficiency in work production. As noted later, this should be correlated to higher cash receipts.

Recommendations:

1. Examine whether client rates can be increased or whether lower-rated timekeepers can be put on certain client assignments.
2. Check the budget to ascertain whether enough hours were budgeted for the higher-rated timekeepers.
3. Make certain that fixed-fee or other alternatively billed work is being properly priced.
4. Keep in mind that this has nothing to do with write-downs, since this represents the gross billable value before any write-downs are taken into account.

Low Billings

Possible reasons:

1. Low billable hours or low billable value, as noted above.
2. Poor billing habits, as represented by the timing of billing as a percentage of billable value built into the firm's budget.
3. Higher than expected write-downs.

4. Higher level of contingent fee, or slower-paying client work than was anticipated.

Recommendations:

1. Consider shifting client management responsibility to those lawyers who do a better job of billing clients on a current basis.
2. As noted above, make certain that fixed-fee or other alternatively billed work is being properly priced.
3. Examining percentage of slower bill versus faster bill work and make certain that percentage is in line with budget. If not, determine what can be done to change it.

Low Receipts

Possible reasons:

1. Low hours, low value, or low billings as noted above
2. Longer pay cycle, as represented by the timing of collections as a percentage of bills rendered
3. Billings made on work that has less opportunity for collection in a short time frame
4. Contingent cases not getting settled on a regular basis
5. Collection process not working, not installed, or not kept up to date
6. Clients not being sent follow-up letters on a regular basis
7. Alternative billing methods not proving successful as evidenced by low receipts per billable hour worked. This is the major test as to whether fixed-fee and other types of billing methods are producing the required level of profitability.

Recommendations:

1. Consider taking the collection process away from lawyers and making it the responsibility of the firm accounting department.
2. Determine whether hiring outside collection lawyers makes sense.
3. Check to make certain that contingent files are being adequately pursued. It should be policy to "touch" every file within a thirty-day to forty-five-day period.

Note that expense issues are not addressed above, for several reasons. First, expenses are the easiest of all the profit factors to control. Second, there is not much that can be done with expenses, once a firm has matured beyond the point where significant cost reductions may result in a major level of service reduction that the firm, lawyers, and clients will not tolerate.

Also, it is a good idea to look at the numbers not only at the firm level but also at the practice group level, and make certain that each practice group is pulling its weight in producing profits. It may be that some areas of the practice should be eliminated because of a lack of current or potential profit. This issue is covered in some detail in Chapter 11.

It is easy in today's technological world to create analyses that analyze the analyses. However, it still takes a human being with knowledge and expertise to decipher the data, explain what it means to those with limited accounting knowledge, and then make recommendations and suggestions so that steps can be taken to correct problems and put the firm on a financial footing where it can meet its financial goals.

Annual Report

In addition to the monthly reports, a law firm manager should also prepare both oral and written annual reports to be given to partners very soon after the close of the year. The oral report covers what has happened in the past year, and what is predicted for the future year in terms of next year's budget. This report also provides some exposure for the manager, letting all of the partners know that he or she is knowledgeable about the financial operations of the firm. Using graphics on significant items is also helpful during the oral report.

This may also be the one time of the year when the legal manager can address the entire partnership. It also may be a good time to discuss any other significant items such as a new telephone system, updated computer equipment, or a move to new office quarters. The firm may also want to consider giving this same report to the associates and members of the administrative management team. People generally work harder and react better to change if they know what's going on.

The written report is simply an extension of the oral report and contains all the information from the prior year and for the upcoming year. It should be prepared so that it is a handy reference tool for the partners on major financial issues, including information on billing rates, capital balances, compensation information, and the like.

The Balance Sheet:
The Statement of Worth | **10**

Now that the review of the income statement has been completed, let's take a look at another important statement: the balance sheet. The balance sheet is a statement of financial position at a given date, usually the end of the month. In many respects, it can be used as the barometer for evaluating a firm's net worth or value. This value is determined by examining the net assets—total assets minus liabilities or claims against these assets.

The balance sheet lists in summary form a firm's assets, liabilities, and capital accounts. The assets primarily include cash, investments, advances to clients, and the net value of capital assets. Liabilities include amounts due outsiders, which is principally debt. Capital is the permanent capital of the partners plus any undistributed profits. Since cash is usually the focal point on the balance sheet, it deserves a certain amount of attention.

Understanding Cash Flow

One of the most difficult concepts for nonaccountants to understand is the concept of cash flow. Most people look at the net income on the income statement, then immediately look at the cash balance and wonder why the increase in cash does not correspond to the year-to-date profit amount.

First, let's dispel some myths concerning cash flow.

◆ *Myth Number 1: Cash earnings and cash distribution are the same.* This isn't true, and, in fact, is usually never true. Cash earnings, for the partnership form at least, are those reported on the partners' K-1 form for income tax purposes. Cash distributions are the amounts the partners receive against those earnings during the year. In many cases, particularly for those firms that are grossly undercapitalized, cash distributions could lag behind cash earnings by as much as 15 to 20 percent. In the professional corporation (PC) environment, earnings are reflected on each shareholder's W-2 form, as for all employees. In many cases, however, bonuses in excess of salary levels can't be paid due to cash shortages. This creates a major problem for the professional service corporation since excess earnings not paid by year-end are currently taxed at the corporate level at a high rate, and then taxed again when finally distributed to the shareholders. For this reason, care needs to be exercised at the end of the year to monitor profits closely and make certain that all profits are distributed either in cash or in the form of notes to avoid any tax liability.

◆ *Myth Number 2: Firms have no capital since all their assets are purchased out of current earnings.* This also is a contradiction. In the partnership setting, if debt repayment and fixed-asset acquisitions are funded through operations and not totally by depreciation, then—whether or not the firm knows it—it has created capital accounts.

Each firm needs to budget its cash flow requirements in the same way that it budgets its revenues and expenses. Included in this budget (which is prepared monthly as well as yearly) is an analysis of additional cash necessary to run the firm over and above funds provided by income and depreciation. This includes the anticipated costs of additional capital items such as computers and leaseholds, as well as an estimate of funds required to support client cost advances and debt curtailment.

Once these determinations are made, a firm must determine how any cash shortfall is to be funded. It can come from funds provided by the partners in the form of additional capital, from a reduction in monthly draw, from the bank, or from a combination of these sources. In many cases, the shortfall is dictated by the percentage of earnings that the firm wishes to distribute in that twelve-month period, in addition to the payment of undistributed profits from the prior period. Firms that are undercapitalized generally won't be able to pay as much of the current year's earnings in the current year. Good cash management will put a firm in a position where 92 to 95 percent of the earnings in any given year are distributed in that year. This reduces the problem of partners not having the cash to pay taxes due on K-1 earnings.

Capital

Many firms say they don't have capital accounts but rather fund their capital-asset acquisitions, client advances, and debt repayment through current earnings. What is actually occurring is an accumulation of undistributed profits that simply rolls over every year and, in effect, forms a permanent capital pool. However, in many instances, the individual partner capital balances have no relationship to partner income percentages. The result is that certain partners are essentially financing the firm disproportionately to their share of the income without any remuneration in the form of interest.

A particular problem exists with PCs when earnings are retained instead of distributed, and therefore increase the net book value of the firm. In most PCs, ownership interest of the stock is not in the same proportion as compensation interests. Thus, when a firm decides to capitalize profits rather than distribute them, the high-income partner with a low-ownership percentage is penalized. The low-income, high-ownership partner receives a windfall.

The result is constant disagreement within the firm about what to do with profits in excess of salary levels. This situation shouldn't occur. If the ownership interests are equal to the income interests, then the partners' share in that year's profits, whether distributed or not, are correct. The undistributed profits are added to the shareholder values of the affected shareholders in the correct relationship, become part of their capital accounts, and are paid out at the appropriate time in accordance with the firm's shareholder agreements.

Funding for capital asset acquisitions, debt repayment, or client advances comes from after-tax capital dollars. Once partners receive their share of profits (not necessarily in the form of cash), they must give back a certain amount to take care of the firm's financial requirements. By holding the cash earnings to finance the firm's operations, the firm is creating capital balances.

To better manage these cash requirements, you can do some or all of the following:

◆ If purchasing fixed assets by bank financing, arrange debt curtailment to coincide with cash generated through the depreciation deduction.

◆ Include significant leasehold improvements in the rental rate, thus deducting the amount currently through the monthly rent expense. However, the landlord will probably charge for this benefit at a rate higher than normal bank interest. The agreement is based on the size of the space occupied and the leverage that your firm may have in striking the initial deal.

◆ Establish more formalized capitalization programs in which all partners make annual capital contributions to help fund the firm's capital requirements. In most cases, the capital balance is determined as a function of the income percentage—all partners contribute in proportion to how much they take out in earnings.

◆ Factor into the ownership equation the accrual-basis assets of accounts receivable and work-in-process. How this is done is another subject. Suffice to say, however, that the movement of partners from firm to firm and the extent of merger activity have prompted firms to examine the question of who owns the assets not usually recorded on the cash-basis balance sheet.

Cash Flow Analysis

Whether a firm has two lawyers or two hundred, cash flow requirements must be a part of the annual forecast of revenues and expenses. Too often, this isn't done, and the firm comes to the end of the year with significant extra net profits but no cash available to make the distribution.

Two principles should be emphasized. First, cash transactions affect the balance sheet and the income statement separately or together. Second, a variety of noncash transactions, such as depreciation, that flow through the income statement must be added to or subtracted from net income to obtain the true change in the cash balance due to operations. In the analysis, all changes in the balance sheet accounts are calculated and accounted for as they relate to their effect on the cash balance.

The cash flow analysis focuses on the sources and uses of funds. Major sources include

◆ *Net income.* This assumes the firm is operating at a profit.
◆ *Bank borrowings*
◆ *Depreciation.* This is a source of funds, in the sense that when recorded on the income statement, there is no actual cash outlay. Thus, the amount must be added back to net income to reflect the real change in the cash balance brought about by operations.
◆ *Capital.* This represents the initial and annual partner contributions to capital.

Major uses or applications of funds include

◆ *Distributions.* Whether a partnership or corporate firm, all payments to partners or shareholders should be excluded from expenses and shown "below the line," after profits have been determined.
◆ *Repayments of debt.* This is not an income-statement entry. The amounts paid to curtail borrowings must be subtracted from the cash balance during the period the payment was made.

◆ *Capital asset additions.* Again, the purchases of fixed or capital assets don't flow through the income statement. They are recorded as assets when purchased (and the payment of cash occurs) and then recovered through the periodic recording of depreciation or amortization on the income statement.

◆ *Capital refunds.* Amounts paid to departing partners are deductions from the cash balance and accounted for separately since there is no income statement effect from this transaction.

In addition to the items noted above, consideration must be given to changes in other asset accounts, such as investments and other liability accounts, principally payroll taxes and related items.

Once a firm has made its net income determination, it must then prepare a cash flow statement and make certain that the cash flow goals can be satisfied based on the projected net income. If a shortage exists, it can then make an informed decision on how to raise the additional funds.

A firm generally sets cash flow goals at the same time it sets its overall income and expense budgets. Able, Baker set five cash flow goals for the year:

1. Maintain a monthly working capital balance of $45,000.
2. Since it is a PC, distribute 100 percent of its total income by the end of the year.
3. Schedule supplemental distributions to shareholders as cash permits.
4. Incorporate a capital budget of $10,000.
5. Pay down debt by $80,000.

When the firm looked at the cash flow analysis for the year as seen in Figure N, it came up with a shortage of $92,363 . In other words, to fulfill its cash objectives with the same net income target, the firm must come up with an additional $92,363 or alter some of its goals. It could reduce its capital expenditures or distributions to partners, reduce its debt payments, or choose another alternative. The key is that the firm is better able to make these judgments now rather than finding out late in the year that there are major cash shortages.

Each firm has its own philosophy about how much equity comes from the partners and the limits on outside borrowing. As mentioned earlier, some firms believe strongly that a firm should be owned by its partners and not by the bank. Others feel just the opposite. There should be some balance; however, at least at this time, there are no guideline ratios for equity and debt. Personally, I believe in a high amount of individual partner capital and low debt to the extent possible.

Able, Baker decided to meet the $92,363 cash shortfall by going to the partners for $75,000 and letting the rest of the shortfall come about through the normal course of the year's activity.

Able, Baker, Charles & Dogg, PC
Cash Flow Analysis
For the Year Ending 12/31/YY

Cash from Operations	
Net Income (Loss)	$1,142,414
Expenses Not Requiring Cash Outlays	
Depreciation	35,000
Changes in Operating Assets and Liabilities	
Decrease (Increase) in Unbilled Client Advances	11,315
Decrease (Increase) in Billed Client Advances	(13,928)
Decrease (Increase) in Other Assets or Liabilities	(5,000)
Net Cash Provided by Operating Activities	1,169,801
Investing Activities:	
Net Purchases (Disposals) of Fixed Assets	(10,000)
Financing Activities:	
Net Increase (Decrease) in Debt	(80,000)
Net Increase (Decrease) in Cash	1,079,801
Cash Balance at Beginning of Year	15,250
Cash Balance at End of Year	(45,000)
Cash Available for Distribution	$1,050,051
Net Income	−1,142,414
Cash Excess (Deficit)	($92,363)

Figure N

There is no magic in arriving at individual partner capital balances. The key is to agree on a strategy to fund the firm's major capital expenditures and then determine each partner's participation in the overall capital goal.

COST ACCOUNTING | **11**

Over the years, I have written and spoken on the subject of profitability several times. My first article on this issue, written in 1975, appeared in a now discontinued publication, *Manual for Managing a Law Office,* published by Prentice-Hall, which at that time was the bible for law office managers. This article was written after I had recently left public accounting, convinced that one could apply the same cost-accounting techniques to the service profession as one did to any other industry. This was not the case, as I later determined once I began attempting to apply various cost-accounting practices to the legal profession.

Many of these types of articles were published in *Law Office Management and Administration Report* (LOMAR), and were designed to illustrate the problems in attempting to perform the cost-accounting function within the service environment, to provide some guidance on how to do it once the problems were recognized, and to list the issues that need to be considered.

The profitability issue has now risen to new levels of interest brought about by the emergence of alternative billing methods that require a more sophisticated approach to developing cost and value. Also, firms are critically examining their practice areas and determining which ones should be discontinued and which ones expanded. In addition, with more emphasis on billing and collection management in the owner-compensation process, firms need to produce some type of profitability analysis at various levels to make certain that resources are being used properly and that the firm is being compensated for these resources on a timely basis.

This chapter updates those earlier efforts to explain how this process is accomplished, recognizing that current spreadsheet and timekeeping system technology makes it much easier to gather the required information, manipulate the data, and produce the answers.

Cost Analysis

The first step in the process is to perform a cost analysis in order to obtain a cost rate for each timekeeper. To do this you need to allocate the various firm expenditures to a group, practice area, or class of lawyers on some consistent basis, and then compare that to some income amount in order to calculate profitability. The most accurate way is to examine expenses in minute detail, and spread the expenses to the individual or group based on an actual allocation. This means measuring each person's office and multiplying by the square-foot rental rate to ascertain occupancy costs, and making the same calculation for any staff who support that lawyer; determining which lawyer attended which CLE function; and figuring out who uses the library more, who uses the telephone more, who uses technology, accounting, and so on.

Obviously, this is virtually impossible to do, although I have known some firms who have gone to this extreme. The better way to deal with the problem of expense allocation is to establish some consistent base upon which the allocation can be made, and where possible make direct charges of significant expenses. This reduces the errors in the analysis.

Be careful when preparing the analysis, and make certain that all the variables are computed properly so that you end up with a defensible and accurate evaluation. Even then, the analysis should be used with much discretion.

One of the first problems you may encounter is that your in-house accounting and timekeeping systems are not capable of providing the abundance of information that is required. Therefore, you may need to adopt a methodology that uses the information available to you, and gives you the minimum amount of grief and the least possible political fallout. Even if you are able to assemble most of the information, depending on how detailed you want to get, you may need to consider using some or all of the following assumptions:

1. The cost attributable to each timekeeper category is the same on all files. This means that whether a timekeeper is a high-paid partner or a low-paid partner, a high-paid associate or a low-paid associate, the cost for an hour of time for each category of timekeeper is the same. An alternative (as seen later in Figure O) is to assign a cost rate for

every timekeeper in the firm. This increases the work involved in doing the analysis, particularly if you are a firm of any size. However, you can do this if you want a lot of detail and you have the information necessary for this level of analysis. But remember that the more detailed you get, the more opportunity there is for someone to pick apart the analysis. For the cost allocation process, discussed later in this chapter, each timekeeper is considered individually (see Figure O).

2. If there are multiple offices, you may need to assume that the cost to produce an hour is the same in each office. Again, it is possible to assign a cost on an individual basis for each office and for each timekeeper in that office, but the mechanical problems involved in doing this create additional work. This computation also tends to highlight differences in lifestyle among offices that generally are kept in the background in most firms. Unless the cost structures in the various offices are extremely out of line with each other, I suggest developing the rates on a global, firm-wide basis. Recognize, however, that timekeepers in satellite offices do not want to be overburdened by what they may see as exorbitant home-office expenses (expensive rent, large secretarial staff, high marketing costs, and so on).

3. There is also the assumption that the cost to produce a product is the same regardless of the product. That means the cost of an hour to generate a will for Mrs. Jones is the same as the cost of an hour to produce a brief for one of the firm's largest clients. To attempt to assign costs to each individual file based on the complexity of the matter is probably impossible and is not recommended. Using the methodology discussed below helps solve this problem.

Even with the all the information available from a firm's timekeeping records, there is still a certain amount of "ball parking" and estimating that goes into the development of statistics of this type. Many assumptions must be made, particularly in a larger firm with a cross-pollination of lawyers working on various files. Therefore, after the statistics have been developed, they must be looked at for what they are—nothing more than a relatively accurate representation of the profitability of the area in question, and not necessarily a gospel fact, or one calculated through scientific methods and proven formulas.

Allocating Costs

The following discussion shows an objective way to perform cost analysis, which should enable a firm to determine the overhead required to perform the analysis, and calculate the corresponding profit or loss.

Exhibits A-G illustrate the steps in the analysis for a sample firm.

The first information you need is the cost and expenses for the year, which come directly from your firm's accounting records and are segregated by major expense function. The next main task is to establish the basis for allocation, which I suggest should be staff levels within the firm.

Let's assume that over a twelve-month period, the sample firm used in the analysis shown in Exhibits A to G had the full-time equivalency of 4.0 partners, 5.8 associates, 3.0 legal assistants, and 15.4 other staff personnel.

The first step is to assign a weighting factor to each of the timekeeper categories for the purpose of calculating the number of billing units. This is the first major assumption that must be made, and one that you can either agree or disagree with. An associate has a billing unit of 1. For partners, the billing unit is $1^{1}/_{3}$; for legal assistants it is $^{2}/_{3}$; for secretaries and other staff it is $^{1}/_{4}$. The basis for these weighting factors has to do with the service and cost utilization that usually accompanies an individual's stature within the firm. For example, partners normally have larger offices occupying more square feet, have better furniture, generally have higher-paid secretaries, and on the average utilize more services than others in the firm. Legal assistants, on the other hand, probably share secretaries, have smaller offices, and utilize cost and services to a lesser degree than do the associates.

There is no magic to this calculation. Each firm must decide what, if any, weighting factor should be applied. These overall assumptions then carry through to determine the point values assigned to the various groups. For the firm shown in Exhibit A, these assumptions produced a total of 17.0 billing units for the year in question.

The next step is to review the various expense categories and determine which of these to allocate on a direct basis and which to allocate on an indirect basis. For those on an indirect basis, make the determination whether or not the expenses pertain to the firm as a whole or just to selected groups. For example, Exhibit A shows that it is easy to determine the total associate and legal assistant salaries, and it may also be easy to determine the secretarial salary expense of the partner, associate, and legal assistant group. For these, you can make a direct allocation. For other expense categories such as occupancy costs, office supplies and services, communications, and so on, you need to determine if they apply to all or part of the groups in question, and allocate the expenses based on the total point value. If secretaries are not assigned to groups or individuals and their services are used somewhat evenly throughout the firm, I suggest including secretarial salaries in the general expenses to be allocated on the billing-unit basis.

Exhibit A shows that occupancy costs pertain to the entire group, with a total expense of $115,300. In this example, the firm pays parking for its partners; thus, $4,000 gets charged directly to the partner group and the remaining $111,300 is allocated among the other groups. When $111,300 is divided by 17.0 billing units, the value per unit is approximately $6,547. This amount, multiplied by 5.3 partner billing units, allocates $34,871 to the partner group for occupancy. Multiply the amount per unit by the point value for each of the other groups to determine the allocation of occupancy costs for the other groups. Note that associates get $38,018; legal assistants, $13,175; and staff, $25,236. For the practice development expense function, you might decide to assign this cost only to the lawyer group. In this case, the $12,500 is distributed to partners and associates at $5,980 and $6,520 respectively. This process continues until all the expenses have been properly allocated.

In addition to expenses, you also need to allocate the miscellaneous other cash-basis income to each of the groups. In this example, the total amount is $25,000. Last, you need to spread the expenses in the category titled Other to each of the groups. In Exhibit A, $321,244 is allocated to the producing groups. This was done using the total units in the groups. It is not necessary to allocate expenses to the Other category and then reallocate them back to the timekeepers; it was done here because the firm in the example wanted to get some idea of the expenses attributable to the non-timekeepers.

In Exhibit A, the net expenses of $1,040,060 have now been allocated to the proper groups. With that complete, it is now possible for the firm to make several other analyses.

Calculating Overhead

To calculate pure overhead, deduct compensation from the total expenses. This provides the firm in the example with the "Overhead Per Salary Dollar" amount necessary for the billing rate computation (discussed in Chapter 4) that is used to set sales prices, and is important in the billing rate model for constructing timekeeper rates. Note the cost of $.96 for associates and $1.04 for legal assistants. What this means is that for each dollar of associate salary, it costs $.96 of overhead support. Is this good or bad? There is no simple answer to this question. The overhead is determined by the firm's culture and the level of service it wishes to provide its clients. This overhead then determines the rates that it will charge to those clients. Obviously, assuming the same level of profit is desired, those with higher costs need to charge higher rates.

By dividing the overhead expenses by the number of people, the example firm is able to calculate the average costs for each timekeeper group as well as to arrive at a cost rate per billable hour. If the firm elects to use overall cost rates, then this rate is recorded on the timekeeper master file and

COSTACCTG
EXPALLOC

PROFITABILITY ANALYSIS FOR   SMITH LAW FIRM PC.
PERIOD ENDING   12/31/XX

	TOTALS	PARTNERS	ASSOC	L/ASST	OTHER	TOTAL	
		5.3	5.8	2.0	3.9	17.0	13.1
COMP:							11.1
ASSOCIATES	291,000		291,000			291,000	
LEGAL ASSTS	91,000			91,000		91,000	
SECRETARIES	153,200				153,200	153,200	
ADMIN	47,000				47,000	47,000	
OTHER	2,500				2,500	2,500	
TOTAL	584,700	—	291,000	91,000	202,700	584,700	
PAYROLL TAXES:							
FICA	86,040	41,310	22,262	6,962	15,507	86,040	
OTHER	5,000	1,567	1,708	592	1,134	5,000	17.0
OTHER PERS CSTS	40,820	12,789	13,943	4,832	9,255	40,820	17.0
DEPREC/AMORT	44,200	13,848	15,098	5,232	10,022	44,200	17.0
OCCUPANCY	115,300	4,000	4,000				17.0
	111,300	34,871	38,018	13,175	25,236	111,300	17.0
PROF EXP	15,000	4,700	5,124	1,776	3,401	15,000	17.0
PRAC DEVEL	12,500	5,980	6,520				11.1
GENERAL STAFF:	5,500	—	—	—	—		17.0
PTR MEETINGS	1,500	1,500				1,500	17.0
EDUCATIONAL	1,000		342	118	540	1,000	17.0
OTHER	3,000	940	1,025	355	680	3,000	17.0
LIBRARY	17,500	5,483	5,978	2,072	3,968	17,500	17.0
OFFICE SUP/SVCS	28,500	8,929	9,735	3,374	6,462	28,500	17.0
TELECOMMUN	22,500	7,049	7,686	2,663	5,102	22,500	17.0
OTHER OPER	65,000	20,365	22,203	7,694	14,738	65,000	17.0
COMPUTER SVCS	22,500	—	—	—	22,500	22,500	17.0
1065060	1,034,020						
TOTAL	1,065,060	163,332	440,639	139,845	321,244	1,048,560	
ALLOC OTH EXP		130,161	141,905	49,177	(321,244)	—	
ALLOC OTH INC	(25,000)	(10,129)	(11,043)	(3,827)	—	(25,000)	13.1
NET EXPENSES	1,040,060	283,364	571,500	185,195	—	1,023,560	
DIRCOMP		540,000					
TOTAL COSTS		823,364	571,500	185,195			
LESS COMPENSATION	382,000	540,000	291,000	91,000			
NET EXPENSES W/O	658,060	283,364	280,500	94,195		658,060	
PER UNIT		70,841	48,362	31,398			
OVERHEAD PER SALARY		0.52	0.96	1.04			
COST RATE		118.13	54.78	41.25			
PARTNERS	4.0	1.3	5.3	6,970			
ASSOC	5.8	1.0	5.8	10,433			
L/ASST	3.0	0.7	2.0	4,490			
STAFF	15.4	0.3	3.9				
TIMEKEEPERS ONLY			13.1				
TIMEKEEPERS AND STAFF			17.0				

Exhibit A

used to compare with the recorded income for purposes of computing profitability on a client, matter, department, or practice area basis. In this example, the cost rate calculated by dividing the total costs by the billable hours for partners, including their base compensation, is $118.13; for associates, it is $54.78; and for legal assistants, $41.25. The overhead cost, excluding compensation, for each individual partner is $70,841; for each associate, $48,362; and for each legal assistant, $31,398.

Determining Profitability

Once the cost rates are calculated and the financial system accepts them, they can then be used to determine profitability at the client, practice area, or billing lawyer level.

There are several questions that generally come up during this kind of profitability analysis. These issues need to be addressed and a consensus reached so that the information that comes out of the analysis is creditable once it is prepared.

Individual or Average Compensation?

The first question has to do with the method for dealing with compensation. There are three different theories for this. The first is that you simply take the compensation for each individual and add it to the overhead cost to get the cost per person. The second method is to use a compensation amount based on an average for different classes; in other words, each associate class may have a different compensation level, and partners may also be divided into classes with an average compensation. The third method is to simply take the average for an entire group and use it as the compensation number for purposes of determining the total overall cost, similar to what was done in Exhibit A.

The method that you use will in many cases be determined by the results that you wish to obtain. If you are looking at profitability strictly at the client or matter level, then it may make sense to look at averages based on different classes within the partner and associate groups. For example, if a matter requires the use of a fifth-year associate, the fact that one of those associates gets paid more than another is not relevant in determining the profitability of the matter. You can use the same argument when it comes partners.

If you are examining profitability at a more detailed level, then you may have to look at the direct compensation of each individual person and not deal with averages. This is the approach used by the firm in the example.

In most cases, the purpose of profitability analysis is not necessarily to look at individuals, but to look at practice area, client, or billing attorney profitability. This information allows a firm to do a strategic review of types of clients, and see how much money is being made from them. Therefore, using averages of the various classes is possibly the best method.

What Is a Partner's Salary?

Even if you assume that averages are the best method when it comes to partner compensation, there remains the question of whether you use the total compensation or some percentage of it. There are some schools of thought that say partner compensation should be divided into various pieces. One piece is the actual salary for being a partner. In other words, if the partner went outside and took a job, what would be that salary? Depending on your compensation levels, chances are you already have that number. The second piece is a return of investment, which is the interest paid on the partner's capital account. The third piece is the amount of profit made from others in the firm.

It makes some sense to use only the salary piece, because if you use total compensation then the cost rate varies directly with the firm's profits. It is better to try to peg the lawyer's imputed compensation based on some salary or worth on the outside, probably in a general-counsel capacity. Again, if you are doing this analysis at the individual partner level, then you may have to use actual compensation. In the example, we used the draws that were assigned to each partner at the beginning of the year in the normal compensation-setting process. Many firms also elect to exclude performance bonuses from compensation for purposes of calculating the cost rate.

Which Revenue Number?

After you have obtained the current cost information, you need to decide which revenue numbers you will use for comparing costs. Three different revenue numbers can be used. One is the accrual-basis revenue number, which is hours worked multiplied by hourly rate. The second is the bills rendered number. And third is the cash receipts number. Keep in mind that you are trying to accomplish two objectives.

First of all, you are trying to ascertain the actual profitability of cost against value of the time worked. In order to have the proper matching of costs and revenues, the revenue side must be the value of the hours worked, which is the accrual-basis gross number. This way you are matching the current year's revenue with the current year's costs and arriving at what should be the current year's profitability, at least on the accrual basis.

Secondly, you are trying to ascertain profitability *vis-à-vis* cash-basis income, which ties back to the financial statements. Here you probably compare the current year's costs with a revenue number based on collections. This does not, however, create the proper matching of costs and revenues. The worst number of all is the bills rendered number. This number really means nothing, and in my opinion to compare costs with bills rendered produces no meaningful information whatsoever.

Keep in mind that when you do the analysis based on the accrual method, as noted in the example, you need to take into consideration net write-ups or write-downs on fees at the time the bill is rendered, and write-offs on fees that reside in the accounts receivable balance.

Should Carrying Charges Be Added?

The last item has to do with whether or not you compute a carrying charge on each and every file, to reflect the costs of work-in-process and accounts receivable until they are collected by the firm. This is a controversial question, and the amounts may be so insignificant that it need not be done. However, there are those who believe that carrying charges are important, and since some people in a firm are better billers and collectors than others, this calculation should be made. In addition, if a client for whatever reason is not being billed and collected on a timely basis, then some carrying charge should be added to the cost so that the firm can determine whether or not it should continue doing work for that particular client. This reflects the fact that there is a cost over and above the normal cost for performing legal work as a result of late billing and collection. The firm in the example opted not to take this approach.

Developing Cost Rates

In order to alleviate some of the problems and potential aberrations that can result from using this rather simple method of cost analysis, I have expanded the illustration somewhat to show a more refined method. This refined method is still fraught with possible problems, but it produces a more accurate result. It is an analysis done at the primary (billing) lawyer level and at the practice area level. Keep in mind that each situation is different, so the assumptions in this example may not necessarily apply to your firm.

The analysis has five steps:

1. *Cost allocation.* This is reflected in Exhibit A as described above, for the calculation of a cost rate for each timekeeper as shown in Exhibit B. Note that as a timekeeper's hours increase, his cost rate decreases. This is how it should be, since the more hours he has, the lower the overhead per hour and thus a greater profit. This coincides with the rules applied in any cost accounting scenario in which the person with the highest level of production has the lowest cost.

COSTACCTG
COSTRATE

DEVELOPMENT OF TIMEKEEPER COST RATE

	TOTAL HOURS	**COST COMP**	**FULL TIME OVERHEAD**	**COSTS**	**RATE**	**EQUIVALENT**	
PARTNER A	1,660	180,000	70,841	250,841	151.11	1.0	(0,000,000)
PARTNER B	1,665	140,000	70,841	210,841	126.63	1.0	
PARTNER C	1,795	120,000	70,841	190,841	106.32	1.0	
PARTNER D	1,850	100,000	70,841	170,841	92.35	1.0	
	6,970	540,000	283,364	823,364			
ASSOC A	1,825	60,000	48,362	108,362	59.38	1.0	
ASSOC B	1,846	57,500	48,362	105,862	57.35	1.0	
ASSOC C	1,868	50,000	48,362	98,362	52.66	1.0	
ASSOC D	1,726	48,500	48,362	96,862	56.12	1.0	
ASSOC E	1,904	45,000	48,362	93,362	49.03	1.0	
ASSOC F	1,264	30,000	38,690	68,690	54.34	0.8	
	10,433	291,000	280,500	571,500			
LEG ASST A	1,542	40,000	31,398	71,398	46.30	1.0	
LEG ASST B	1,363	28,500	31,398	59,898	43.95	1.0	
LEG ASST C	1,585	22,500	31,398	53,898	34.01	1.0	
	4,490	91,000	94,195	185,195			

TOTAL COST:
COMP	922,000	NET INCOME RECONCILIATION:		
OVERHEAD	658,060	RECEIPTS	1,713,426	
TOTAL	1,580,060	EXPENSES	(1,040,060)	
	NET	673,366		

ALLOCATED ABOVE
COMP	922,000	PTR COMP	(540,000)	
OVERHEAD	658,060			
TOTAL	1,580,060	NET	133,366	

DIFFERENCE 0

Exhibit B

2. *Hours allocation.* In order to allocate the costs appropriately to each billing lawyer, it is necessary to determine the distribution of the time-keeper hours to each billing lawyer and calculate the cost attributable to these hours.

The hours distribution among the billing lawyers is shown in Exhibit C. For example, Partner A has 1,660 billable hours, of which 1,258 are charged on his own files; 150 are charged to Partner B; 175 to Partner C; 65 to Partner D; and 12 to those billing lawyers who are not partners.

COSTACCTG
HRSDIST

DISTRIBUTION OF HOURS TO BILLING ATTORNEYS						
HOURS	**PARTNER A**	**PARTNER B**	**PARTNER C**	**PARTNER D**	**OTHERS**	**TOTAL**
PARTNER A	1,660	1,258	150	175	65	12	1,660
PARTNER B	1,665	200	1,410	21	25	9	1,665
PARTNER C	1,795	610	225	900	50	10	1,795
PARTNER D	1,850	1605	125	60	50	10	1,850
	6,970	3,673	1,910	1,156	190	41	6,970
ASSOC A	1,825	1525	125	100	55	20	1,825
ASSOC B	1,846	1240	150	400	26	30	1,846
ASSOC C	1,868	250	1,375	240	0	3	1,868
ASSOC D	1,726	275	936	422	70	23	1,726
ASSOC E	1,904	323	427	1,125	20	9	1,904
ASSOC F	1,264	975	42	200	35	12	1,264
	10,433	4,588	3,055	2,487	206	97	10,433
LEG ASST A	1,542	1,258	125	125	34	0	1,542
LEG ASST B	1,363	100	1052	205	6	0	1,363
LEG ASST C	1,585	235	357	980	13	0	1,585
	4,490	1,593	1,534	1,310	53	—	4,490
TOTAL T/K	21,893	9,854	6,499	4,953	449	138	21,893
TOTAL OTHERS	500	225	148	113	10	4	500
OVERALL TOTAL	22,393	10,079	6,647	5,066	459	142	22,393

Exhibit C

3. *Allocation of costs to billing lawyers.* Using the cost allocation and hours allocation described above, and taking into account the individual compensation for the period and the cost rate calculated in Exhibit B, the costs can now be allocated to each group being examined, as shown in Exhibit D.

By spreading the costs in this manner, it is possible to determine the total costs necessary to support the time on each billing lawyer's files. In Partner A's case, it costs $758,205 to support 10,079 hours of time. On a per-hour basis, it costs $75.23 to produce an hour on Partner A's cases and $69.96 for Partner B.

In many cases the cost per hour, dictated both by the number of hours and by who performs them, varies with the practice area. General litigation work generally has a lower cost per hour than, for example, corporate or tax work. This is one reason why the lawyers in

COSTACCTG
COSTDIST

	HOURS	COST RATE	TOTAL COST	PARTNER A	PARTNER B	PARTNER C	PARTNER D	OTHERS	TOTALS
\multicolumn{10}{l}{**DISTRIBUTION OF TIMEKEEPER COSTS TO BILLING ATTORNEYS**}									
PARTNER A	1,660	151.11	250,841	190,095	22,666	26,444	9,822	1,813	250,841
PARTNER B	1,665	126.63	210,841	25,326	178,550	2,659	3,166	1,140	210,841
PARTNER C	1,795	106.32	190,841	64,854	23,922	95,686	5,316	1,063	190,841
PARTNER D	1,850	92.35	170,841	148,216	11,543	5,541	4,617	923	170,841
			823,364	428,492	236,681	130,330	22,921	4,940	823,364
ASSOC A	1,825	59.38	108,362	90,549	7,422	5,938	3,266	1,188	108,362
ASSOC B	1,846	57.35	105,862	71,110	8,602	22,939	1,491	1,720	105,862
ASSOC C	1,868	52.66	98,362	13,164	72,403	12,638	—	158	98,362
ASSOC D	1,726	56.12	96,862	15,433	52,528	23,682	3,928	1,291	96,862
ASSOC E	1,904	49.03	93,362	15,838	20,938	55,164	981	441	93,362
ASSOC F	1,264	54.34	68,690	52,985	2,282	10,869	1,902	652	68,690
			571,500	259,079	164,175	131,229	11,568	5,450	571,500
LEG ASST A	1,542	46.30	71,398	58,248	5,788	5,788	1,574	—	71,398
LEG ASST B	1,363	43.95	59,898	4,395	46,231	9,009	264	—	59,898
LEG ASST C	1,585	34.01	53,898	7,991	12,140	33,325	442	=	53,898
			185,195	70,634	64,159	48,122	2,280		185,195
TOTALS			1,580,060	758,205	465,015	309,681	36,769	10,390	1,580,060
AS ABOVE			1,580,060						
TOTAL HOURS				10,079	6,647	5,066	459	142	22,393
COST PER HOUR				75.23	69.96	61.13	80.11	73.17	70.56

Exhibit D

a business or tax section may have higher billing rates than those in litigation, assuming the compensation is similar. Insurance defense work has a lower cost per hour because of the individuals performing the work, but has a higher value of time because of higher billable hours. In the example, the overall cost to produce an hour of time for the entire firm is $70.56.

4. *Determination of billable value.* Along with developing the allocation of expenses, you need to develop the gross value of time based on the standard hourly rates of each of the timekeepers. This is illustrated in Exhibit E. In Partner A's case, his files produce a total value of $1,147,555, or 48.3 percent of the total for the firm. This partner is the largest producer of work in the firm and correspondingly has the most files to manage and is the most highly compensated. Keep in mind that this is gross value, prior to any consideration for rate reductions that may result from special arrangements with a client. The

COSTACCTG
TKVALUE

DISTRIBUTION OF TIMEKEEPER VALUE

	HOURS	RATE	TOTAL	PARTNER A	PARTNER B	PARTNER C	PARTNER D	OTHERS	TOTALS
PARTNER A	1,660	205.00	340,300	257,890	30,750	35,875	13,325	2,460	340,300
PARTNER B	1,665	180.00	299,700	36,000	253,800	3,780	4,500	1,620	299,700
PARTNER C	1,795	175.00	314,125	106,750	39,375	157,500	8,750	1,750	314,125
PARTNER D	1,850	150.00	277,500	240,750	18,750	9,000	7,500	1,500	277,500
ASSOC A	1,825	100.00	182,500	152,500	12,500	10,000	5,500	2,000	182,500
ASSOC B	1,846	95.00	175,370	117,800	14,250	38,000	2,470	2,850	175,370
ASSOC C	1,868	90.00	168,120	22,500	123,750	21,600	—	270	168,120
ASSOC D	1,726	90.00	155,340	24,750	84,240	37,980	6,300	2,070	155,340
ASSOC E	1,904	70.00	133,280	22,610	29,890	78,750	1,400	630	133,280
ASSOC F	1,264	70.00	88,480	68,250	2,940	14,000	2,450	840	88,480
LEG ASST A	1,542	60.00	92,520	75,480	7,500	7,500	2,040	—	92,520
LEG ASST B	1,363	50.00	68,150	5,000	52,600	10,250	300	—	68,150
LEG ASST C	1,585	40.00	63,400	9,400	14,280	39,200	520	—	63,400
OTHER	500	35.00	17,500	7,875	5,180	3,955	350	140	17,500
TOTALS			2,376,285	1,147,555	689,805	467,390	55,405	16,130	2,376,285
PERCENT				48.3	29.0	19.7	2.3	0.7	100.0

Exhibit E

$2,376,285 represents this gross value. On a net value basis, the amount is $2,255,995. The difference of $120,290 represents the "rate variance." The rate variance is a significant number, since it illustrates whether or not the firm's rates are too high and not supportable given its client base. For example, reducing rates on insurance defense clients is a part of the rate variance. These are not write-downs. Rather they represent value that is recorded in the system each time a timekeeper puts an hour on his or her timesheet, based on the hourly rate structure agreed to between the lawyer and client at the time the engagement is obtained.

5. *Calculation of profit.* After the revenue and expense sides are determined, it is then possible to calculate profitability. This is illustrated in Exhibit F. Profits can be calculated on several bases. At the billing lawyer level, it can be done using the accrual method (the preferred way) or the cash method. At the working lawyer level, it is usually done on the cash basis. Note that on the accrual basis, Partner A produces a profit of $217,057.

COSTACCTG
BILLINGATTY

BILLING ATTORNEY PROFITABILITY FOR THE YEAR ENDED				12/31/XX	
	PARTNER A	**PARTNER B**	**PARTNER C**	**PARTNER D**	**OTHERS**	**TOTALS**
STANDARD VALUE OF						
BILLABLE TIME	1,147,555	689,805	467,390	55,405	16,130	2,376,285
RATE VARIANCE	(28,689)	(13,796)	(74,783)	(2,217)	(805)	(120,290)
NET VALUE	1,118,866	676,009	392,607	53,188	15,325	2,255,995
WRITE-DOWNS	(95,104)	(60,842)	(5,889)	(1,064)	(1,530)	(164,429)
WRITE-OFFS	(48,500)	(22,650)	(10,000)	(1,500)	(1,000)	(83,650)
					—	
NET ACCRUAL GROSS	975,262	592,517	376,718	50,624	12,795	2,007,916
					—	
COSTS OF BILLABLE TIME	(758,205)	(465,015)	(309,681)	(36,769)	(10,390)	(1,580,060)
					—	
NET ACCRUAL BASIS PROFIT	217,057	127,502	67,037	13,855	2,405	427,856
					—	
WIP BEG OF PERIOD	191,325	80,825	56,871	45,269	19,266	393,556
WIP END OF PERIOD	321,325	140,852	80,555	39,568	41,936	
NET CHANGE	(130,000)	(60,027)	(23,684)	5,701	— (22,670)	(230,680)
A/R BEG OF PERIOD	152,986	60,360	20,357	11,257	14,173	259,133
A/R END OF PERIOD	222,630	95,633	40,835	10,524	14,699	384,321
NET CHANGE	(69,644)	(35,273)	(20,478)	733	= (526)	(125,188)
(-INC) DECREASE IN WIP						
AND A/R	(199,644)	(95,300)	(44,162)	6,434	= (23,196)	(355,868)
CASH BASIS NET	17,413	32,202	22,875	20,289	= (20,791)	71,988
RECEIPTS	775,618	497,217	332,556	57,058	(10,401)	1,652,048
COSTS	(758,205)	(465,015)	(309,681)	(36,769)	(10,390)	(1,580,060)
PROFITS	17,413	32,202	22,875	20,289	(20,791)	71,988

Exhibit F

The reason why the accrual method is preferred, although it is harder to understand, is because it properly matches costs and revenues. *Remember: Expenses are being incurred to support billable hour production and not cash collections.* In addition, the timing of collections can materially affect profitability in any given period.

Having said that, it is still important that your cash-basis profits be as high as possible since this is what determines when everyone gets paid, including the owners. The cash-basis numbers take into account the timing issue of converting hours into dollars. To the extent that a lawyer's receivables or work-in-process increases, his cash-basis net income decreases. In Partner A's case, his net increase in work-in-process and accounts receivable is $199,644. This is a result of an increase in work-in-process of $130,000 and an increase in accounts receivable of $69,644. The result of this calculation produces a net cash-basis profit of $17,413. Note that Partner A has write-downs of $95,104 and accounts receivable write-offs of $48,500 in addition to his rate variance of $28,689.

The working lawyer profitability, which is always suspect because of its dependence on factors normally not under the control of the working lawyer, is determined by subtracting the overhead and compensation costs from the receipts at the working lawyer level. This analysis is fairly simple to make once the costs are determined at the timekeeper level and are then compared to the receipts on his or her own time. This analysis also enables the firm to determine the realization rate attributable to each timekeeper, which is an essential element in calculating billing rates.

You need to recognize that write-ups, write-downs, and write-offs that may occur in the future have an affect on cash-basis profits only to the extent that cash receipts projections based on accrual-basis profits will not materialize. They will have an affect on accrual-basis profits during the period that the transaction occurs.

The overall profit of the firm in the example is $71,988, which is a bonus pool above established draws that can be distributed as the firm sees fit. In some cases, a lawyer or practice area could have a bad accrual year but still have high cash-basis profits. This results from collections from one year offsetting increases in work-in-process and accounts receivable in another year, thus not seriously affecting cash-basis profits. The eventual write-offs will materially affect the accrual-basis profits and affect future cash-basis profits by not having the time value in the system to collect at some date in the future. The effect is dramatized at the working lawyer level, assuming that the problem is controllable by the working lawyer. Remember that if the correct compensation amounts are used for the partners, zero profit is good. That means that a billing lawyer or those in charge of a practice area are able to cover all of the costs, including their own compensation in completing the work.

Marginal Income

One important consideration to keep in mind is that while profitability is important, each billing lawyer unit contributes "marginal income" that is used to offset the indirect overhead expenses. If a billing lawyer terminates, the indirect expenses do not disappear when he leaves, but rather must now be borne by all of the other billing lawyer units. Whether or not the lawyer was profitable, the fact is that he contributed this marginal income that reduced the indirect-cost portion of the cost to produce each billable hour. Thus, upon his termination, and assuming his practice leaves as well, each remaining billing lawyer has his billable-hour cost increase proportionately.

Another important advantage of this type of analysis is that it can be used to examine profitability at the practice area level as noted in Exhibit G. By creating a report that allocates billable hours by practice category rather than by billing lawyer, and computing the cost rate in the same manner as illustrated above, it is possible to make the exact same calculations at the practice category level. In the example, we examine the profitability of four major practice areas of the firm. On a cash basis, Business/Corporate is the most profitable and Commercial Litigation is the least. This type of analysis makes it easier to identify those practice areas that are profitable and those that are not, and is important as the firm goes forward in an atmosphere where emphasis will be on improved profitability and partner earning levels.

COSTACCTG
PRACAREA

PRACTICE AREA PROFITABILITY FOR THE YEAR ENDED			12/31/XX		

	GENERAL LITIGATION	BUSINESS/ CORPORATE	INSURANCE DEFENSE	REAL ESTATE	OTHERS	TOTALS
STANDARD VALUE OF						
BILLABLE TIME	1,147,555	689,805	467,390	55,405	16,130	2,376,285
RATE VARIANCE	(28,689)	(13,796)	(74,783)	(2,217)	(805)	(120,290)
NET VALUE	1,118,866	676,009	392,607	53,188	15,325	2,255,995
WRITE-DOWNS	(95,104)	(60,842)	(5,889)	(1,064)	(1,530)	(164,429)
WRITE-OFFS	(48,500)	(22,650)	(10,000)	(1,500)	(1,000)	(83,650)
NET ACCRUAL GROSS	975,262	592,517	376,718	50,624	12,795	2,007,916
COSTS OF BILLABLE TIME	(758,205)	(465,015)	(309,681)	(36,769)	(10,390)	(1,580,060)
NET ACCRUAL BASIS PROFIT	217,057	127,502	67,037	13,855	2,405	427,856
WIP BEG OF PERIOD	191,325	80,825	56,871	45,269	19,266	393,556
WIP END OF PERIOD	321,325	140,852	80,555	39,568	41,936	
NET CHANGE	(130,000)	(60,027)	(23,684)	5,701	(22,670)	(230,680)
A/R BEG OF PERIOD	152,986	60,360	20,357	11,257	14,173	259,133
A/R END OF PERIOD	222,630	95,633	40,835	10,524	14,699	384,321
NET CHANGE	(69,644)	(35,273)	(20,478)	733	(526)	(125,188)
(-INC) DECREASE IN WIP						
AND A/R	(199,644)	(95,300)	(44,162)	6,434	(23,196)	(355,868)
CASH BASIS NET	17,413	32,202	22,875	20,289	(20,791)	71,988
RECEIPTS	775,618	497,217	332,556	57,058	(10,401)	1,652,048
COSTS	(758,205)	(465,015)	(309,681)	(36,769)	(10,390)	(1,580,060)
PROFITS	17,413	32,202	22,875	20,289	(20,791)	71,988

Exhibit G

Alternative Billing Methods

Those firms who have made the progressive move toward billing clients other than on an hourly basis (as discussed in Chapter 12) will find this type of analysis extremely useful. Should a firm decide to bill a matter on the basis of a fixed fee or a blended rate (the more popular of the alternative billing arrangements), it now has the information available to determine what that amount should be based on the cost information. This assumes that the matter is one which can be budgeted based on the work to be performed and the estimated time to completion.

For example, suppose it is estimated that in order to complete a particular matter, it will take 100 hours and that these hours will be distributed as shown in Figure O below: to Partner A, 10 hours; Partner D, 25 hours; Associate D, 50 hours; and Legal Assistant B, 15 hours. Figure O also shows the cost to produce this work based on the cost analysis.

It is now possible to estimate the amount to be quoted to the client. It is also possible for the responsible billing lawyer to track the time on the file to make certain that it does not exceed the cost estimate, and if it does, to see what is causing the overrun and what corrective measures must be taken.

The information provided by this analysis can be used to make certain that the alternative billing arrangement meets the profit expectations of the firm and provides a tracking mechanism so that these profit goals are achieved.

Use as a Compensation Device

Some firms are beginning to use this type of analysis as a compensation tool. It should be emphasized that this analysis in and of itself does not provide information as to whether a lawyer is overpaid or underpaid. Rather, it reflects the ability of the lawyer to manage those files under his or her

Partner A	10 hours @ 151.11	$1,511.10
Partner D	25 hours @ 92.35	2,308.75
Associate D	50 hours @ 56.12	2,806.00
Legal Assistant B	15 hours @ 43.95	659.75
Total Costs	$7,285.60	

Figure O

responsibility in a manner that produces the most profit for the firm. This means timely billing and collection, proper utilization of lawyers and non-lawyers, alternative billing arrangements where possible, and a minimum level of write-downs and write-offs.

The profitability issue is simply another of the criteria that is used by the firm to determine the level of compensation paid to each lawyer. It should be used along with all other established criteria and given its proper consideration in ascertaining the contribution that the lawyer makes to the overall good of the organization from a financial, organizational, and managerial perspective.

Miscellaneous Issues

Improper Recording of Billable Hours

The question arises from some firms as to whether this analysis can be performed in those instances where timekeeper hours are either not recorded on a regular basis or perhaps not recorded at all. The answer is that it can still be accomplished, assuming that the timekeepers in question are assigned to one specific billing lawyer or practice area. If this is the case, then their costs as determined above can be directly charged to the appropriate category and total costs obtained. The cost rate is required because most timekeepers spread their time over a variety of matters and the cost rate is the only way to track their costs to specific clients, which can only be accomplished through proper recording of billable hours.

Disproportionate Cost Rate

When this analysis is prepared, oftentimes there are one or two timekeepers whose cost rate for whatever reason is disproportionate to their actual costs. This generally occurs when there is an "expert" in the firm who does not have significant hours, is paid relatively well, and who is only called upon in certain situations to assist in client matters. In this case, it is possible to "impute" a cost rate, recognizing that this individual's cost is generally offset by a higher-than-normal billing rate due to the expertise offered in the situation.

Guidelines for Profitability

Once the cost analysis has been prepared either at the billing lawyer or practice area level, the next issue is to establish policies and procedures to improve profitability in the future. Law firm managers have continually been searching for the ultimate solution to improving profitability in their firms.

Unfortunately, there is no cookbook available that provides the solution. However, years of experience in working with firms has permitted me to establish a certain set of guidelines, which if followed by a firm in most of its practice areas, will go a long way to improving profitability and providing a greater income stream to the owners. Not only will profits improve, but this plan also permits more efficient and cost-effective services to the clients and provides for more communication and cooperation among the various lawyers participating in a client project.

It is recognized that the nature of a practice may necessitate certain deviations from any plan in unusual or extraordinary circumstances. The plan is devised to take care of the majority of the services provided by a firm, with exceptions clearly documented and substantiated by the billing lawyer. Here are the guidelines:

♦ *Lawyer involvement.* All initial client inquiries are referred to a lawyer before setting up an appointment. This permits the lawyer to attempt to get sufficient information in advance to determine the complexity of the matter. In more complex matters, before the appointment the lawyer sends the client a questionnaire with a cover letter and brochure designed specifically for the practice area. The letter requests that the questionnaire be returned before the appointment if possible, or brought to the appointment by the client. As soon as possible after a potential client is obtained, all lawyers involved in the assignment are made aware of the client's situation, and a plan for completing the assignment is developed. This communication occurs at the time of the initial meeting with the client. If this is not possible or practical, then it occurs as soon as all of the facts are known concerning the client's situation and the work that is to be performed has been identified. Again, where possible and practical, associate lawyers, and in certain cases legal assistants as well, attend meetings with the client, including the final one when the documents are presented for review and signature.

♦ *Budgetary constraints.* In most cases, the billing lawyer prepares some estimate of the costs involved in completing the project. These cost estimates are communicated to all of the lawyers on the assignment. This enables them to understand when or if certain work should be performed and also provides some measuring device in the event that the work is expected to significantly exceed budgeted estimates.

♦ *Communications with client.* To the extent possible, and for the majority of work performed by the firm, the client is informed of the estimated costs to finalize his assignment. Where possible within certain practice areas, written fee guidelines are developed for similar assignments such as estate plans, will preparation, business formations, and so on. While it is recognized that this is an inexact process, prior assignments on similar matters should enable the primary lawyer to provide an estimate of the final costs that is close to actual. This communication also includes the billing and payment policies of the firm and provides for some level of retainer against the final cost estimate. When possible, except for certain clients who would likely seek other counsel if required to pay a retainer, retainers are secured.

◆ *Progress billings.* The firm establishes a policy of sending progress bills on all regular matters if the estimate is expected to exceed a threshold amount set by agreement of the lawyers. The progress bills generally coincide with the delivery of tangible evidence of progress on a case, such as a draft of documents associated with the assignment. The clients are informed of this policy as part of the communications outlined in item 3 above. Progress bills are the rule rather than the exception, and the billing lawyers understand that they may be required to submit written explanations to the firm's management for not sending out bills on a current basis.

◆ *Billing policy.* In addition to the practice of issuing progress bills as outlined in item 4 above, the firm establishes a policy of submitting bills each time documents are delivered to the client. Again, not following this policy will be the exception rather the rule, and the same accountability from the billing lawyer regarding progress billings applies.

◆ *Standard forms.* Where possible, and within certain practice areas, the firm develops standard forms that can be used for a majority of client assignments that are similar in nature. The members of a practice area agree to use them and to not make changes unrelated to the fact situation of a particular client unless these changes have been approved by the chair of the practice group, who has responsibility for maintaining the standard forms database, making any changes, and communicating the changes to the other members of the group. The practice-group chair is also responsible for making certain that the forms continue to adhere to current legal requirements, although each member of the group has the responsibility to report any nonadherence to legal requirements that may become apparent.

◆ *File review.* It is a policy of the firm to "touch" each file at least once during a thirty-day period. This is evidenced by a time entry on the file. This ensures that matters get attention quickly and that the turnaround time to completion and signing of the documents occurs on a timely basis. This, in turn, helps the firm more quickly realize revenues from the work performed. The billing lawyer keeps a list of pending files that is reviewed and updated every thirty days as a means of moving the files to conclusion.

◆ *Staffing.* It is recognized that work is most profitable when performed by the lowest-paid person who can perform the work in the best possible manner. The billing lawyer on each assignment makes every effort to use associate lawyers or legal assistants where possible in order to reduce the overall costs for the project.

◆ *Client rejections.* It is understood and agreed that the selection of clients for which work is performed undergoes a much greater scrutiny than in the past. Extra care is exercised because those clients who refuse to pay a retainer or who appear to be concerned about the estimated charges should probably not be retained. There is a recognition that clients who complain about fees initially usually continue to be problem clients, and the firm is better off without them.

The subject of profitability at other than the firm level is one that is very difficult to grasp for those not fairly versed in cost-accounting concepts. Whatever methodology is used, it should be agreed to by a consensus of the partners so that the results are accepted once the methodology is applied to the actual information from the firm's accounting and timekeeping systems. Make certain that everyone buys into how the process is going to be done, and more importantly, why it is being done and what decisions will be made from the information once the analysis is completed.

ALTERNATIVE BILLING: IS THERE A BETTER WAY?

12

While billing rates may continue for a long time to be the easiest and most understandable way to bill clients on an ongoing basis, I would be remiss if I didn't present some thoughts on alternatives to the almighty hourly rate.

Years ago, before timekeeping systems and the now-indoctrinated concept of the hourly rate, lawyers rendered bills primarily on the basis of some value that was placed on the work performed. In most cases, it was based on a relatively subjective judgment that there would be more clients that produced a profit than produced a loss. Thanks mostly to the computer and the neat software packages that can prepare bills in 237 formats, the hourly rate became the objective standard for most professional service firms. The problem, particularly in the legal environment, is that firms have become more and more mechanized in the area of standard practices and forms. In addition, the law itself is perhaps more difficult, so that productive, nonbillable time must be spent on research and development of legal matters, which then later translates into client assignments.

Everyone talks about efficiency and productivity, but if the legal profession isn't careful, it will "efficiency" itself right out of business. If a lawyer performs a client assignment that previously took twelve hours in only eight hours, then he or she must bill at a value close to the twelve hours or lose four hours' worth of income. Or, without producing any additional revenue, the lawyer finds another four hours to take the place of the lost time, or utilize the excess time to perform work that would be done by others, thus reducing the number of lawyers required in the firm overall.

Value Pricing

The concept of value pricing, or premium billing, takes on several forms. The objective is to find a way to recoup both the expertise and the prior work product that lawyers have accumulated during their years in practice. Clients and lawyers need to be sensitized to the fact that firms are now producing a better product in less time. Yet firms still must be compensated as they were when the work took more time.

In my lifetime, and certainly in the lifetimes of many people reading this book, we will see a shift away from hourly billing to some other method in a majority of the work performed by lawyers and other professional service organizations. Billing by the hour will be the exception rather than the rule.

I stopped billing by the hour years ago when I found out that the more efficient I got, the less money I made. This did not make any sense to me. A $5,000 project is worth $5,000. Oftentimes I quote a price for a project, and the client asks me how much time the project will take. I then ask if the price is fair for what the client will receive; if the client says yes (which he generally does), then what difference does the amount of time make? As long as the client feels he is getting the service he requires at a fair price and in a timely manner, how long the work takes is irrelevant. In some cases, this approach doesn't work; however, a firm should not automatically assume that a pricing system not based on hourly billing couldn't be used for a particular project or in a particular practice area.

Making Value Billing a Reality

Clients are clamoring for change, and competition is forcing firms to become more creative in how they price their services. The time has come for the legal profession and their clients to begin thinking about billing and paying for what is produced, and not for how long it takes to produce it.

When this change happens, it can create many internal problems for law firms. But make no mistake; the change is going to happen. The question is whether your firm is going to follow the lead or lead the way. This is a judgment that each firm must make in light of their position in the area where they operate, the services they provide, and the clients they serve.

There are certain ingredients that must be available to a firm in order to make value billing a reality:

- ◆ Similar assignments
- ◆ Prior work product, and the technology to use it
- ◆ Cost analysis, to establish a price that produces the desire profit level
- ◆ Changes in firm culture

Each of these elements helps in allowing a firm to begin using alternative billing. A firm will never use value billing 100 percent of the time, but it can at least begin making the transition away from an hourly rate system.

Determining Value

I am often asked how value is actually determined. Unfortunately, there is no formula for that. As noted earlier, you need a practice that repeats itself either in whole or in part, or a practice whereby your knowledge or work product in one area assists you in solving problems in another. When I have said this to law firms, many are immediately turned off. They think their firms are different, that nothing ever repeats in their practices, and every assignment is a reinvention of the wheel.

Obviously, this is not true. Technology permits firms to save prior work product, which can be used over and over again. Somehow you need to be compensated for the work that is used for Client B, even after you have used it for Client A. Also, when the work was done for Client A, perhaps it was billed at a discount to take into consideration the learning curve for the person doing the work.

Everyone talks about how technology improves productivity and profits. It does. But it only helps those that have a fixed selling price so that as the cost goes down, the profit margin goes up. Unfortunately, professional service firms have a floating sales price, based not on what was produced but how long it took to produce it. Thus, productivity gains are passed onto the consumer and the firm gets little or no benefit. Law firms who specialize in plaintiff work have been the most successful in taking advantage of technology, because they have a fixed sales price, such as one-third of x. As they reduce their costs, they increase their profit margins.

How many times has one of your fellow professionals walked into a partner's office with a question, knowing that a brief conversation with the knowledgeable partner can save hours of time? And how many times has the partner then looked back over his day and logged .1 or .2 hours for that conversation, rather than increasing his rate or time because of the bargain the client just received? This is value billing.

I noted earlier that I stopped billing by the hour many years ago. Now, I admit that I have projects that do repeat themselves, but each has some special feature that makes it different than the one before. Generally, I price the work twice, using two different methods. The first method assumes I have no major knowledge, experience, or prior work product relating to the project; the second assumes I that I do. The fee I quote is somewhere between the two amounts. Using this system, both of us get a good deal.

Here are some of the subjective factors I use in determining fees:

- How complex is the assignment? Am I one of only a few people who can solve this problem, or am I one of many?
- Do I want to encourage further business from this client? If so, I can't charge him so much that I scare him away.
- Is there any travel involved? Will I be away from my family for a long time?
- What is the time frame for the project? Will I have to work long hours to get the work done because of the client's time schedule?

All of these go into the mix when determining what value to put on the work.

Overcoming Obstacles to Alternative Billing

There are certainly problems and challenges that occur when implementing a new billing structure that is a major departure from how firms have operated for the past thirty years.

- *Getting the professionals to try something different.* This is always a problem, even if it only means changing the way that expense reports are completed.
- *Getting the clients to try something different.* Believe it or not, this is less of a problem than the professionals believe it to be. In fact, most clients welcome a system that allows them to better predict what their legal costs will be.
- *Better and more efficient management of the work.* Obviously, if there is a fixed price, the billing lawyer needs to make certain that the file is managed so that is stays within a prescribed budget.
- *Sacrificing quality for efficiency.* There has to be a balance here. There is some fear that the stress of attempting to stay within a budgeted price causes lawyers to cut corners and not do a complete and accurate job. With the threat of malpractice hanging out there, this should not be that much of a problem. At the end of the day, the work must be done properly and correctly, even if the costs exceed the price quoted.
- *Establishing new budgeting systems.* This occurs over time, as firms get more history on the effect of value billing methods.

◆ *Revising reward systems.* Firms who gravitate to value billing change their reward criteria away from billable hour production and toward realized profits, regardless of the time it takes to produce those profits.

Determining Rates

At the time of this writing, a variety of methods are being used by firms to deal with the change to value billing. They are included here for information, although I'm sure that several more will be developed in the years to come.

One-Time Increase

Some firms simply add *x* dollars to every lawyer's rate. In theory, this one-time increase effectively pays for the technology investment throughout the firm. This simplistic approach might work if you can rationalize adding a few more dollars to the rate and if the use of the technology is uniformly distributed so that all clients effectively bear their appropriate fair share. But I believe this is a cop-out that doesn't deal with the issue of using skills and expertise to create a better product in less time, thus justifying additional charges in an objective way.

Range of Rates

Some firms have adopted a range of rates. When an entry is placed on the time sheet, a code is placed next to it that indicates the rate to be charged. This works if you can identify the value for the service and if lawyers are diligent enough to input the code. The main objection to this system is that clients have become more sophisticated in dealing with their lawyers. They are asking them to render services at the lowest rate available to all other clients. It may not be possible to use a floating rate if the client receives a commitment to use the lowest rate charged. Obviously, the lowest rate won't reflect the use of technology. In addition, lawyers are inevitably tempted to use it to avoid write-downs.

Padding Hours

Some firms simply pad hours. In other words, if a project used to take four hours but now takes one, a lawyer may record two or three hours on the time sheet. Again, while this may work, it's still a cop-out in dealing with the real issue. It significantly distorts the statistical information that is so prominently used in the compensation process. In addition, some lawyers will always have the ability to use technology whereas others will not. I would have a problem penalizing one who can't and trying to explain why one associate has five hundred fewer billable hours than another—difficult enough even when most of the facts are known throughout the partnership. Padding hours also raises some ethical questions.

Surcharge Rate

Another method, which may be somewhat of a compromise, is to code the time according to a surcharge rate. Instead of the code identifying a different rate, the code automatically increases the standard rate by some predetermined percentage—in effect, placing a surcharge on the work performed. For example, an *A* beside a time entry might mean to increase the rate by 25 percent; a *B* by 35 percent, and so on. The problem of coding the time still exists; however, a firm avoids the problem of having multiple rates. The standard rate is retained and an overrealization condition exists when the rate is actually billed.

Flat Charge

Still another method is to code into the computer systems a flat charge to be used any time that a prior work product is used on a client assignment. This could be a brief, a memorandum, or an opinion that is stored in a firm's work-product database, or a standard form such as a will or articles of incorporation that is stored in the word-processing system. In effect, each time these items are accessed, an automatic charge is made to a client's file. This procedure allows a firm to recapture some of the research and development time that was expended creating work products or standard documents. This way, a firm is actually selling a commodity—the document—and it charges a fixed price to all who use it.

Fixed-Fee Pricing

Some firms use fixed-fee pricing or blended rates, which seems to be the most popular alternative billing method. Here you quote one rate for all partners, one for all associates, one for all legal assistants, and so on, or a rate for all timekeepers combined. The billing lawyer then tries to manage the manpower based on the budget that is produced for a particular matter.

Keeping Time Records

Some discussions about the move to more value-based billing have raised the question of whether the keeping of detailed time records will still be necessary. Many lawyers see the change away from unitized billing as a first step toward getting rid of one of the administrative tasks they dislike the most: keeping a record of what they did and how long it took to do it. But this long-honored tradition will undoubtedly continue, regardless of the billing systems used, for the reasons listed below:

- *Profitability analysis.* One of the key features in any type of profitability analysis is to calculate the cost rate assigned to each timekeeper. To make this calculation, total costs such as compensation and overhead are divided by billable hours to compute the cost rate. Without the hours record, it becomes difficult to compute the cost rate for purposes of cost allocation.
- *Traditional work.* Regardless of the billing system used, there will continue to be traditional work situations where the firm needs to record time in order to get paid. This could be in connection with bankruptcy proceedings, family law matters, and so on. In addition, chances are that for the foreseeable future, insurance companies will continue to want their lawyers to keep accurate time records.
- *Estimated value.* Almost every assignment has some threshold level beyond which further work produces little, if any, additional revenues. By keeping time, the lawyer stays aware of the value of time on the file. By comparing this time value against the potential receipt, regardless of how that is calculated, he is better able to determine when the matter should be brought to some type of conclusion. It makes little economic sense to continue to work on a file that has a collection limit of $10,000 if the time value has already exceeded that limit.
- *Buy-out of departing lawyers.* With lawyers now moving from firm to firm in great numbers, there has been an increase in the number of firms with buy-out agreements with their partners. Generally, these agreements contain provisions whereby a departing lawyer retains some interest in the work-in-process and accounts receivable balances that remain at the time of his departure. This departure may occur due to withdrawal, death, disability, retirement, expulsion, or a move into public service as a judge, corporate general counsel, and so on. Time records provide a logical basis for determining the extent to which the terminating partner receives his due share of these amounts that were created while he was an owner. Without these records, it is difficult, if not impossible, to determine the value to the departing lawyer. Oftentimes one of the parties ends up in litigation to make certain that the allocation of the proceeds of these files, when collected, are adequately and fairly shared.
- *Asset valuation.* One of the major assets of most law firms, and one that is usually missing from the cash-basis balance sheet, is the value of work-in-process and accounts receivable. These values cannot be obtained without time records, which are the basis of this valuation.

Oftentimes, banks lend money based solely on the value of these accrual-basis assets, so knowing the value increases a firm's borrowing power. This value is also used in buy-outs, as noted above.

◆ *Legal record.* Due to the mounting public pressure to reduce lawyers' fees, many jurisdictions require some type of evidence of fees accumulated on a particular client assignment. Keeping time records provides a firm with some evidential material of the time value charged on behalf of a client, and may, in some cases, provide justification for the fees requested. This record also serves another important purpose. In some cases (more often than I would have thought) a client becomes dissatisfied with his lawyer, and decides to change counsel before a matter is completed. When that occurs, the original lawyer oftentimes places a lien on the eventual collection for what he considers his reasonable share of the eventual proceeds. Good time records can provide evidence of the amount due under these circumstances.

Changes in billing practices will definitely alter the method by which lawyers are measured for performance, not the least of which is compensation. Actual receipts will probably replace billable hours as one of the main criteria, since fees, in many cases, will bear no relationship to hours production.

Convincing the Client

I mentioned earlier the need to sensitize the client to the alternatives to the hourly rate. This should be done in the engagement letter. Below are two paragraphs that can be used in an engagement letter to address the issue of billing for services other than by the strict applications of hours and rates. While the second paragraph doesn't fully address the technology issue, the "unusual skill, experience, or factual knowledge" comments can be interpreted that way.

1. While we will generally be rendering bills on an hourly basis, there may be instances where we will be using prior work products, computer models, simulations, or spreadsheets that have been developed specifically to perform services relative to your assignment. Since it is both to your benefit as well as ours to utilize these tools in providing services to you, the amount billed may not necessarily correlate with the time involved to perform all or part of the project. In all cases, however, the charges will be less than if we had to perform the tasks or services without the benefit of these tools.

2. Our bills are not always determined solely by the mechanical application of standard hourly rates to the number of hours worked. We endeavor to charge fairly for the value of our services and hope that our clients will perceive our fees to be reasonable for the services rendered. Where appropriate, our fees are subject to adjustment to reflect lower charges, for example, for start-up or learning time. The fees may also reflect a premium if we are engaged on matters of extreme complexity or importance, or which impose unusual demands on the firm's resources, or for which we possess unusual skill, experience, or factual knowledge.

Dick Reed is an old friend, a former senior partner at Reed, McClure, Moceri and Thonn, and a consultant at Altman Weil. In 1985, Reed published an article in which he discussed the "true measure of value of a lawyer's services." He addresses so-called value billing in the article, saying:

To value a lawyer's services to a client based primarily upon hours spent ignores the true worth of the lawyer's services and rewards incompetence. It is unfair to both the client and lawyer to do so. To value a lawyer's services to his or her firm primarily based upon production of the total hours spent likewise fails to recognize properly the criteria for true value to the firm for the lawyer's contribution.

Reed later edited two books in which he expanded upon the theme of value billing: *Beyond the Billable Hour: An Anthology of Alternative Billing Methods,* and *Win-Win Billing Strategies: Alternatives That Satisfy Your Clients and You.* In addition, he also wrote *Billing Innovations: New Win-Win Ways to End Hourly Billing* (1996). All three books are published by the American Bar Association Law Practice Management Section and may be useful to readers.

For additional reference on this subject, I recommend a book published in 1989 by the ABA's Task Force on Alternative Billing Methods, *Alternative Billing Methods,* and the more recent publication, *Winning Alternatives to the Billable Hour: Strategies That Work, Second Edition,* also published by the ABA Law Practice Management Section (2002).

JUSTIFYING THE COST OF TECHNOLOGY | **13**

After spending millions of dollars on technology, most of it with after-tax money, many law firms still cannot produce a meaningful cost-benefit analysis of these expenditures. Instead, they continue to spend, thinking, "We have to, if we want to remain competitive."

In fact, most attempts to justify the cost of technology are still based on expense reductions. In other words, firm leaders say, "If we spend x dollars on technology, and we save y dollars on secretaries, then the decision was a good one, since we are further ahead that we would have been without the investment."

But this type of analysis is flawed and produces inaccurate results. Why? Among other things, it fails to take into account key issues such as the enormous cost of training and back-office support as well as the constant need for software and hardware support and upgrades. In fact, what generally happens is that technology allows a firm to replace a secretary or two, but the firm must now hire skilled technology workers whose salary and benefits far exceed that of the secretaries the computers supposedly replaced.

Chapter 12 addresses the issue of using technology to change billing habits. This is one of the ways lawyers can use technology to produce a better product in less time for their clients, and still be rewarded with the same level of revenue.

What Should Technology Do for You?

The question to ask about technology in a law firm today is not "do we need it?" but rather "how much of it do we need?" Answering this question correctly is especially important if there are people in your firm who always want the latest and greatest technology, and think that having all the bells and whistles makes the firm competitive.

Technology offers a payback when it allows your firm to do all, or a majority, of the following:

- Work more efficiently (however that is determined)
- Work more productively (however that is measured)
- Produce more billable hours
- Increase the effective hourly rate
- Produce a better product
- Produce a better-looking product
- Compete for business with other firms
- Keep clients that might have been lost
- Get new clients that otherwise might not have been obtained
- Use alternative billing methods
- Have more personal time

Surveying Your Computer Users

The following is a questionnaire that I use for my law firm clients to help me determine the level of technology they need, so they can purchase the minimum yet have maximum return. Before investing heavily in additional technology, you may find it useful to distribute this questionnaire to the lawyers and other computer users in your firm so that you can better understand what technology they need to provide your firm's desired level of client service.

QUESTIONNAIRE FOR COMPUTER USERS

1. On a scale of 1-10 (10 = highest), in relation to your coworkers with the same job title, rate yourself with respect to your computer literacy.
2. When you are not in meetings with clients or coworkers, how much time each do you use your computer for business-related issues?
3. Check the applications below that you use frequently.
   ___a. E-mail
   ___b. Word processing
   ___c. Spreadsheets
   ___d. Databases

___e. Electronic research

___f. Internet (business use only)

___g. Firm accounting (time sheets, reports, etc.)

___h. Specialized applications (please list)

___i. Other

4. Listed below are some benefits that should come from using technology. Please indicate those applicable in your situation.

___a. Made me more efficient

___b. Made me more productive

___c. Has increased my billable hours

___d. Has increased my effective hourly rate

___e. Enabled me to produce a better product

___f. Enabled me to produce a better-looking product

___g. Has allowed me to compete for business with other firms

___h. Has allowed me to keep clients that I may have lost

___i. Has allowed me to get clients that I may not have obtained

___j. Has allowed me to use alternative billing methods

___k. Has allowed me to spend more time with my family

___l. Other

5. List below those clients that you have lost or did not obtain because the level of technology in the firm was below that of other firms competing for the same business.

6. List below those clients that you have gained or been able to keep due to the level of technology in the firm being above or equal to that of other firms competing for the same business.

7. Check below those reasons why you may have not fully taken advantage of the technology available to you.

___a. Have little or no interest

___b. Can't type and do not want to learn

___c. Software available not sufficient to handle my requirements

___d. Hardware available not sufficient to handle my requirements

___e. Lack of available system and service support

___f. Need more training on what is available and how to use it

___g. Other

8. Comments:

BUDGETING IN THE PLAINTIFF FIRM | 14

Unlike general practice firms—that bill their time on an hourly basis—most plaintiff firms don't keep time and are paid a percentage of any eventual settlement that is received. This percentage, negotiated when the client is obtained, is in the 25- to 40-percent range. Because there's no correlation between time worked on an assignment and the fee to be received, plaintiff firms have taken the attitude that it's not necessary and, in fact, is counterproductive for its professionals to keep detailed time records. Although some plaintiff firms do keep time, they are in the minority.

First, I'm going to make a case for those lawyers involved in plaintiff work to keep time records on the same basis as their peers involved in general practice. Because the number of converts may be few, I'll then discuss budgeting methods that can be used if time is not recorded. With a little imagination and ingenuity on the part of a firm's financial manager, many of the analyses used in a general practice firm can be applied to a plaintiff firm, whether or not accurate time records are kept.

The Case for Timekeeping

Plaintiff firms need to keep accurate time records for the same reasons as general practice firms—it provides a method for measuring the success of a firm internally and against the competition,

161

as well as enabling a firm to operate on a sound basis of financial management. Other benefits, some specific to a plaintiff firm, are detailed below.

Profitability

In most cases, a plaintiff firm has little, if any, method of measuring profitability, or lack thereof, at the completion of an assignment. Since hours aren't kept, the cost related to a client project can't ever be obtained. Thus, a firm receives its share of the settlement proceeds but has no method of determining whether the assignment produced an adequate profit in relation to the time devoted to it. In most firms, large settlements produce a high degree of euphoria among the partners, with the lawyer in charge becoming "king for a day." However, if a firm keeps adequate records of its costs, it might discover that certain projects, regardless of the settlement amount, produce a loss rather than a profit. Many firms wonder why, despite continually obtaining good settlements, they always fall short of profits available for distribution to owners or lack the cash to keep the firm in operation.

Some firms view small cases as loss leaders that must be taken on to attract larger ones. While this may be true, good management still dictates that a firm be cognizant of just how much is being lost with the smaller assignments and the extent to which they are using firm resources.

Evaluation

The evaluation criteria for lawyers in a plaintiff firm generally concern number of clients obtained, number of settlements achieved, and perhaps the average settlement per case closed. While these are adequate, they may not properly evaluate productivity. Thus, certain lawyers may settle many cases at better-than-average levels but don't work the requisite amount of time commensurate with their compensation levels. If nothing else, timekeeping provides a good indication of a lawyer's industriousness and work ethic, both of which are major performance standards in setting compensation levels.

Settlement Point

Almost every file in a plaintiff firm has a threshold beyond which further work produces little, if any, reward. By keeping time, a lawyer remains aware of the value of time on the file. By comparing this time value against the potential settlement level, he or she is better able to determine when the settlement option should be vigorously pursued.

Buying Out Terminated Lawyers

With lawyers now moving from firm to firm in great numbers, many are attempting to formulate some type of buy-out agreement with their partners. Generally, a departing lawyer retains some interest in unsettled cases. Time records provide a logical basis for determining the share of settlements that a terminating partner receives on files that were in process prior to his leaving the firm. In such cases, a lawyer receives a share of the settlement based on a percentage of the value in the case at the time of departure, compared against the total time on the file when the settlement occurred. Without these records, it's difficult, if not impossible, to determine the value to the departing lawyer. This oftentimes ends up with one of the parties litigating to make certain that the allocation of the settlement proceeds are adequately and fairly shared.

Asset Valuation

One of the major assets that most law firms have—usually missing from the cash-basis balance sheet—is the value in work-in-process for unsettled cases. Time records form the basis for the valuation. This relates to the buy-out issues referred to above.

Legal Record

Due to mounting public pressure, many jurisdictions require some type of evidence of fees accumulated on a particular client assignment. Keeping time records provides a firm with some evidence of the time value charged on behalf of a particular client and may, in some cases, provide justification for the fees requested.

This record also serves another important purpose. In some cases, more often than you would think, clients become dissatisfied with their lawyers and decide to change counsel prior to their cases being settled. When this occurs, the original lawyers often place a lien on the settlement for what they consider their reasonable share of the eventual settlement proceeds. Good time records can provide evidence of the amount due under these circumstances.

There is no question that keeping time records is not a favorite activity of most lawyers. In fact, many have told me that the reason they enjoy the plaintiff type of practice is that they don't have to keep time. While I agree that this will never become anyone's favorite pastime, the fact is that the benefits of keeping time records far outweigh the costs, including the time it actually takes to record the hours.

Particularly significant are those situations where a firm has both a general and a plaintiff practice, something that is becoming more the norm than the exception. With only half the firm keeping time, it has a major problem in preparing realistic budgets, monitoring its financial performance, and evaluating the work of its lawyers.

Today's economy forces every firm to manage its resources soundly to meet the desired goals and objectives of its partners. While the $10 million and $20 million settlements get all the headlines, the truth is that most plaintiff firms survive on turning over many cases in small amounts. A firm needs all the information it can get to make certain that these files are handled profitably and that the lawyers are at a state of productivity commensurate with the culture of the organization.

Alternate Budgeting Methods

If, after reading this chapter, plaintiff firms still believe keeping time records is "against all that is right and proper," can they still benefit from the budgeting process? The answer is yes, although it requires making more assumptions and probably being less accurate. However, 50 percent of something is better than 100 percent of nothing, so what follows are some budgeting concepts plaintiff firms can use. This discussion focuses primarily on the income side, since expenses can be budgeted as in a general practice firm.

The income produced in a plaintiff firm is a product of the number of cases that can be settled and the amount of settlement per case. The number of cases that can be settled is a function of how many cases are available to be settled and the average length of time it takes to settle a case.

In this regard, the number of cases in a firm's inventory can be correlated to value of hours in a general practice firm's inventory. Thus, a plaintiff firm's income budget can be computed as in Figure P.

Number of open cases at beginning of year	300
Number of new cases estimated to be received	1,200
Total cases available to be settled	1,500

Figure P

If, on the average, it takes three months to settle a case, then at the end of the year, a firm will have three months of new cases open, having settled 1,200 during the year. If the average settlement value is $3,000, then the expected fee income for the year is $3,600,000. If it takes four months to settle a case on the average, then 400 cases will remain in inventory, and only 1,100 would have been settled for a total value of $3,300,000.

Firms need to examine historical patterns of obtaining and settling cases. Once this is determined and the fee income is estimated, the manager can then calculate the firm's financial activity on a monthly basis to determine whether projections are being met. If not, what are the reasons? Is it because cases aren't being settled in the same time frame as in the past? Is the number of new cases higher or lower than anticipated? Is the average settlement value higher or lower than historical averages? After reviewing each one of these areas, steps need to be taken to correct problems so that income expectations can be met. Obviously, one huge hit—or a major loss—can significantly alter the budget amounts. For most plaintiff firms, however, these numbers are fairly predictable and can be used as a yardstick by which to measure the firm's financial plan for the year.

As manager of a plaintiff firm, you should also examine, if possible, whether cases settle at different times of the year. This, too, can be predicted for those firms that have been practicing for some time. If seasonal variations can be predicted, then you can more accurately calculate when cash flow will be affected, possibly altering the amount of compensation partners receive.

It's a cop-out to simply assume that, since a firm doesn't keep time records, it can't prepare a realistic and sound budget. Although certain assumptions need to be made—which may not be as accurate as when time records are kept—you can prepare some type of budget and use it to measure a plaintiff firm's progress during the year.

Compensating Lawyers

There is another issue that is relevant to the plaintiff practice—determining compensation for lawyers. If time records are not being kept, it is aftertimes difficult to evaluate the amount of dollars attributable to a timekeeper; so some other method must be used as an evaluation tool when it comes time to determine a lawyer's contribution to the overall profits of the firm.

One method of doing this is to correlate settlements by individual lawyers with some expected billable value that would have been created had they been keeping accurate time records. For example, if a third-year lawyer would normally have 1,800 billable hours at a rate of $150 per hour, he or she would expect to have working lawyer receipts of approximately $270,000. Thus, in evaluating a similarly situated lawyer in a non-timekeeping plaintiff firm, the settlements of this lawyer should be close to that amount. If not, then questions should be raised as to why not. There could be many compelling reasons why these amounts are not being met; however, this method can serve as one evaluation tool in the event it is not possible to track receipts from hourly billing at the working lawyer level.

Originations, should they be part of the compensation criteria, can be tracked in the normal course of recording case information in a firm's case management system. There are several systems that are particularly adaptable to the plaintiff form of practice.

USING OR MISUSING STATISTICAL SURVEYS | **15**

One way to obtain comparable information for analysis purposes is through the use of recognized surveys available specifically for the legal profession. There are several that offer information on rates, hours, and financial performance. But before you consider using surveys, you should understand what they mean in general, how you should go about completing them, and, most importantly, how to analyze the results.

Why Participate in Surveys?

The first question most people ask is "why participate in a survey at all?" Often, not a week goes by that someone doesn't call you asking for information to complete some kind of survey. When I was a law firm administrator, I received calls from long-distance telephone service providers, computer vendors, paper manufacturers, and anybody else who decided they wanted to get some information for marketing purposes. However, there is only so much time in the day, and, if you are as busy as I was, you simply don't have time to deal with surveys. So therefore, when you take the time to complete a survey, you want some assurance that the results of your efforts are going to bear some fruit for your firm and not simply add to some sponsor's database of information.

You need to ask yourself this: can I operate my firm in a vacuum? Can I go about the business of practicing law without knowing what's going on in other firms in my area that are similar in size and practice? If the answer to these questions is yes, then don't fill out surveys. It's simply a waste of time for you since regardless of what the survey says, you're not prepared to alter any of your habits to change anything within your firm.

If, on the other hand, the competitive marketplace in which you practice requires you to keep abreast of what is happening in the legal profession, then you need information about the competition.

But where do you get that information? Well, if you're the administrator and really good friends with some of your colleagues, you may be able to share information about settlements, billing rates, compensation, staff ratios, expenses, and such. If you do that and word gets back to your respective firm, you'll soon be looking for work. But you can do it.

You can also read legal publications that are devoted primarily to general practice firms and glean information about the profession from these publications. The problem is, of course, that they are not specific to your geographical area, and, in many cases, not to your practice specialties or size of operation.

Therefore, the easiest and best way to obtain comparable information is to participate in a structured survey from a reputable organization. The information is obtained on a consistent basis; it's accurate; it's specific to your practice area, size, and geographical location; and it compares your information with the norms of the other participants to give you a feel for the competition.

Once you decide to participate, you have to deal with filling out the surveys. My experience has been that many of the small and even some medium-sized firms simply don't have the ability to retrieve the kind of information required for these surveys. While you might think that it's easy to determine the average settlement per case, you would be amazed at how many firms simply don't know how to do that. There are many firms that simply live out of a checkbook and never know from month to month or year to year how much money they really make. They simply distribute whatever cash they have, and that is the extent of their financial management process.

How to Use a Survey

Obviously, one of the benefits of a survey is that it forces you to come to grips with the process of dealing with financial management. It makes you deal with income issues, expense issues, staffing issues, and so on. It forces you to put together some type of annual financial plan that gives you the opportunity to focus on areas where expense adjustments could occur. It forces you to take a look at a realistic capital-asset budget and to focus on where the cash is going to come from to buy the new computer or move into that new office building. It tells you whether or not you can do all those things and still make sure that your partners have enough money to meet their compensation expectations. So if nothing more, the simple process of completing a survey will go a long way towards assisting your firm's long-term profitability objectives.

The obvious next questions are "what do I do with the information once I get it? Specifically, how do I evaluate my firm's performance against others in the survey? What do I do to improve my results from year to year, and how does it help me manage better?"

It is difficult to analyze surveys, regardless of who sponsors them. I spent fifteen years with my firm; every year I attempted to analyze our results and found it very difficult. Every firm maintains a certain lifestyle with which it is comfortable. The fact that a law firm across the street or in the next city makes $20,000 or $30,000 more per partner than your firm perhaps isn't relevant, particularly if those lawyers are at the office every weekend while your lawyers are coaching their children in Little League or driving racecars.

There is no right or wrong lifestyle; however, all partners in a firm must be tuned into the same one. If not, conflicts arise among certain groups who believe other people are not working hard enough and not making the same contribution, but still receiving as much or more compensation. This frustration festers and then begins to divide a firm.

Surveys tend to activate these frustrations. So when you look at your results, look at them on the basis of what your particular firm is trying to accomplish. If everybody in the firm is on the same wavelength and satisfied with the firm's goals, then a survey may not mean much. If that's not the case, then a survey sometimes points out what changes in lifestyle have to be made if the firm is going to survive and increase its profitability relative to firms of similar size and location.

I have often thought of a survey as a test. When you look at your results, you decide whether or not you've passed. Actually, it's several different tests. There is a test to see whether or not the price you charge is competitive, and a test to determine if you get the most out of your partners, associates, and support personnel. There is a test to determine whether you understand the concept of leverage, utilizing nonlawyers as much as possible to perform the work, so that income can be distributed to fewer partners. There is a test to determine whether you are controlling expenses.

By looking at a survey you are able to decide if, in relation to other firms, your expense lifestyle is above or below that of comparable firms. There's nothing wrong with not being equal with the other firms, if, in fact, that's the level of service that your firm wants and has come to expect. The expense side of a survey in many cases brings out the differences that create the most problems but can also create opportunity for increased net income.

So the survey is a test. Each year you take an examination for your firm and by making the proper comparisons, figure out whether you made the dean's list or the dunce list.

Many surveys also provide other useful information, such as the extent of automation in firms of comparable size, employee benefits, lines of credit, and the success or lack of success of marketing programs.

Surveys often have sections on ratios of staff-to-lawyers. This, to a certain extent, relates to the expense question. If your firm's lifestyle is supported by a high ratio of staff to lawyers, then your firm must decide if that's the way it's going to be run, recognizing the effect it has on the bottom line. You also have to examine whether or not you're receiving service commensurate with the number of people you have.

One note of caution in comparing your information to that in the survey relates to those statistics that are prepared on a per-lawyer basis. This would primarily include receipts, expenses, staffing numbers, and so on. The problem is that many firms often employ several nonlawyer timekeepers who require service and support, are included in the expense numbers, but are not included for purposes of calculating the per-lawyer averages.

Thus, a firm with several of these types of employees tends to look bad in the survey in relation to the averages. If your firm is staffed in this manner, then you need to examine these statistics in light of "lawyer equivalents" rather than just the number of lawyers. Generally, paralegals and other non-lawyer timekeepers are given a weight of .6 or .5. Thus, at a .6 ratio, ten paralegals would translate to six lawyer equivalents. These should then be added to the number of lawyers in order to produce comparable statistics with those averages included in the survey.

After participating in a survey over a period of years, a firm may find that it becomes an excellent tool—not only as an analysis and a test, but also as a way to force your firm to deal with significant gut issues. Remember, as the person in charge of the financial operations of your firm, whether you are the financial partner or firm administrator, you can install the best telephone system in the world, install the most up-to-date technology, and hire the greatest secretaries, but a manager's overall success is determined by his or her ability to help the partners make more money. I'm not in any way suggesting that participating in a survey is going to make your firm any more money. However, it forces you to look at the process, to make a strategic assessment of strengths and weaknesses, to determine where changes need to be made, and helps start you down the road to profitability enhancement.

PROBLEMS OF MULTIOFFICE FIRMS | 16

As illustrated throughout this book, the financial management process in a law firm is not all that difficult. This is particularly the case in the one-office firm. However, once the process is expanded to include other offices, certain problems are encountered. This chapter deals with some of those problems and how to begin addressing them.

I have always urged caution in dealing with the profitability and cost accounting of satellite offices. The divisiveness that this information can cause if the analysis is incorrect may create more problems than it solves. Still, office-by-office profitability data—like partner, client, or department profitability data— should at least be available for analysis and action if necessary.

The problems associated with branch office profitability are similar to those encountered in examining other specific areas of the firm, as discussed in Chapter 11:

- Should the analysis be prepared on an accrual basis, cash basis, or both?
- How should you handle interoffice transfers of time?
- How should you deal with expense allocations for direct and indirect expenses?
- Should an office be treated as a profit center or a cost center?

Accrual Basis versus Cash Basis

I've always emphasized the accrual basis of accounting. This method is particularly important when dealing with office-by-office financials. It permits you to examine the gross income of those timekeepers assigned to a particular office regardless of whether or not the files are located there. Lawyer A in Office A who works on files in Office B should have his or her time credited to the accrual-basis gross income of Office A where it rightfully belongs.

While it may be equally important to prepare the financials on a cash basis, when determining the overall contribution to profit by an individual office within a multioffice firm, the accrual basis may be the best indicator of performance.

Interoffice Transfers

The problems that most firms have with the accrual-basis concept is developing a system that allows them to track "exported" and "imported" time to each office by the various assigned timekeepers. These transfers must be tracked and the accounting system should permit the calculation of net transfers. That way, you can assign proper credit to the sending office on an accrual basis and to the receiving office on a cash basis.

In preparing the budget, the net transfer information should also be included on an estimated basis so that the cash-basis net income can be calculated. Various office statistics such as turnover can't be made unless this transfer number is determined.

Transfer numbers should be tracked for practice management purposes also, by ascertaining the amount of time that offices perform work for each other. Since one of the benefits of a multioffice firm is its ability to assign people wherever the work exists, a firm should be able to gauge the extent to which a smaller office is attracting those clients that a larger office can service.

Expense Allocation

While it is fairly simple to track the income side of these statements, the expense side presents problems, which probably creates the most controversy within a firm.

The direct expenses are easy to determine and generally account for the majority of the expenses. These include compensation of the lawyers, secretaries, and staff assigned to that office; benefits; rent; and all the other expenses normally necessary in a law office.

It is the allocation of the indirect or "firm" expenses that oftentimes creates the most controversy. These expenses include malpractice and other insurance, meetings, recruiting costs, contributions, marketing costs, administrative salaries, and, to a certain extent, costs of lawyers and staff who devote significant time to firm-related committees.

Obviously, you could spend a lifetime attempting to arrive at an absolute expense allocation system. When completed, chances are it wouldn't be significantly different from the system that estimates these expenses on a rational, practical, and consistent basis. In my opinion, this method relates to establishing a system that correlates an expense to the people, project, or category where it can be traced. For example, recruiting costs could be allocated on the expected number of new lawyers to be hired during the year in each office; malpractice costs on the basis of the number of lawyers; other insurance such as personal liability, fire, and theft on the total number of people or perhaps even on a square-foot basis; partnership meetings could be spread on the basis of the number of partners, and so forth.

The allocation of administrative salaries, although perhaps less straightforward, can be achieved by determining the extent to which individuals serve the firm as a whole and then on the basis of the total number of people assigned to various offices.

Let's take, for example, accounting personnel who serve an entire firm, as noted in Figure Q. First calculate the extent to which these people perform work solely for the office in which they are located, which in this example is $20,000. The balance of the expense of that department, or $40,000, is then spread to other offices on the basis of the number of people.

Make this calculation for all those people who perform duties that benefit the firm as a whole. This would include the personnel department, the accounting department (assuming it's centralized), recruiting, library, marketing, technology, and general management.

Allocation of Indirect Costs on an Office-by-Office Basis				
Offices	A	B	C	Total
Number of People - %	50	25	25	100
Accounting Dept. Costs				$60,000
Home Office Costs	$20,000			$20,000
Allocated Costs	20,000	$10,000	$10,000	40,000
Total	$40,000	$10,000	$10,000	$60,000

Figure Q

Profit Center versus Cost Center

One of the more significant issues that must be addressed in office-by-office financial management is the philosophical decision of whether the offices will be treated as profit centers or cost centers. As profit centers, the exporting office receives credit for the full net transfers of time that it exports to all the other offices. Thus, if Office A transfers $100,000 of time to Office B, Office B, in effect, "pays" $100,000 to Office A, recording the item as a cost on the books of Office B and as income on the books of Office A.

This reimburses Office A both for the expense in generating the time as well as for the profit. Under this scenario, if the time is billed by Office B at 100 percent of its value, then all the profit remains in Office A's accounts, and there is a wash with respect to the financial condition of Office B. To the extent that Office B *either* writes-up or writes-down the time (bills at rates above or below standard value), then that profit or loss is charged or credited to Office B, with Office A bearing none of the billing and collection risk.

Under the cost center concept, Office A is reimbursed only for its costs to produce the time that it transfers to Office B. Assuming an accrual expense ratio of 60 percent, Office B would in effect pay $60,000 to Office A for the cost to produce the $100,000 worth of time, with the entire $40,000 of profit remaining in Office B. It is then Office B's responsibility to bill the time at the value that realizes the greatest profit. Office A is thus made whole and effectively ends up with no profit or loss.

There is no right or wrong way to handle the profit and cost center idea. It's strictly a matter of preference within the firm. Keep in mind that this is a cash-basis adjustment and has nothing to do with determining the income of Office A or B on the accrual basis. The full $100,000 would be credited to Office A under the accrual-basis scenario, with Office B receiving none of the credit until the file has been billed and collected.

Another method is allocating cash receipts on a working lawyer basis, and crediting them to the office where the timekeeper has been assigned. The problem with this system is that the lawyer from Office A then becomes subjected to the billing and collection habits and philosophy of the billing lawyer in Office B. If the billing lawyer decides to bill only 90 percent of the value of the time, and if this 10 percent write-down is then prorated overall, the assigned timekeeper in Office A receives credit at 10 percent below the actual value, even though he or she may have done an outstanding job in performing the work on the file under the responsibility of the lawyer in Office B. In addition, if the lawyer in Office B is a poor biller, the lawyer in Office A will effectively never get credit until the Office B lawyer decides to bill the file. If it takes a long time, this could result in significant underrealization or accounts receivable write-offs.

The preparation of financial statements by office is simply another tool that the manager can use to evaluate the contributions made by the various offices within the law firm. In my opinion, this shouldn't be used as a compensation issue but simply as a management tool for the purposes of allocation, expense control, and service to clients. This analysis is particularly useful when a firm decides to open a new office in another area and, through the preparation of *pro forma* statements, must determine whether the new office will contribute to the overall profitability of the firm or become a drain on the existing partners.

Having said that, however, the lawyers in the satellite offices must fulfill the goals and objectives that the firm has set for their performance. If the firm believes that the resident partners should support themselves and also contribute additional profits to the rest of the firm, then the profitability of the office is important and is used to determine compensation levels. There are certain benefits to having this mentality since it creates incentives for the satellite office lawyers to originate good, profitable work that inures to the benefit of everyone.

OWNER COMPENSATION 17

The subject of owner compensation is worthy of a book all of its own, and in fact many have already been written. I believe that owner compensation needs to be addressed in this book as well, if for no other reason than to share my years of experience in working with firms in the critical areas of law firm growth, success, and continuity. Additionally, the subjects of financial management and owner compensation cannot be separated; one is dependent upon the other. A firm cannot set owner compensation until it knows the size of the net income profit pool. This book addresses how to determine the profit pool, and this chapter discusses how to deal with the issues that result from that determination.

Let's first address the compensation issue. As most law firm managers already know, nothing evokes more emotion in a law firm than how much each partner is paid. The subject consumes hours of time and has caused many a firm to split up and partners to go their separate ways.

In consulting with clients over the years, the following problems have been identified that hinder the development of a fair system that everyone can buy into.

- Those making the decisions are not representative of a firm's owners. This could be in terms of age, practice group, seniority, office, and so on.
- Committee members often remain the same for long periods of time without any changes, despite the changes that are occurring within a firm. Committee members get stale and the process gets stale as well.

- The criteria for determining contribution to a firm are either undefined or ill-defined; if defined, they are generally not properly communicated to everyone concerned.
- The criteria, if there are any, often change without notice. What everyone thinks is important suddenly is not important any more, and no one was told about the changes.
- There is too much emphasis on objective data without consideration of those other contributions that are more subjective in nature. Unfortunately, this is a trend that has developed over the past several years as younger partners have assumed more control over the compensation process and want to shed themselves of those partners who they believe are not productive.
- There is too much self-interest among certain groups without concern for the best interest of a firm as a whole. This occurs primarily when the decision-makers do not change for long periods of time.
- A firm fails to address changing goals and values of the firm.

Unfortunately, a consultant is usually called in after a crisis has occurred and after some individual or group has threatened to leave the firm if something is not done to change the method for allocating profits. Thus, a hostile atmosphere already exists from the beginning, making it very difficult to arrive at the consensus required to institute any new system.

The first lesson to be learned is to be ever mindful of how the system is currently operating, and not to be afraid to change it or tweak it from time to time, even if you believe that it is working properly.

Before you can even begin to evaluate or design a compensation system for your firm, you must first make certain that each of the partners shares the same visions and values and are all pointed in the same strategic direction. For example, if a group of partners within a practice group is interested in devoting a substantial amount of time to an area that may be less profitable than others, such as a new practice area, or becoming involved in a major contingency matter that may not settle for several years, then the firm must decide if this is a worthwhile endeavor deserving of its support. Major questions need to be raised concerning how this will be credited toward the contribution effort and what will happen if the experiment goes sour. Or, if the philosophy of the firm is to practice as a confederation sharing expenses, the system that you adopt will be far different from that for a firm with an institutional perspective.

Above all the criteria used in this process, remember that compensation is driven by the firm's culture. If it is the firm's culture not to hold people accountable for their actions, then that will be reflected in the compensation system that is developed. There is nothing wrong with this type of culture, assuming everyone buys into it. Problems arise when certain members of a firm no longer accept a system where there is an indirect relationship between contribution and compensation.

The job of a firm's manager is to find out when that situation is occurring and to do something about it. A manager needs to be ever mindful of the time bomb that is about to explode. It must be found and diffused as quickly as possible. Once it goes off, it probably is too late. Problems tend to fester in strange ways and then explode before you realize it.

It is not my objective to provide you with that one great system that can instantly be used in your firm. In the area of compensation systems, probably more than in any other, there is no right system that satisfies every situation. Each firm is different based upon its history, culture, and overall philosophy, so the system in each firm may be different. What I want to accomplish is to make you aware of the key issues involved in the process so you have a basis for preparing whatever type of system best fits with your firm's culture. Then I want to address some practices that I have found to be the most successful in the many firms with whom I have worked.

Objectives of a Compensation System

Assuming that a firm has determined its overall goals and objectives and wants to move forward in an institutionalized way, then some of the following issues need to be addressed.

As noted by Tom Clay of Altman Weil, Inc. several years ago, and still true today, a compensation system should satisfy the following objectives:

- *Internal equality.* Partners must believe that their compensation is fair in comparison with others in the organization. This relationship issue is important and will be addressed further.
- *External equality.* There needs to be a perception that when compared to others outside the firm, either inside or outside the profession, the partners' compensation is equitable.
- *Integration with firm goals and objectives.* This relates back to earlier comments concerning shared values and visions. A compensation system must be geared to accomplishing the goals and objectives that partners collectively have for their future and that of the organization. For example, it is difficult to satisfy compensation objectives if a firm as an entity elects to pursue a specialty that does not produce sufficient profits for allocation, or if personal cash requirements of one or more partners are of a magnitude that cannot be satisfied with the level of firm profits available for distribution.

◆ *Ease of administration.* A system must be easy to administer within the confines of the current procedures that a firm uses to keep track of the information required for financial analysis.

◆ *Understandable.* Partners must understand how the system works and how they fit into it. They should not be surprised at the compensation that is set for them.

◆ *Sustainable.* Lastly, a system must be sustainable. In other words, it should stand the test of time and continue to work whether a firm gets larger or smaller. The design should sustain itself as a firm changes its current configuration, whether in size, location, number of partners, specialties, and so on.

Implementing a Compensation System

Once everyone recognizes and agrees on the objectives of the compensation system, a firm can begin getting into some of the details of implementation, and discuss the following issues:

◆ *Who makes the decisions.* A firm must determine whether a managing partner, managing committee, separate compensation committee, or the partners as a group make the final determination of the income allocation. With five or six partners, it might be feasible to have everyone involved; eventually, as the group grows, this is no longer possible.

◆ *Subjective or objective.* The criteria used to develop the compensation schedule can come from an examination of purely objective data, without regard to some of the more intangible contributions that are made by individual partners; or can be purely subjective, with or without assignment of numerical values to the subjective elements; or it can be a combination of the two, with the final judgment made by those who make the ultimate decision. In the past, I have not been in favor of a formularized compensation system because I believe it may put incentives in the wrong place, but many of the smaller and medium-sized firms are gravitating in this direction. In my opinion, there needs to be a balance between the use of objective and subjective information.

◆ *Retroactive or prospective.* There is a continuing debate as to whether an individual is paid for what he has done in the past or for what he is going to do in the future. Many of the more successful firms set compensation at the end of one year for the next year, expecting that performance will continue at the same level as in the past period. Firms that make compensation decisions on a prospective basis reward truly extraordinary performance (and I emphasize extraordinary) with some type of bonus arrangement. I know of at least one firm that sets percentages for two years at a time.

◆ *High to low ratio.* Some firms attempt to set a realistic ratio between the highest and lowest paid partners in the firm. A ratio that is too high creates a negative feeling among the younger partners that the senior owners are being unduly paid at the expense of the working efforts of the younger ones. A ratio that is too low creates disincentives for the older partners and does not give them adequate financial goals to achieve in their later years with the firm.

◆ *Number of levels.* The number of compensation levels needs to be examined and, if possible, reduced to a minimum. The amount between levels should be significant enough to make a difference. Separations of $1,000 or $2,000 create more problems than differences of $7,500 or $10,000. The latter are usually much easier to justify.

An additional issue includes deciding whether a bonus pool will be created to reward the super-achiever or super-performer. In the more institutionalized environments, bonuses are very difficult to determine since success or lack thereof is not necessarily attributable to a specific person but rather to the firm as an entity.

The criteria that is set for determining levels of contribution varies from firm to firm, and need to be set in conjunction with the firm's goals and objectives. If the firm believes that being president of the local or state bar association does nothing for it and in fact is counter to the objective of serving clients, then all the partners need to buy into this idea. Thus a partner who does want to achieve this office recognizes the effect it may have on his compensation if this activity detracts from other more important compensation criteria, such as billable hour production, originating business, and so on.

General Partner Criteria

Broadly speaking, a partner in any professional service firm is paid based on a set of criteria that evaluates his individual contribution to the firm. These are as follows:

◆ Functions as a working professional and charges billable time
◆ Functions as a manager with file management and billing and collection management
◆ Develops new business for others to perform
◆ Solidifies and increases business with existing clients
◆ Assists in firm management

◆ Represents the firm on outside activities, to the extent that this representation has been agreed to by the firm as important to his status in the community or profession

◆ Serves as mentor and trainer for other professionals

If you were to survey partners in most firms today, particularly younger partners, you would find that many of them want a more performance-based compensation system with an increase in individual accountability. As stated earlier, I am not in favor of a strict formula-based system because under that process there is little or no credit given for some of the important attributes that make the firm successful, including many nonbillable but necessary activities, such as firm management, training and mentoring, marketing, and outside business and community activities. For example, in the area of firm management, a partner usually spends a considerable amount of time managing the affairs of the firm. This can seriously impact his ability to produce new clients or billable hours, yet he needs to be compensated for this work.

In an effort to consider all of a partner's contributions, many firms have gone to a self-evaluation report that lets an individual partner evaluate how he has done in relation to the criteria established by the firm. An example of this form is provided at the end of this chapter. Once this form is completed, it then serves as the basis for review by the compensation-setting group as well as a vehicle for counseling the individual partner on his performance for the year. The report covers both objective and subjective criteria used to determine the overall contribution that a partner makes to the success of the firm, in the short term as well as in the long term. This form can also be used by other lawyers to assist them in setting their goals and objectives for the year and beyond.

The Compensation-Setting Process

The compensation-setting process goes something like this, recognizing that the size of the firm dictates which of these steps are necessary:

1. The firm gets whatever objective data it requires, which in many cases is determined by the extent to which this data is used in the compensation setting process. I suggest that to avoid aberrations in any one year, the information should be accumulated on a three- or five-year rolling average basis. Generally, this information includes originations, working lawyer receipts, realization statistics, and billable hours.

2. Each partner prepares a self-evaluation report for review by all of the other partners, or by a committee established for this purpose.

3. The compensating-setting group meets with each partner to review performance from the prior year, and to review goals and objectives for the coming year. If no committee is established for this purpose, then this performance review is done with the entire partner group.

4. Compensation levels are established, based upon these reviews and objective data.

5. The first draft of the proposed compensation plan is prepared and distributed to each partner for his comments and review. If necessary, further meetings are held with individual partners in the event someone wants to discuss his own compensation or that of another partner. If partner compensation percentages are set correctly and are reflective of net income, adding to one partner means subtracting from another. This keeps changes to a minimum, since no one is willing to ask for an increase if it means cutting someone else.

6. Once all of the comments are received, the total package is then presented to the entire partner group for their approval.

Contrary to what many may believe, the initial compensation-setting process doesn't set a guaranteed salary. One of the problems with professional corporation firms is the perception that since partners have a salary, they must be entitled to it regardless of firm profits. The fact is that owners simply get whatever is left over, and there is no guarantee. Regardless of their tax status or organizational structure, law firms operate as partnerships that divide the excess profits after all expenses, excluding compensation, have been accounted for. The amount established by the compensation-setting process is what a partner would get if he received a regular salary, but his actual compensation is driven solely by his eventual percentage share of net income. It is the percentage which determines relative worth and relative value.

The initial compensation-setting process establishes profit percentages, sets monthly draws at 100 percent or some other amount depending on cash flow, and in some cases sets ownership, voting, and asset-percentage share. After that, the salary has little if any meaning. Again, there is no guarantee, and salary should not be regarded as such.

Setting Monthly Draws

There are three elements to determining the monthly draw amounts:

1. *Realistic net income budget.* This is set at the beginning of the year and provides a basis for knowing how much a firm and thus each partner is going to earn. There are financial models presented in this book and elsewhere that enable a firm to accurately forecast net

income within 2 to 3 percent, assuming that a firm has historical information to rely on.

2. *Cash budget.* The cash budget takes into account all of the cash flow issues, and determine how much cash will actually be available for distribution.

3. *A realistic draw schedule.* This is set as a percentage of available cash, and is usually conservative in nature to account for historical monthly receipt activity.

Most firms set partner compensation at the beginning of the year and pay a percentage of this on a monthly basis as draws against the total amount. This way, each partner can plan his personal finances with some idea of his total annual compensation. Supplemental distributions are made as cash becomes available.

If a firm is going to change its current system, it must focus on the *evaluation process* and spend less time on the *mechanical process.* The problem is that most firms spend their time trying to change the mechanics, which is generally the easier way out. If I am a partner, I do not care how much I get paid, providing I get paid what I am worth. What I am worth is an evaluation question, not a mechanical one.

Relationships

When you are done dealing with all the details of a compensation system, you get down to one concept: relationships. How much a partner makes can only be determined with reference to someone else. Most arguments about compensation do not arise from the dollars one partner gets, but rather the dollars he gets in relation to another partner.

In setting compensation, a firm must focus on relationships, generally the relationship of each partner's compensation to that of the highest-paid partner in the firm. Each year you either maintain the same relationships, or move people up or down depending on the evaluation process. As a practical matter, once the relationships are established, you only have to deal with those partners who have done exceptionally well and must move up in relation to the top earner, or those have not done so well and must be further away. The rest of the partners, in relation to the top earner, remain the same. Every firm with a history has already established some relationship among the owners. It is just a question of looking at the relationships each year, and making the appropriate adjustments to a small percentage of the group.

In order to make all this happen, however, a firm must have an internal financial management reporting process that accurately projects net income and provides the objective data required for the evaluation process to take place. Once the budgeting process is in place for a few years, a firm can predict its net income *and* cash flow with a very high degree of accuracy.

The methodology described above goes a long way toward allowing a firm to better understand and explain the compensation process. It also permits those entrusted with the responsibility to have the mechanics available for reviewing all of the partners as a group and in relation to one another, and providing a more realistic and fair comparison.

Merger Compensation Issues

A peripheral issue to the compensation question, and one that I seem to be asked about more and more frequently, is dealing with compensation when two firms are getting ready to merge. Often the incomes of the two firms are not equal, and simply to put the firms together without some consideration for this inequality can lead to animosity among the partners, and to the failure of the merger.

There is a process that permits a firm to deal with the potential disparities in earnings among the participants as well as the uncertainties of how each of the respective entities will perform. Under this plan, the partners are assigned income percentages that are applied against the total net income of the combined entity. The percentages are developed as follows:

1. The net income of the two firms for the past three years, (or longer if desired), is determined, combined, and a percentage relationship developed based on the contribution each firm made to the total net income of the two firms. For example, as illustrated in Figure R, Firm A with two partners had average income of $750,000, and Firm B with four partners had $400,000. Thus, Firm A had 65.2 percent of the average net for the period and Firm B had 34.8 percent. The due diligence performed prior to the merger ascertains whether there are any aber-

---

Merger Compensation Plan

Average Net Income for the Two Firms for Three Years is Determined.

Example:

		%
Firm A Net	$ 750,000	65.2
Firm B Net	400,000	34.8
Total	$1,150,000	100.0

Figure R

rations in the net income amounts in the years used to create these averages. If so, then adjustments in the averages are made.

2. After the net income budget for the combined firm is determined, each firm then separately sets compensation for *their* own partners by allocating their percentage of the estimated net income as set for the year. If the merger is a good one, chances are the net of the combined entity will be more than the totals of the two firms calculated separately. Thus, in this example, assuming the same net income budget for the new entity, Firm A sets compensation for its partners totaling $750,000 and Firm B, $400,000. From this exercise, percentages can be calculated for each partner. To make it easy, Figure R assumes that the partners in each firm are of equal status from a compensation standpoint. Each partner in Firm A receives an income percentage of 50 percent, and each partner in Firm B receives 25 percent. There is obviously an expectation that at least this much net can be achieved in the next year by the combined firm, assuming that the amounts used to calculate the averages are historically correct.

3. The individual percentages are then factored by the percentages developed in determining the average net income contributed by the two firms during the period as noted in Figure R. Thus, Firm A's percentages are factored by 65.2 percent, and Firm B, by 34.8 percent. The range of percentages are now 32.6 for Firm A and 8.7 for Firm B. Note that Firm A's percentages add up to 65.2 and Firm B's to 34.8. These then become the percentages to be applied against the budgeted net income of the new combined entity. (Figure R-1)

Calculate Revised Firm Percentages

Combined Firm then Factors Net Income Percentages by 65.2 and 34.8 to Calculate Individual Percents.

Example:

Partner 1	50.0	32.6
Partner 2	50.0	32.6
Partner 1	25.0	8.7
Partner 2	25.0	8.7
Partner 3	25.0	8.7
Partner 4	25.0	8.7
Total		100.0

Figure R-1

There are several advantages to this system:

◆ The relationships that were in existence in the old firms get preserved in the new entity and are set based on actual past results of the firms. It is assumed, of course, that as part of the due diligence process, the net incomes used in the calculations are realistic, representative of the firm's normal net income experience, and not materially affected by any unusual transaction, such as a large unusual one-time fee that may never reoccur, or a fee from a major client who has now gone away.

◆ Once the percentages have been set, the "we-they" mentality disappears. Everyone is now working toward a common goal of producing as much net income as possible. There is an incentive to exceed the projections, since everyone benefits proportionately. If the projections are not met, then everyone suffers on the same basis.

◆ It is possible under this proposal for some type of bonus pool to be established for exceptional performance in terms of billable hours, originations, and so on. It would be allocated if everyone agrees that a special bonus be paid to one or more of the partners. If not, then this bonus pool goes into the net income stream and is allocated the same as all other income.

◆ At some point in the future, the firm can then establish a different system if they want. I suggest that the newly merged firm adopt this type of system for at least three years; once some history is available for the new firm, refinements of the percentage plan can be adopted. Chances are if the net income used in the initial calculations is accurate, over time you probably find that the percentage relationships do not change that significantly.

Documenting a Compensation System

One issue that comes up many times is how a firm's compensation system should be documented. In my opinion, many firms make the mistake of including the compensation setting process within the body of the firm's main operating agreement. This is not a good idea, and here is why.

Whenever an agreement is made between owners of a professional service firm, many issues need to get resolved. The result is a series of compromises arrived at after many hours of discussion and debate. Generally, once this is done, this agreement usually stays in force for many years into the future.

The compensation system, however, changes more frequently. If you include the compensation process within the body of your agreement, then what happens is that every time you change the compensation plan, you end up having to rehash old issues that took hours of time and many compromises to conclude. Thus, you are better off making some brief statement in the agreement concerning the fact that compensation is set by a manager or by committee, and then refer to a separate plan that can be changed as necessary without affecting the body of the firm's main operating agreement.

There is another important point. Your compensation plan should be geared to establishing or altering the behavior patterns that the firm is attempting to instill in its professionals. If you are emphasizing new client development and this is the behavior you want to instill, then your plan should be geared to rewarding originations. If you are more concerned with increasing billable hours, billings, and so on, then you need to gear your plan to reward those behaviors.

Whatever plan you adopt should encourage hard work, encourage originating new work, and encourage participation in those administrative, management, or outside activities that allow the firm to operate and market itself to the outside world.

Potential Problems

As noted earlier, I have no particular compensation plan to share with you. If you do change what you have now, chances are you will gravitate more to an objective rather than a subjective plan. If or when you do that, you need to recognize certain problems. None of these are insurmountable, but they need to be considered.

◆ A firm must have an accounting system that can accurately produce objective information on a timely basis. There are several types of accounting systems that can do this.

◆ There must be strict rules regarding write-downs of unbilled time and write-offs of accounts receivable. If a firm is not careful, write-down and write-off decisions will be made strictly with compensation in mind. Thus, when given a choice, the billing lawyer (in most cases also the originating and working lawyer) will first write down the time of other people working on the files before writing down his own, thus retaining his share of the credit when the file is eventually collected. This type of system works best when *all* write-downs and write-offs are assigned to the originating lawyers. In most firms using this type of system, the rule is that the reductions are always allocated to the working professionals on the basis of their percentage of time on the project. Thus, if a partner has 40 percent of the time on a given client assignment, he would receive 40 percent of the write-down or write-off. Most time accounting systems can easily perform this mechanical function.

♦ At some point, which lawyer originated a particular client or matter becomes muddled. There is also the question of the length of time that a lawyer receives credit for an origination. It could be as little as three years, to as much as for the remainder of a partner's career. This becomes more of a problem as a firm grows, and clients come to the firm because of its reputation for good work and not necessarily because of any one professional in it. Segregating introduction credit from origination credit can help alleviate this problem, as well as using a system that provides for a gradual reduction in origination credit over a period of years to a maintenance level. This is a particular problem when there are new originations in a different practice area that arise from the good work of a person that has nothing to do with the original person who brought in the work in the first place.

♦ Most plans assume that the type of work in a firm is such that the costs associated with completing a project is approximately the same for all files. In other words, two individuals who generate $100,000 worth of revenue should basically have the same level of profit. The issue of profitability of different practice areas, and indeed of different billing lawyers, is a very complicated subject and is covered in other chapters in this book. If a firm believes that there are wide disparities in the costs involved to produce income, then this difference must be taken into account in the overall compensation scheme. (See paragraph on Dispelling the Originations Myth)

♦ In some cases, there are projects that have longer payouts than others. This affects certain of the receipts criteria used in the plan, whether it relates to receipts at the individual working lawyer or originating lawyer level.

♦ There is also the situation where one lawyer is working for another who happens to be a poor biller and poor collector. This again impacts the working lawyer who has no control over when files are billed or how they are collected.

♦ Lastly, there is the start-up problem. At the time a new plan is adopted, originators of business already in house need to be identified, if they have not been already. This may not be a problem if the firm kept good records in the past. If not, it may want to start fresh from some point forward.

Keep in mind that in designing any compensation system, you will never solve 100 percent of the problems. You try to get to 90 or 95 percent, but probably will achieve 80 to 85 percent. You need to deal with the exceptions as they occur.

Bonuses

I discussed the bonus issue previously. A firm needs to decide whether some portion of the net income is set aside for bonuses. Again, I emphasize that this needs to be for exceptional performance, to the extent that this can be measured. In the event no bonuses are given, then the amount goes back into the normal profit pool to be allocated on the basis of the established income percentages.

It is important in determining the criteria for a bonus that individuals do not get credit multiple times for the same level of performance. For example, originations are generally rewarded in the overall compensation plan. Therefore, a lawyer should not be given additional credit for bringing in new work unless there is a process whereby new originations are tied to some historical average, or the new work is extremely significant and produces excessive amounts of profits in the year under review. Those who exceed their averages are rewarded in the bonus system. This same argument can be made for those with unusually high billable hours. Criteria that could be used for a bonus include excessive out-of-town activity, identification of a significant technical issue that assisted the firm in resolving a client's problem and created a very favorable result, firm-related activities that cannot be fully evaluated in the subjective area of the normal compensation plan, and so on.

Expectations of Partners

I am often asked what to expect as a partner. Here is the list that summarizes the answer to that question quite well:

Participation in equity, primarily from excess profits

A certain level of autonomy

Right to become a part of the decision-making process

Tenure to some degree, although in today's world this may not always be possible

Net income increase, usually—although I have seen situations where associates make more money than younger partners

External status and recognition

Recognition among one's peer group, which is very important to lawyers

Unfortunately, in many firms, this is what a partner sometimes gets:

Missed paychecks
Large capital contributions
Guarantor on huge firm debt balances

Charging for Good Will

Since I work mostly with small to medium-sized firms, one of the issues that comes up frequently in the compensation area is a situation where two or three founding partners want to bring in new blood, but are concerned that the new people will reap a large bonanza in their early years. The older partners want new lawyers, but at the same time do not want to give up significant portions of the net income to those who were not responsible for building the business.

A solution to this problem is to create a category called "special equity shareholders" and use a system of profit tiers. This divides the profits into tiers that are allocated differently. Tier One is allocated on the basis of income percentages. Tier Two is allocated only to the special equity shareholders, and Tier Three to all equity shareholders based on a consensus of the group. This type of system generally satisfies most of the individual groups at each level, since there is a belief that everyone's interests are being addressed and protected.

The key is to protect the older partners who built the firm, took all of the risks, and allowed the younger partners to come along and enjoy the income levels that the older partners have reached. This type of system provides that protection and creates a situation where there is less reluctance to bring in new partners who have done a good job and who have the potential to help the firm achieve additional success.

A Plan that Works

If I were to suggest a plan that I have seen work well in many firms of all sizes and practice disciplines, it would be a "democratic plan" which would operate somewhat as follows:

1. The firm first of all prepares a net income budget based on the process previously described, which will provide a realistic estimate of the capacity of the firm to create profits.
2. Based on historical performance and compensation history and by a consensus of the shareholders, amounts are assigned to each share-

holder by each shareholder, totaling to the net income projection. This amount creates a percentage that is used for excess compensation above budget, or for other matters where income percentages are important. If desired, some portion of the budget could be set aside for bonuses for exceptional performance. This would alter the amount of net income available for allocation. This process also permits examination of and credit for some of the subjective criteria that may not be taken into account in a more formula-driven system.

3. Approximately 90 percent of the amount in item 2 above is paid as a monthly draw during the year. If there is a concern about available cash, less may be paid in draw, with the balance paid in supplemental distributions as cash permits.

4. The remaining 10 percent is set aside for a bonus pool, to be awarded monthly based on individual performance against some predetermined goal, or quarterly to individuals or groups, or annually to individuals or groups, using some criteria geared to performance, profitability, and so on.

The benefits of any supplemental bonus programs are designed to alter behaviors in these ways:

♦ To encourage billable hour production
♦ To encourage billings and collections of one's own time as well as the time of others
♦ To place emphasis on originations and practice development, and reward those who make the extra effort to produce business
♦ To create monthly incentives so that emphasis is year-round on making the firm profitable
♦ To permit those who excel above their budgets to participate in the additional net income in an amount disproportionate to their income percentages
♦ For those bonuses that are rewarded monthly, to eliminate the possibility that one bad month can ruin the entire year since each month effectively stands on its own

Capitalization

I want to address the capitalization issue that was also discussed in Chapter 10. Many law firms continue to struggle with how much capital a new owner should contribute upon admission, attempting to strike a balance between what is required and how much a newly elected partner actually can afford.

I grew up in an environment where the capital requirement was very simple to calculate. The firm prepared its cash flow forecast for the year, calculated the amount of new capital that was required, and added it to the total capital already in the firm. A partner's income percentage was then applied against that balance and a balance due or balance to be refunded was calculated.

New partners, with no previous balance, paid the full load—which could be in the $40,000 to $50,000 range. Those partners who had compensation reductions or received few increases could actually receive a refund.

My experiences, particularly with small and medium-sized law firms, has been that this is no longer the method by which capital contributions are calculated. Some have a fixed amount, generally in the $15,000 to $20,000 range; others have a graduated amount, rising over time to $30,000 or $40,000. Then there are others that have no capital requirement. Some base the amount on stock value, using cash-basis numbers only. Others use stock value based on accrual-basis numbers, such as work-in-process and accounts receivable balances.

Unfortunately, as noted elsewhere, the issue of cash flow is still a mystery to most professionals. They do not understand why principal payments on debt are not expensed, do not understand the concept of depreciation, and cannot understand why the bank balance does not correlate with the amount of net income.

Also as noted, the issue of capital is a cultural issue as much as it is a financial one. Some firms believe that the firm should be owned by the partners, and thus require heavier capital commitments and less dependence on bank borrowings. Other firms believe that the firm should borrow any funds it needs, rather than have the owners make contributions with after-tax dollars. Usually, the partners in the latter firms are those who are the least knowledgeable about how the cash flow system actually works, and are the younger ones who have grown up with a credit-card mentality that says, "If you cannot afford to pay for it, then charge it."

I favor tying income percentages to capital percentages, which is similar to the method that I am accustomed to. I do not favor purchasing any of the accrual-basis assets, but rather having them accrue during the lifetimes of the owners.

Dispelling the Originations Myth

I cannot discuss the compensation issue without making some comments about the practice of many firms in overvaluing individual originations in determining contribution to the firm.

If you were to go into most law firms, large or small, review the list of owner compensation, and then ask why one person's or group's compensation is much higher, you would probably get the same answer: the highest compensated owners are the "big business producers." You would seldom be told they are the "big profit producers." The reason is because firms have become increasingly enamored with the idea of producing business in terms of billable hours and value, and perhaps even collections, but have paid very little attention to whether this business is bringing income to the bottom line from which the owners are paid.

Having now spent several years stressing the importance of profitability at all levels, perhaps I am more sensitive to this issue than others are. However, it does not take a CPA to understand that unless someone originates business that, after the cost of production, leaves something left over to distribute as earnings to the shareholders, these originations are worthless. Thus, to the extent that this statistic is a measurement of contribution to the firm and given significant value in the compensation criteria scheme, the compensation system is flawed.

There are several ways to determine whether originations are producing the desired profits. One is to perform a complete profitability analysis, a subject that has been addressed in previous sections in this book. This can be done by originating lawyer, by billing lawyer, by practice group, by office, and so on. Another is to perform some "quick-and-dirty" analyses which, while not 100 percent accurate, provide some indication as to the profitability of originations submitted by the various lawyers in your firm.

This analysis can be performed by following these steps:

1. Obtain a schedule of cash receipts from originations recorded for each lawyer in the firm.
2. Obtain a list of net write-ups, write-downs, and write-offs for each lawyer and add that to the originations total from item 1 above. This will give you the total value of time attributable to that lawyer for the period under review. Recognize in doing this that there may be some timing differences; for example, the net write-ups, write-downs, and write-offs may come from a different accounting period. This does not render the analysis any less accurate, since net originations is the number you are seeking for analysis purposes, which include the reduction (or addition) of adjustments to billing value.
3. Calculate the expense ratio for the year by dividing the total costs and expenses, not including owner compensation, by the total receipts for the year.
4. Apply this ratio against the total time value calculated in item 2 above, and subtract that result from the actual cash originations.

5. By comparing the result from item 4 to the total time value from item 2, you can compute the actual profit on the originations.

As you can see in Figure S, although Lawyer A produced 33 percent more cash originations, he produced only $130,000 in actual profit for the firm, due to the adjustments to his origination total brought about by work that was performed but could not be either billed or collected at recorded rates. Lawyer B, on the other hand, with a better quality of originations, produced $279,000 of profit on $250,000 less in originations than Lawyer A.

Performing this analysis shows whether those with the highest originations are in fact those with the highest level of net income, or whether a lawyer with fewer originations may actually be producing a greater level of profit. Thus, his or her contribution to the firm may be more significant and therefore should be reflected in the compensation scheme.

Anyone can generate originations. The real business producer is the one who can generate originations that add something to the bottom line, given the use of the resources to perform the work. This is the person who is making the greater contribution to the firm. Examining only the dollar amount of originations may not bring to light the true profit producer as opposed to the lawyer who is simply producing originations without regard to whether these receipts are contributing to the income of the owners.

The ownership problems in a professional services firm are difficult and time consuming. I hope that this chapter provides some guidance on dealing with the issues that create those problems.

	Lawyer A	Lawyer B
Cash Originations	$1,000,000	$750,000
Net Write-ups/downs/offs	450,000	35,000
Total Time Value	$1,450,000	$785,000
Expense Ratio	60%	60%
Expenses	870,000	471,000
Net Income	$130,000	$279,000
Cash-basis Net Income %	8.9%	35.5%

Figure S

M E M O R A N D U M

TO: ALL PARTNERS
FROM: COMPENSATION COMMITTEE
RE: PERFORMANCE EVALUATION FOR PARTNERS
DATE:

GENERAL INSTRUCTIONS

Each partner of the firm is required to prepare a report setting forth the information requested below. The report should be delivered to each member of the Compensation Committee no later than _____.

Unless otherwise specified, all information should be given for the period from January 1, 20__ to the present. If the report is not received by the due date, the Committee will proceed with its deliberations concerning compensation without the relevant information respecting each partner.

The report should be typed on 8 1/2″ × 11″ paper with the caption "Evaluation Report for Partners." It should contain the name of the partner and the numbers and captions of each informational item. The text of each item as it appears in this memorandum should be omitted.

Each partner should bear in mind that the purpose of this report is to assist the Compensation Committee in recommending partners' compensation for the year ending December 31, 20__.

We request that no report exceed four pages, double spaced, plus an annex listing information respecting certain professional association memberships and offices, publications, firm committee assignments and like information.

PERFORMANCE EVALUATION FOR PARTNERS
INFORMATION TO BE INCLUDED

PART I PROFESSIONAL ABILITY AND ACCOMPLISHMENT AS A LAWYER.

Item 1. Type of Work
Describe the type or types of projects handled by you personally or under your supervision, indicating (if more than one type), the relative quantity or importance of each.

Item 2. Self Improvement
Describe your efforts to increase your expertise in the areas indicated under Item 1, including seminars or other formal education attended and/or in which you were a participant and any significant professional achievements relating to your knowledge and expertise.

Item 3. Organizational and Team Effort Abilities
Indicate any evidence of your ability to organize and perform professional work and to work efficiently with other partners and non partners on client-related matters.

Item 4. New Clients
List here, or on a separate annex, any new substantial clients produced by you, solely or in conjunction with other members of the firm. Give some indication or estimate of the significance to the firm of each such client both in terms of current, ongoing or referral work. Also, if applicable, list any prospective substantial clients that you declined because of a conflict on other reason.

Item 5. Client Retention
Describe, as to substantial clients of the firm, your role and the role of others who work with you in retaining those clients as satisfied clients of the firm. Give some indication or estimate of the significance to the firm of each such client.

Item 6. Recorded Time
State whether you believe your recorded billable and non-billable hours adequately portray your industry and productivity. If not, explain.

Item 7. Billing Management
With respect to matters for which you are billing manager, describe your efforts to utilize other partners who have the required expertise and non-partners who have lower billing rates. Include an assessment of your ability to delegate work for which you are responsible, to the persons who may perform it most efficiently for the firm and the clients.

<u>Item 8.</u> <u>Billing and Collection Practices</u>

Evaluate your billing and collection practices during the period in relation to your ability to manage the files for which you are billing manager. If you believe that these practices require improvement, outline the steps you plan to take over the next year to effect that improvement.

PART II   <u>STANDING IN THE PROFESSION AND IN THE COMMUNITY</u>

Include in your response relevant information for the current year, and two preceding years, where such information is helpful in demonstrating continuity of effort or progress in the activity over a period greater than the current calendar year. Use the attached annex to <u>list</u> the requested information; any <u>discussion</u> or explanation about the activities should be included in this report and not in the annex.

<u>Item 1.</u> <u>Bar Activities</u>

List on the attached annex the names of any committees on which you serve and offices which you hold in the Bar, either local, state or national.

<u>Item 2.</u> <u>Community & Civic Activities</u>

List on the attached annex any memberships, offices and other positions that you hold in civic, social, charitable, educational and religious organizations.

<u>Item 3.</u> <u>Miscellaneous Information</u>

List on the attached annex other miscellaneous information that support a favorable view of your standing in the profession or the community. This would include teaching positions, publications, speeches, etc.

PART III   <u>CONTRIBUTIONS TO THE FIRM</u>

Include in your response relevant information for the current year, and two preceding years, where such information is helpful in demonstrating continuity of effort or progress in the activity over a period greater than the current calendar year. Use the attached annex to <u>list</u> the requested information; any <u>discussion</u> or explanation about the activities should be included in this report and not in the annex.

<u>Item 1.</u> <u>Committees</u>

List on the attached annex any committees of the firm on which you serve.

Item 2. <u>Special Firm Assignments</u>
List on the attached annex and describe in your report any special assignment you performed for the firm.

Item 3. <u>Internal Client Relations</u>
Describe any actions taken by you that tend to broaden the relationship of clients with the firm, for example, passing on of clients to younger partners or exposing the clients to a broader cross section of the firm. Also include here a description of your efforts to involve other partners in the management and servicing of clients for which you are responsible so as to insure their continuing as clients of the firm in event you are no longer able to service them.

Item 4. <u>Overall Cooperation with Firm Policies and Practices</u>
Describe your efforts to promote and adhere to prescribed firm policies and procedures, including responding to internal requests for information, submitting information on a timely basis, etc. If deficient in this area, what steps will be done to improve in the ensuing year.

Item 5. <u>Practice Development</u>
To the extent not mentioned elsewhere, describe the practice development (marketing) activities that you have engaged in during the current year and the results of such activities.

Item 6. <u>Other Firm Activities</u>
Describe any other contributions you have made to the firm such as in the recruiting, retention, or training of non-partner accounting personnel and staff personnel.

PART IV   <u>GENERAL</u>

Item 1. <u>Other Information Relevant to Compensation</u>
Describe any other information you deem relevant in the determination of your compensation.

Item 2. <u>Satisfaction with Existing Status</u>
State whether you are presently satisfied with your role respecting the type of work and responsibilities in the firm and activities outside the firm. If not satisfied in any of these areas, indicate what change should be made to better utilize your capabilities and/or what action you anticipate taking with respect to outside activities.

Item 3. <u>Compensation Level</u>
Assuming a top compensation level of $100,000, what do you believe is a fair level for you in relation to other partners in the firm and in relation to your contribution over the period.

PART V   SPECIFIC PROFESSIONAL GOALS

<u>Item 1. Practice Development Goals</u>

If not already included, describe your goals and plans for practice development efforts over the next year. This should include developing additional business from existing clients and plans to seek business from individuals or entities that are not currently clients. In terms of hours, how much time do you expect to devote to this effort during the next year.

<u>Item 2. Devotion of Time and Energy to the Practice</u>

Describe your plans and goals for the coming year with respect to anticipated billable hours. Do you plan to exceed or fall below the firm's average for partners.

Signature:_____

Date: _____

ANNEX TO PARTNER EVALUATION

CIVIC ORGANIZATIONS—Community activities including significant clubs.

NAME   OFFICES HELD

PROFESSIONAL SCHOLARSHIP

Teaching Assignments:

CLE, Other Lectures Given:

Articles, Books Published:

CONTINUING EDUCATION

Seminars Attended:

CONTRIBUTIONS TO FIRM

Membership on Firm Committees:

Special Assignments for the Firm:

THE MULTITIER OWNERSHIP STRUCTURE AND ALTERNATIVES

18

$\mathbf{A}$ corollary to the compensation questions discussed in Chapter 17 is whether you have partners at all, and if you do, whether or not there is some status below equity partner to which individuals can aspire. The multitier partnership structure bears a great deal on the question of ownership, capitalization, and compensation, and thus needs some attention. This chapter discusses some of the issues related to this structure and whether there are other alternatives for firms to consider.

As part of the compensation process, the firm must ultimately come to grips with the owner-admission process in general and whether some other level of partner needs to be developed. One of the alternatives that many firms have used since the mid-1970s has been the creation of the nonequity partner. This is an individual who is essentially paid as an associate, but gets some status internally as well as with outside peers, and usually has an increase in his overall compensation due to a change in base compensation as well as participation in a bonus pool. This position has become very popular over the past several years as lawyers have been searching for alternative lifestyles, which in the lawyer world translates to fewer hours and fewer administrative and management responsibilities, and with that a compensation schedule that is significantly different from the harder-working, more involved equity partner.

Most firms, even those that have some type of alternate structure, do not fully understand how they are supposed to operate and cannot articulate to the partners or the staff members how the structure works and how people get from one tier to another. I realize that this is a controversial subject with many firms and there have been many articles written on the subject. Some of the articles address whether this is still a viable solution to the partner admission process. Some believe it is not. Within the profession, it still remains an important consideration. Therefore, some understanding of the issues may be important to you, particularly in light of the alternative work styles that many professionals are now seeking.

Keep in mind that a multi-structured partnership system in many cases may simply be a cop-out due to the firm's inability to deal adequately with compensation at the partner level and to terminate those lawyers who are not performing. The firm creates this "other" partner category, hoping that eventually the management problems will go away.

Assuming that you must have two tiers, primarily to keep good people while not filling up the equity ranks, then there needs to be general agreement and consensus as to what the second tier represents and more importantly, the time and criteria for moving into the equity class.

Making a Multitier System Work

Following is some guidance on the mechanics of the multitier structure as seen in other firms who have successfully implemented such a system.

It is important that all lawyers understand early on that there is a life with the firm other than being an owner and that, in order to protect the interests of those who have paid their dues and assumed all the risks, there is another category below the equity level to which they can aspire and that will give them a very successful and rewarding career. When you think about it, professional service firms are the only organizations in the country where you are not perceived as being successful unless you are an owner. This is far from actual fact.

One of the problems with going to a multitier partnership is the inability of a firm to sell this concept to the associates and in many cases to their own partners. There are several aspects of this organizational structure that must be incorporated to make the scheme work. Some or all of them must be adopted in order for the multitier partnership to become a reality.

- There must be a realization that being elevated to a status other than equity partner does not make one a second-class citizen. There are certain differences between the equity and nonequity partner: first, the nonequity partner does not usually have a vote; second, he does not contribute capital; third, he does not have an income percentage upon which his compensation is based and makes him eligible for a bonus; and fourth, he does not participate in the accumulation of the accrual-basis assets represented by changes in work-in-process and accounts receivable. Other than this, a nonequity partner has basically the same rights and privileges as a full partner. Generally, he is given the same size office, is given the same benefits, is invited to all partner functions, has access to all firm financial information, and for all intents and purposes is a partner both to the inside and outside world.

♦ It must be understood that the nonequity partner position is not a place for those lawyers who for whatever reason cannot make equity partner or worse yet who no one wants to terminate. The same basic qualifications necessary to be an equity partner must be present for those who are elevated to nonequity status Those partners must have the right stuff, whether they are admitted to nonequity or equity status. I have seen situations where partners say that an individual is eligible for admission as a nonequity partner but not as an equity partner. This obviously creates a second-class citizenship attitude that is difficult to sell to everyone else.

Each time a person comes up for partner consideration, the firm must ask itself this question: If we did not have a two-tier system, would this person still be admitted as a partner? If the answer is no, then he should not be admitted to the nonequity class.

One of the premises of this concept is the recognition that promoting someone to partner is an *evaluation* question. What type of partner they are going to be is a *compensation* question. Therefore, the first decision is whether a person should or should not be elevated to partner status. Once that decision is made, then the question is "how will he be paid?" The answer to that determines whether he is in the equity or nonequity class.

♦ Equally as important is the realization of the possibility that a nonequity partner could make as much or more money than some of the equity partners. This may be difficult for some people to come to grips with. However, over time, a firm will have certain partners who, for whatever reason, are not ever elevated to equity partner status. Assuming that economic considerations are taken into account in elevating partners, then it is conceivable that a nonequity partner could make more money than an equity partner. In some respects, the nonequity partner has the best of both worlds from a compensation standpoint. He has a guaranteed salary that protects him during bad years, and in good years he participates through some type of bonus system.

If the firm comes to a realization about these items, then I believe it is possible to sell the program to associates and partners and create an atmosphere wherein the two-tier system can operate.

In order to appreciate fully why the two-tier system is important, one must look at the elements of an owner's compensation:

+ Salary, which is commensurate with a person's experience, age, position, and so on, as set by the profession in similarly situated firms
+ Return of capital, which is the interest on the capital accounts (assuming that your firm pays interest on capital, as many firms do)
+ Most importantly, profits made from others. This is the concept of leverage. Some firms do a better job of this than others. This leverage comes from associates, legal assistants, and younger partners.

Anyone who has studied the economics of a professional service practice recognizes that the only way to protect partner earnings is to maintain the pyramid relationship. This means there must be a larger group of associates and young partners supporting the equity partner base. To the extent that the pyramid starts looking like a rectangle, then the dilution of partner earnings maximizes. There are many publications that address whether or not this leverage is still a means to increase profitability. The contention is that more money can be made by partners with more hours at higher rates. In my opinion, this will not occur until some rate reconstructing is done along with obtaining a better understanding of how value billing is to be accomplished. Until that happens, leverage is still the key to more profits, although perhaps not in the same magnitude as in prior years due to escalating salary and overhead levels, lower billable hours, and depressed rates.

Another fairly common axiom is that very shortly in his career, at least in a firm of any size, a partner ceases to support himself. In other words, the gross income generated by taking that partner's billable hours, multiplying by his hourly rate, and subtracting his appropriate expenses, is generally less than his distributed share of income. At that point, there must be a certain number of young partners and associates generating profits to support those partners who have now crossed over this magical threshold.

A firm must take a serious look at this problem and, by making some calculations, decide whether it is possible to make new partners in relation to the amount of work available so as to continue hiring more staff who can then support the higher earnings base.

There is one other aspect of a two-tier partnership that is important. A firm becomes more attractive to either potential merger candidates or lateral entries if it demonstrates an awareness of the realities concerning unlimited entry into equity ownership. The number of mergers and movement of lawyers between firms continue throughout the country. Those firms that are able to show potential entries into the firm that they have addressed and have begun solving the partner issues will be those firms that are better able to attract people with a sizable client following who will be beneficial to a firm over the long term.

The ownership question also bears on the issue of how the firm raises capital. There may be a tendency to want to admit equity partners simply to get more capital. While this may be a short-term benefit, it will be a long-term mistake if you admit those into equity ownership who do not possess the characteristics that the firm believes each equity partner should have.

Equity vs. Nonequity Partners

I am often asked to articulate the criteria for equity and nonequity partnership. This is not often easy to do.

If you believe in my idea that elevation to partner is an evaluation question, then the basic criteria is the same regardless of what type of partner you are admitting. He must pass all the tests such as being a good technician, be a hard worker, be a good administrator and manager of people and clients, have potential for getting business, be good in the community, be a good teacher, and so on. Once those tests are passed, then comes the issue of how he or she is paid: as an equity or nonequity partner? In my opinion, here is where the issue comes down to satisfying one of the following two criteria:

1. Does the individual have a client base that supports him and others?
2. Is the individual so smart that every time there is a major technical issue in the firm, he gets consulted?

Assuming one of these criteria is passed, then this person should be paid like an equity partner.

As I stated at the outset, there have been many articles that have addressed this issue. Some recently have said that the multitier structure may not be necessary if you can control compensation. The fact is that with changing career goals and standards among younger people, the nonequity partner or shareholder is still going to be popular as a way to provide status to those people who should be and want to be partners, but for whatever reason do not pass the "origination and smarts" test.

There is no question that a danger exists if the firm becomes top heavy with worker bees and does not bring along those who can bring new business to the firm. In addition, you need to make the judgment of whether you want to have someone just filling a slot who does not generate business, at the expense of getting someone who can also fill the same slot but generate business as well.

Alternative Structures

In addition to the nonequity partner, there are several other forms of leverage that firms are using to their advantage: part-time lawyers and contract lawyers. Whatever you call them, the key word is leverage and how best to provide income that will inure to the owners of the firm without substantial dilution. If you can accomplish that, then you have succeeded in developing a profitable structure, regardless of its name or its characteristics. Several firms have successfully used part-time or contract lawyers. In today's technology world, it is very easy for someone to operate out of his home or elsewhere off site and be in constant contact with the firm on a particular issue. This is a very profitable method for handling certain work, and I believe that it will become a definite trend for the future.

Having described how the multitier organizational structure functions, the next question is whether this structure is really necessary. Are there alternatives that fulfill the same overall objectives? Invariably, the decision to admit equity owners rests in large part on the willingness of the current equity group to admit additional owners who will share in the firm's income pot. This is an even larger problem if the pot is not growing sufficiently, and everyone's piece of the income stream is being reduced as new owners are added and the percentage share is diluted.

As noted earlier, the problems with the multitier system are twofold: First, it creates a position where the firm can "park" all those associates who for whatever reason do not pass muster as a partner, but whom no one wants to terminate outright. Second, even if the right people are placed in this category, the firm then faces the problem of how long to keep them in this group and establish the criteria required to move them into a full equity position.

There are several reasons, some already discussed, why firms establish the nonequity partner position.

- *The firm does not want to share extremely good years with other equity partners and thus dilute the current partners' share of the profits.* This has already been addressed and will be discussed further.
- *The firm does not want others to share in the decision-making processes of the firm.* There are partners who enjoy the power that comes with being an owner and who are not willing to share that power with others. Again, there is a solution to this, which will be addressed later.
- *Younger partners cannot afford the requisite capital contribution so they are left in the nonequity status until their personal financial situation*

changes. This can be a problem but can be resolved easily by either re-quiring no capital contribution for a period of years after equity part-ner admission, or by allowing the individual to borrow the money from the firm's bank, with the firm guaranteeing the debt and receiving re-payment through payroll deductions.

◆ *The firm does not want to fire someone, so they are made a nonequity partner.* Of the ones listed, this is the worst reason to elevate some-one to this status, since very soon the firm ends up with a group of highly paid lawyers, none of whom could pass muster to be full own-ers and who end up preventing the firm from growing at the bottom where new owners are initially created. At some point, the firm needs to bite the bullet and terminate these lawyers. It is better to do it early on so that the individual can find other, more suitable employ-ment rather than later when that employment may be more difficult to find.

In today's law firm, one either needs to be an outstanding finder (busi-ness originator) or outstanding grinder (great legal skills) to achieve a status whereby one can participate fully in the financial success of the firm.

Developing New Partners

This then leads back to the question of how a firm moves lawyers into the eq-uity ranks without completely diluting the income shares of the current equity owners.

The truth is that if firms can control compensation, difficult for many firms to do, there really is no need to have a multilayer system. By limiting the compensation of the new equity partners, a firm can avoid the dilutive effect of new owners as it relates to the diminishing of the profits left for the other owners.

This can be accomplished by doing two things: First, create another clas-sification called something like "senior equity partner" that distinguishes the more senior shareholders from the junior shareholders. Second, establish an income tiering system whereby the total income of the firm is divided into three tiers as discussed earlier.

In addition, by tying ownership percentages to income percentages, the senior equity owners with the largest overall income still retain a greater share of the decision-making power, which they may be reluctant to share with those junior to themselves. Thus, another reason for the nonequity group goes away.

This process permits the firm to control new owners' compensation while at the same time allowing new owners to earn significantly more than they did as associates. It permits them to reap the benefit of becoming equity partners and, through some level of capital contribution, to obtain the right to participate in the firm's overall economic successes.

As stated earlier, this issue impacts capitalization, ownership, and compensation and must be part of the strategic planning process of every law firm. Whatever the firm decides, it is absolutely imperative that the partners buy into the concept and that a communication process exists so that everyone, whether new and old, understands the system and how it affects them and their future with the firm.

ACCUMULATING EQUITY IN A PROFESSIONAL SERVICES FIRM

19

For the past twenty-five years or so, I have been one of the few individuals within the law firm consulting community who has advocated a supplemental payout system to law firm owners. This is a payout over and above the usual amounts, consisting primarily of capital balances and in some cases an arbitrary payout for good will and long-term service, or whatever else you care to call seniority or longevity.

The reasons for not having such a scheme are not grounded in logic but are based on emotion, and because remaining owners are not willing to accept what they perceive as the liability of those who no longer are making financial contributions to the firm.

To properly understand why I continue to advocate for a payout policy, you need to step back and educate yourself on the foundation upon which this type of policy is developed.

The Right to Accumulate Equity

First of all, recognize that owners of professional service firms have the same right to accumulate equity in the organization that they own as do the owners of any other type of business. If I am the owner of the XYZ Widget Company, I expect over time to accumulate equity in that company and upon my death, retirement, or termination for any reason, there is an expectation that I will receive some value over and above that which I have invested. Heck! This is the American way!

For whatever reason, law firm owners do not appear to have this expectation and thus do not spend the time and energy necessary to develop a process that permits their equity to accumulate for payment at some date in the future.

If you are among the few who believe that equity accumulation in a professional services firm is appropriate and necessary, or if I have now piqued your interest in developing such a program at your firm, the next question is "how do you set up such a system?"

Implementing an Equity Accumulation System

Once again, you need to buy into some concepts which are generally not understood or recognized in an environment that functions by selling services in terms of time value rather than Barbie dolls or software. These concepts are of an accounting nature, and focus attention on some very old accounting methods that have probably been in existence since the beginning of time: accrual-basis versus cash-basis accounting.

Most professional service firms operate on the cash basis of accounting; Receipts are accounted for in the time period in which the mailman delivers the checks, and expenses are accounted for when the check to the vendor is written. When the services were actually performed or the products or services were actually received is not relevant. This type of accounting has fostered an attitude among owners that compensation and related ownership issues only count when cash is physically transferred in or out of the organization. This is the first myth that must be dispelled.

The fact is that the better and more successful law firms operate internally (though not for tax purposes) on the accrual basis. Revenues are not represented by cash receipts but rather by the value of billable hours. When a time entry has been recorded on a time sheet, then a sale has been consummated with a willing purchaser of the service. The fact that this time is in "inventory" and not billed or collected is not important to the recognition of the revenue stream. Thus as an owner, my share of the net income is not the difference between cash receipts and expenses, but rather between the realizable value of the billable time of all the timekeepers in the firm, accounted for in the appropriate accounting period, and the expenses incurred to support and produce that billable time.

If you buy into this concept, then in reality, on an annual basis an owner actually receives a cash distribution or draw against his accrual-basis earnings. The difference between the share of profits on an accrual basis and that on a cash basis becomes his equity in the firm. The equity (call it deferred compensation if you like) is accumulated in an account to be paid out according to the owners' agreement upon the occurrence of an event such as death, disability, or retirement.

Since accounts payable does not change much from year to year, the major difference between accrual-basis net and cash-basis net is the accumulation that occurs in the balances of work-in-process and accounts receivable. The accumulation of this difference over the lifetime of ownership in the firm creates a pool of equity that was created but not converted into cash and made available in cash distributions. This assumes that in most successful law firms, these balances generally increase from year to year as the number of timekeepers and value of time increase accordingly.

The Opposition to an Equity Plan

Now that I have really piqued your interest, you are probably wondering why there has been such opposition to developing payout plans when they make such good logical and accounting sense. There are two major arguments against this type of payout system, neither of which can be logically supported, if you buy into the underlying methodology discussed earlier.

First, there is the argument that the amounts due are equivalent to an unfunded pension plan. A partner leaves the firm, and there is a perception that the amounts to be paid out over a ten-, fifteen- or twenty-year period is a liability that is not supported by any firm asset. This, of course, is not true. The total liability *is* supported by the pool of work-in-process and accounts receivable that has accumulated to the credit of the terminated partner. Thus, this argument is unfounded. The safeguard against overstatement of these assets is to periodically value the work-in-process and accounts receivable balances and set up a reserve that reduces the amounts to a realistic value. Generally, the firm agrees on some percentage to be applied against the gross amounts.

Second, there is the argument that the firm does not want to subject itself to long-term payments to a terminated partner, thus depriving the current partners of their earned share of the firm's profits. This argument is also unfounded, if you agree with the position stated earlier: an owner's profit share is not on the current year's cash receipts, but rather on the current year's billable time value, a share of which is *not* allocated to the terminated partner, but rather only to the remaining partners as a proportion of their income percentage interests. Law firms should not look to prior value to earn their income; rather, they should be concerned with the value that is generated during the current year, and how they can convert that to cash as quickly as possible to increase their earnings in that current year. The safeguards against being strapped with payments for long periods of time include having a vesting schedule and tying payments to terminated partners to a percentage of the firm's net income. I have also seen some firms, in states where this is legal, attach a non-compete clause to the payout agreement.

Does this same system apply to those firms who do not keep time records? The answer is yes, with the deferred value represented not by work-in-process and accounts receivable, but rather by the expected value of future cases to be settled, less the costs to be incurred to settle those cases.

The mechanics of developing and administering a payout system are somewhat complicated, and in many cases dependent upon getting the firm to agree on certain assumptions prior to instituting the process. Thus, the mechanics are not included in this book, though they have been described in other writings. One article that may be of particular use is "Who Owns Your Work-in-Process and Accounts Receivable?" (published in *Law Office Management and Administration Report*). Please refer to the list of articles at the end of this book for information on obtaining a copy of this article.

MERGERS AND LATERAL HIRES **20**

Law firms either grow by hiring young associates, lateral owners, or associates who are already practicing, or by merging another firm with their own. Law firm expansion is a subject that is not directly connected to financial management, but because of its financial implications, it is important in the context of this book.

The strategic plans of most firms will at some point include the issue of expansion. Expansion can be further subdivided into establishment of branch offices either by the firm itself or through the merger route. Mergers can be with other practices in the city where a firm already has offices, or into areas where a firm wishes to have a presence. Expansion also involves lateral hiring of individuals, from other firms or out of government service or industry, who can assist a firm in enhancing its profitability.

A major fear of most small and medium-sized firms is the movement of larger firms into their area. However, this should not be a great fear if a firm has nurtured their clients well, has given them good service at a good value, and has been able to develop an expertise in those areas necessary to satisfy clients' demands. To the extent that a firm cannot provide a particular service, then it has to acquire it through merger, lateral hires, or association with correspondent firms in the geographical area of the client so it can still control all of the client's legal business.

To fill specialties they currently lack or to compete with medium-sized or large firms, smaller firms have to begin some type of expansion. Care must be taken, however, that synergism takes place. This means that the total is greater than the sum of the parts, or that 2 + 2 = 5, or better yet, 6. It means that when you put together a group of firms, the combined firm should make more money for the owners than if they had stayed separate entities. This is easier said than done, and depends upon the goals for the merger, the kind of planning that goes into it at the beginning, and the size of the firms that are being merged.

What happens unfortunately in many cases is that firms enter into an expansion without really understanding its objectives. The result is that problems occur and the synergism never takes place.

Mergers

In order for synergism to occur, the firm must set certain goals for the merger. These goals include:

- Developing a network of practice and client management that results in a 2 + 2 = 5 situation
- Substantially expanding the firm's presence in a particular area or region of the country
- Attracting clients that neither firm had developed before the merger
- Enhancing the ability to attract regional or national business
- Enhancing the ability to attract new business in the area where the new offices are located
- Offering expanded legal capabilities to clients in the current area
- Enhancing recruiting at all levels
- Giving the firm an edge in competing with larger firms moving into the area
- Expanding financial resources to fund future expansions, defensive posturing, and increased owner earnings
- Expanding and strengthening major practice areas

These are just some of the goals that each firm can set when a merger is contemplated. Some of them will be met early on, some will take time to develop, and some may never materialize. The important thing is that some definitive plan needs to be in place before a decision of this magnitude can be made. There are several issues that are important leading up to and including the merger itself.

Understanding the Reason for the Merger

A firm must first make sure that it knows why it wants to merge before the process begins. This is part of the goal-setting process. All the owners in a firm must reach a consensus that the merger is important to the firm's long-term success. Everybody has a friend who has a friend who wants to be with a particular firm. There is a tendency sometimes for that to take precedence rather than what that particular person or group brings to the table. The merger must take place for all the right reasons.

Sometimes the methodology that is used is a little backwards. A firm decides to merge with another firm in location X and then concludes that the reason for the merger was that it wanted to be in location X in the first place. The methodology should be just the opposite. The firm should first decide that it wants to be in location X for whatever reason, and then go out and find the very best firm in location X that it can merge with. The firm must study the area, determine whether or not the business is there, and then go out and decide which firm can best suit their ultimate goals and objectives.

Once a merger starts down the track, it should be consummated very quickly. Word about mergers gets out within a few days after the first meeting. This is not healthy for either firm. There are a certain amount of conflict problems that may develop where one firm is representing one side and the other firm is representing the other. If possible, the merger should be consummated within a two- or three-month period at most, one way or the other. Keep in mind that turning down a merger is not all that bad and some of a firm's very best friends will be those firms with whom talks were held but a merger did not materialize.

Resolving Important Issues Early

The major issues must be placed on the table very early on in the negotiations, and resolved. A firm does not want to waste a lot of time on some of the minor issues, only to find out in the eleventh hour that the nepotism policy, or the owner-admission policy, is a deal-breaker.

The success or lack of success of most mergers is often a result of how the firms deal with their cultural differences. Culture relates to how the owners deal with some of the gut issues of the firm. For example, how does each firm deal with compensation? Is one firm in a lock-step system and another firm on a formula-based system? Does one firm regard billable hours as the number-one criteria for compensation while the other firm uses a combination of hours, marketing, management, and so on? Does one firm have a two- or three-tier ownership system and the other firm a one-tier system? Does one firm bring in its owners after four or five years while the other brings theirs in at seven or eight years? Does one firm believe that the committee system should be utilized to run the firm, and the other one believes that there should be one leader to make all the major decisions?

These are the kinds of cultural differences that exist within firms that must be resolved very early on during the discussions, or they will come back to haunt the firm should the merger take place.

If either firm has some unusual procedures or policies that must be maintained, these should come up early in the negotiations. If there is a problem and no compromise can take place, then the discussions should be broken off immediately. There is no reason wasting time for both firms.

Changing the Name

Obviously, the name of the merged firm is an issue. Changing a name can be either a problem or an opportunity. It can be a problem in the sense that an institution that has become known to the outside world now has a different name. It is expensive because of everything in the firm that must be changed to reflect the new name; and believe it or not, it is a time waster because lot of people will spend hours worrying about what the new letterhead is going to look like.

Other people view a name change as an opportunity, in the sense that it is a new beginning. A firm can make a lot of good marketing points with a change of name and all of the hoopla that goes along with it. But based on my experience, I would not suggest a name change unless it is absolutely necessary.

Staff Issues

There are other areas of concern in addition to those recognized as major issues. These are smaller, but they must be dealt with. Most owners can see the big issues in a merger, like partner compensation, name change, and deciding who is going to run which department, but sometimes they fail to be concerned with staff issues. Few people realize that if the troops are unhappy, this mood is going to be communicated to the owners. The owners then start grousing and before you know it, you have a major problem on your hands. Staff issues should be addressed very early on and resolved so that when the merger takes place, there is no question about how things will be handled or whose policies are going to be followed. This includes primarily compensation, benefits, working relationships, and so on.

Using Consultants

Consultants can be helpful in a merger. However, in some cases the firm can probably manage the merger themselves, assuming (and this is a major point) that the firm has people on board who understand the issues and can deal with them objectively. What the consultant does is look past local issues and concentrate on the real problems that need to be addressed. Consultants are good facilitators, and can be invaluable assets in making sure that the merger goes through quickly and easily and stays focused on the right issues. Most lawyers cannot relate to the problems involved in a merger; they just want to get the merger over with and worry about the problems later.

The Negotiating Team

The negotiating teams should be kept small. The major players from both firms should be involved, but certainly not everybody. A firm should choose a negotiating team that has the confidence of the owners and let that team go about its business. The negotiators cannot operate if they are constantly bombarded with other people's better ideas. Obviously, the owners should be kept informed about what is going on. They should be encouraged to make suggestions, but the negotiations have to be carried on by a small group who has the confidence and credibility of the rest of the owners.

Sharing Financial Information

A major part of the pre-merger review is financial information, compensation systems, and information on clients. This should be exchanged very early, usually after the first or second meeting. These are the areas that cause most of the problems and these are the areas that have to be addressed at the very beginning of the discussions.

In connection with the financial information, there are certain issues that need close scrutiny. These issues, when interpreted properly, provide a better understanding of the financial health of the firm.

- *Gross revenues per lawyer.* This should be done on a three- or five-year basis and should identify a healthy growth situation as opposed to a stagnated or reducing trend. It will also identify whether or not one year was unusual as a result of a particular client. A higher gross per lawyer usually means more money to invest in the firm and more money for an owner.
- *Expenses per lawyer.* Again, this is basically looking at trends. Here you should look particularly for extraordinary expenses that may be continuing or may have serious impact on the future operations of the firm. With the trend toward more paraprofessionals, this statistic should also be produced for lawyer equivalents. Keep in mind that economy of scale usually does not work, and the merger should not be seen as a way to cut expenses. While to a certain extent you may be able to reduce some administrative expenses, the merger should be used more to create additional opportunities for generating more revenues.
- *Net income per owner.* This number should be reviewed not only as an average for the firm, but also within owner peer groups. There should be equal compensation at various groups in order to avoid a situation where a ten-year owner in one firm is making substantially more or less than a ten-year owner in the other firm. A rule of thumb is that profits per owner should be equal to two times the revenues per

lawyer. Thus, if the revenues per lawyer are $150,000, the net income per owner should be $300,000. This can only occur in those firms that have a significant amount of nonowner leverage.

◆ *Billable hours.* The firm must examine the extent to which people are willing to work hard. It is not going to be a good merger if one firm is accustomed to averaging 1,800 or 2,000 billable hours per year per lawyer, where the other firm is producing 1,300 or 1,400. This will be a definite deal breaker. The two firms must each be prepared to work hard enough to generate the kind of income envisioned by the owners at the time the merger decision is made. This is especially relevant with respect to the use of nonlawyers. This should be done not only at the owner level, but at the nonowner level as well. If the pyramid system is to work, then obviously those individuals below owner must be working the hours necessary to generate projected revenues.

◆ *Billing rates.* The rate structure must be examined within various peer groups, along with looking at realization. There may be several reasons why the rates are different, some of which depend upon the client base; one firm may have a high concentration of clients in a high-paying practice area while the other firm may have a high concentration in a low-paying area. It could be that a firm is either way above or way below market, and in many cases, the firm's culture determines the rate philosophy. If the firm has multiple rates for individual timekeepers, then an examination must be made as to how these rates are applied to specific clients.

◆ *Work-in-process and accounts receivable.* These balances should be examined carefully and an aged analysis prepared to determine whether the amounts being brought over to the combined firm can be converted into cash in a relatively short period of time. In many cases, this says much about the firm's future financial health, and the turnover statistic of the firm can highlight problems that may be developing.

The firm must examine the nature of all liabilities, potential liabilities and the debt structure of the firm. This will in many cases be related to the capitalization policy. If a firm is more debt-oriented than owner-capital oriented, its debt will be high as opposed to a firm that may derive most of its working capital and funds for asset acquisition from the owners.

Other Merger Issues

It is important that the tail not wag the dog. Whichever is the surviving firm should take charge. They should compromise when necessary, but not give away the store. Besides those listed above, other major issues that need to be addressed include the following:

- Investments that the owners may have in other businesses which either could not or should not be integrated into the merged firm, such as a title company or an office building
- Major personnel issues such as a nepotism policy. This is particularly important if married couples already exist in either of the firms.
- Ownership admissions policy and standards for admission
- Ancillary benefits such as parking, automobiles, marketing allowances
- Retirement plan issue. Here you have to determine whether or not bringing in old owners will significantly affect the amounts that the younger owners will have to pay in the future. In this area, the firm may need to make some actuarial computations. There may also be tax considerations that must be addressed.
- Substantive administrative systems. This has to do with the personnel compensation system, time and accounting systems, payroll policies and practices, fringe benefits, and so on
- Compensation in general, particularly at the owner and associate level to include major cost of living differentials
- Potential malpractice claims against the firm as well as any major conflicts that exist between the two firms
- How institutionalized the firm is with respect to outside income earned by the owners such as director's fees, teaching fees, writing fees, and so on
- How the firms are going to handle the capital requirements. If one has a major capital requirement and the other does not, how is that going to be handled and what is the process going to be to get up to prescribed levels?
- Last, but not least, is how the new merged firm will be represented on the major committees, such as the executive committee, associates committee, recruiting committee, and so on, and who will head up the various practice departments or sections

The Integration Process

Once a merger takes place, then each firm must begin the integration process of the merged entity. The first step is to establish a transition team to deal with the major issues. Generally, the firm assigns one member of the new executive committee to a specific area and then he appoints another committee to deal with the problem. This way the individuals on the various committees are responsible to a member of the executive committee, who then reports to the executive committee. Timetables must be established that specify when various aspects of the integration will be done, and those who do not do their jobs should be called to task.

Once assigned to the team, each person is then given a time frame within which he is to complete his particular task and prepare a report for the executive committee for action. Needless to say, some of the projects get done and some of them don't.

There has to be care and feeding at all levels. Feelings get hurt very quickly if there are changes in procedures or policies that people have lived with for many years, and that people think are as good or better than the larger firm's. It is generally wise to compromise on the smaller issues so that the larger ones are an easier sell.

An important aspect of the merger is having some exchange of people. One recommendation for a firm merging with one in another city is to transfer an owner or a senior associate on the track to ownership to the other city to head that office. This promotes a feeling of oneness within the merged firm and allows the other owners to come to grips with the new policies and procedures. If a firm does not do this, then the "we-they" situation may continue, which does not promote profitability or institutionalization.

A firm must be prepared to lose owners, associates, and clients. Mergers, particularly large ones, inevitably upset certain people to the extent that leaving is their only way out.

One of the questions that frequently gets asked is how to attempt to meld the compensation in a merger situation, particularly one in which you have several owners on each side. In many cases, this depends on the size of the merged firm. If it is only one or two lawyers, then they can be slotted into the normal compensation system, and their compensation depends on their prior earnings history, book of business, and so on.

In a larger firm, it is necessary to examine the history of the merging entities and then calculate the owners' net income history and base compensation on this history, at least for a two- to three-year period. There are various models based on this type of system. In some cases, each of the merging firms sets compensation for their owners based on a projected pool of income, and these amounts are then reviewed and approved by the executive committee of the new combined entity. This issue is detailed in Chapter 17.

A firm must determine early on who is ultimately in charge. This is presumably the chairman of the firm, whoever that person may be. It should be agreed to up front that if and when a merger does take place, the chairman or the benevolent despot is in charge of the merged entity, and that he will continue in that position unless he is removed by a majority of the owners.

A firm must be prepared to spend a lot of time on a merger, because a lot of time is involved. There is a significant reduction in billable hours during a merger period, particularly because many of the lawyers with the highest hourly rates are involved in putting the merger together. Hopefully, it all pays dividends in the end, and synergism takes place. If all goes according to plan, the firms will, in fact, end up making more money together than they would have made separately.

Lateral Hires

There is a corollary to the merger question that deserves some discussion: the question of lateral hires.

There has been unprecedented movement of lawyers among firms over the past several years, both individual lawyers and groups (in addition to mergers). This comes from changes in local, state, and national government; the break-up of firms; and business producers' desire to find a place where their books of business are better appreciated, which translates into them making more money.

Most successful firms receive phone calls, résumés, and inquiries from people who want to be associated with the firm. Unfortunately, in some cases an analysis to determine if a person is good for a firm in the long run is not fully performed. Depending on who gets a call or who is pushing a potential lateral, decisions are made on the basis on a candidate's being a "nice guy" or a "good lawyer," or having many contacts that will generate business for a firm.

The point here is that if a proper review is not made concerning a lateral hire into a firm, it can seriously affect the attitudes of the owners and the morale of the associates. Each lateral must be looked at for what that person brings to the table in terms of expertise or in terms of clients, depending on what a firm is looking for.

As discussed earlier, to the extent that a client or service is on your list of items that you want but do not currently have, you must search outside your firm. This search must be handled properly, and the right questions must be raised. Too often, personalities enter into a decision, which tends to mask problems until after the lateral hire is on board.

Some of the questions that need to be raised when hiring laterals include:

- If a lawyer is bringing business to your firm, have the clients been interviewed to provide some assurance that they will actually go with the lawyer? Many clients become institutionalized to the point where they relate to a firm and not to an individual lawyer. If this is the case with a potential lateral, the expected client base may not be there. Also, potential clients may have a problem with your firm or your individual lawyers that would preclude giving you their legal business. This must be determined beforehand.
- If clients come with a lawyer, how will they be serviced? Is there enough free time among the current complement of lawyers to service new client projects? If not, then where will the hours come from?
- If new lawyers are hired, does the firm have room for them in its current space? Consider support staff, technology, telephone service, and so on.

- If a lateral is bringing associates with him, will they receive the same level of review that is given to all new associates to see how they will fit into the firm? Does this create a compensation problem when the new associates are compared to those already in the firm? What about prospects for ownership? Keep in mind that associates may be around long after an owner is gone.

- If a lateral is coming from government or the judiciary, does he understand the economics of law practice as it exists today? In other words, has he been away so long that he doesn't understand all the nuances of law firm management, like keeping time records and sending out bills?

- How will the lateral hire affect benefits, particularly the pension plan? If the lateral is older, will hiring him cause an expense in the future for the existing owners? Will former pensions be offset against the firm pension?

- Will he be brought in at full equity status, or as a contract owner? If full equity, what is his capital contribution and how is that to be satisfied?

- How will the firm deal with the conflict issues? Will these mitigate against the new business that has been promised?

- Can the firm fund the additional overhead until the lateral's clients start paying their bills?

- Finally, how will the lateral's compensation be determined? Where does he fit in with the other owners?

The firm needs to quantify the levels of contribution by the lateral and create a compensation scheme that takes each into consideration. Once a total number is determined, then the firm divides it into pieces in such a way that both the lateral and the firm share in the risk. For example, the firm may decide to pay a lateral $200,000 per year, $100,000 of which is salary, 60 percent of the remainder coming from a percentage of fees from new clients, and 40 percent on time that the lateral charges personally. This can be adjusted periodically once some history has been developed.

Somewhere in every successful law firm's history, a lateral was hired who played an important part in the firm's success. Each decision, however, must be carefully weighed, using as much information as possible, to make certain that the lateral hire is truly in the best interest of the firm over the long run, and is in keeping with the overall strategic plan of the firm.

Contract Lawyers

One of the concepts popular among firms is the contract lawyer, an individual who comes to the firm laterally but is on a contract for a defined period of time, usually one or two years. A contract lawyer is generally on a fixed income during that period of time, and at the end of the period his contract is renewed, terminated, or brought into the regular ownership. This reduces the amount of risk for the firm, and it is usually more palatable to younger owners and other associates. At the conclusion of the defined period, if the contractor has not been able to develop the kind of business base that was expected, then he can be terminated with little difficulty. This works in most cases; but if a firm brings in a former governor or senator, or a high-powered lawyer from another firm, a contract like this may not be feasible.

Marginal Income

Another related issue that may be helpful in the evaluation process is the method used to determine the economics of a lateral hire. This is the concept of marginal income.

It is important to recognize that when someone joins a firm laterally, there is generally no increase in the regular overhead of the firm. In other words, the space already exists, the number of support people will not increase, the library will stay the same size, and so on. So when a person comes to a firm, his expenses are only those that relate directly to him and do not include overhead expenses that would exist whether he was there or not.

Therefore, In order to project the amount of income to be generated by the lateral, it is important that only an individual's direct expenses be taken into account in determining his profitability. Generally, this includes only salary and benefits, partial cost of a secretary, malpractice insurance, and some minor expenses such as bar dues, telephone, subscriptions, and so on. By determining the lateral's contribution to profit on this basis, it is then possible to ascertain the amount of marginal income that will actually inure to the remaining owners. This is the only fair and accurate way to examine the potential financial impact of a new lateral hire.

HOW TO SURVIVE AS A LEGAL MANAGER

In 1987, I gave a presentation at the Association of Legal Administrators Convention in Orlando, Florida on "Governance and Role of the Legal Administrator." Many of my ideas on legal administration came from that speech and are the ones I share with you now. I decided that it would be a good idea to add "survival" to the title, simply because the roles that administrators play and the methods by which their responsibilities are dispensed often determine their ability to survive in this difficult, frustrating, and pressure-packed profession.

I hope that lawyers reading this will gain insight into their relationship with their legal administrators, and that administrators will gain some additional knowledge on how to survive in a tough job.

For many years, I've advocated improving the image of the professional legal manager. A legal manager should be well rounded in all aspects of his or her position, because that is the only way to gain credibility in the legal profession. Unfortunately, over the years, the ranks have been diluted by individuals who, while they call themselves administrators, really aren't in the true sense of the word. As a result, the roles that administrators play within their respective organizations may be so different that what I suggest may not be practical. But most readers will relate to much of what I say.

Even after all these years, the role of the professional legal manager is still fairly undefined. As a consultant, I have known of searches for administrators by some of the largest firms in the country where a good portion of the time is spent trying to agree on an appropriate job description. A large percentage of firms still really don't understand where the legal manager fits within the overall governance and management structure of a firm.

What you do and how you do it depends on many factors, including the size of your firm; the location; its philosophy, culture, and personality; and, to a certain extent, the level of sophistication that is employed by other legal managers within your own community. Let's deal with these issues as a starting point for describing and defining the aspects of the administrator position.

Large versus Small Firms

There is a school of thought that says that legal managers from large firms, in many cases, enjoy a level of responsibility and authority that is not present in small to medium-sized firms. There are two reasons for this line of thinking. One is that the larger a firm gets, the less time the lawyers are willing and able to devote to administration and management, and, thus, the manager picks up more responsibilities. And, second, because a firm is large, for some magical reason, there are duties and responsibilities that somehow don't exist in small firms. Therefore, legal managers from small firms don't have the same opportunity to participate in important and perhaps more sophisticated activities as managers of larger firms. While this may be true, my experiences have told me that, in many respects, legal managers in small firms may, in fact, have a greater variety of activities within their firms than do those from the larger firms.

The legal manager from a small firm must, by necessity, be a jack-of-all-trades. He or she must have expertise in virtually every area of administration and management, whether it's technology and telecommunications, staff compensation and benefits, financial management, or the variety of administrative and partner issues that are faced on a day-to-day basis The small-firm manager isn't surrounded by individuals who are experts in these areas. The result is that the small-firm legal manager may be more of what I would call the true manager than some of those from large firms.

In addition, the small-firm manager may be only the first or second manager that a firm has ever had. The systems and procedures at the large firms are fairly well established, and the manager is more of a caretaker. Small firms need doers and developers of new ideas and concepts, so the performance expectations may be higher than at large firms, where managers have come and gone for many years.

I've known many large-firm managers who, quite frankly, probably couldn't survive at a small firm. They're used to creating empires, surrounding themselves with highly paid people, and delegating many of the major responsibilities to them. I don't believe in this theory. To survive in this business, you must take a hands-on, roll-up-your-sleeves approach and work in the trenches along with your people to get the job done. Those who have created empires are those who, over the long haul, won't survive in these situations.

Personally, when a partner calls down and asks a question, I like to be able to give him the answer and not simply refer him to somebody else. What happens in many cases is that, over a period of time, someone else is always answering the questions. Soon the partners begin wondering, if someone else has all the answers, what are we paying this legal manager for? Many administrators have lost their jobs as a result of this phenomenon.

There is little question in my mind that managers from small firms have equality with those from large firms and certainly have the same amount of overall responsibility, although perhaps at a lesser scale.

Having said that, I don't want to give the impression that large-firm administrators are nothing more than empire builders, creating fiefdoms and not working. Rather, I want to dispel the theory that you must be from a large firm to be a successful legal manager. True, there is a certain amount of sophistication at a large firm that can't be found at a smaller firm, simply because larger firms have more financial resources available. In addition, legal managers at large firms have staff available to perform many of the day-to-day tasks, such as personnel administration, automation, records management, and benefits administration. This frees up the legal manager to devote time to a firm's strategic issues, which include partner compensation, financial management, office lease negotiations, space planning, expansion, and others.

Thus, the size of the firm does, in many respects, determine how the legal manager dispenses his or her duties. Because of the diversity of responsibility, it's difficult to discuss the subject of governance. Yet, there are even more differences that determine a legal manager's role in a firm, as well as the scope of responsibility.

Other Differences

The philosophy, culture, and personality of your firm, whether large or small, also dictate the manner in which the manager's duties are dispensed. If your firm is basically run by older partners, your role may be fairly restricted; older partner groups sometimes find it difficult to give up the more important and perhaps more interesting aspects of management to a nonlawyer.

Conversely, if your firm is run by a young partner group, perhaps a little more progressive, the opposite may be true. In this situation, the administrator oftentimes deals at the very highest levels of the firm, simply because the partners recognize the role that the professional manager plays in the overall successful operation of the firm.

While this is somewhat of a generalization, my experience has been that those firms managed by young partners are more adaptable to change than those run by older partners. For example, even in some of the larger older firms, legal managers are not give the responsibility to sign all checks, simply because this has always been done by the partners. I know of many large firms where cosignatures are required on all checks over $1,000—a very archaic method of operations.

Another aspect that affects administrator duties is the level of sophistication employed by other legal managers in the same geographic area. Lawyers get together and they talk a lot, and in many cases, they discuss the role of the legal manager. If you are in an area where most legal managers aren't given much responsibility or authority, chances are you won't have much either. Local firms tend to emulate each other in many respects, including this one.

While traveling around the country to different areas, I have noted this phenomenon. It is interesting to sit with a group of managers from one area and hear basically the same kind problem from all of them—that they aren't given enough authority or responsibility within their respective firms. I can go to another town and find just the opposite. It's not too often that I find, particularly in the small city, a situation where some of the managers have a tremendous amount of responsibility and authority and some have very little.

What all this points out, once again, is that it's very difficult to discuss the governance issue, because of the various factors that affect the manner in which the legal manager role is fulfilled.

Issues of Authority

Let me now address some aspects of the position that are critical to surviving. These thoughts may be helpful to you in your current firm with respect to making changes. Or, if you are in the process of changing positions, these may help you determine whether or not a particular position is appropriate for you.

First of all, I don't believe there is any issue in the firm that the legal manager isn't privy to. As a matter of fact, there are probably many things about a firm that the legal manager knows that some of the other partners don't know, including some of those on the executive committee. If a legal manager is to function properly, he or she must have access to all information, from how much the partners make, to which partner is having an affair with the fourth-floor receptionist.

In this regard, I believe that the legal manager should have partnership status immediately. By this I mean he or she attends all partnership meetings, is privy to all partnership financial information (and probably prepares most if not all of it), is involved in all lateral hires and mergers, and generally is regarded as a partner in and outside the firm. The only way this person can gain credibility and respect from the lawyers and staff alike is to be on equal par with the partners.

Perhaps one of the most critical issues is reporting responsibility. A legal manager can't be the lackey for every partner in the firm; he or she must report to one person or one committee. One of the essential elements of being able to do the job correctly is to have one person or one group of people to whom you are accountable. It just simply makes no sense for every partner to be badgering the manager every day for information about the firm or other partners. Not only is it dangerous to the manager, but it's dangerous to the firm if individuals receive information and act on it without really understanding its implications.

In addition, other partners shouldn't have the right to give the manager orders—or instructions to do something out of the ordinary—unless it has been cleared with the managing partner or committee. This, too, muddies the chain of command. The additional danger is that if you become aligned with a certain person or group within the firm and that person or group falls out of favor, you fall out of favor with them.

The legal manager should have broad authority in many areas to make decisions. It's no good to have the responsibility to do something if you don't have the authority to do it as well. Here I am talking about making major decisions within the firm, for example, deciding on word-processing systems or reprographics equipment, setting staff salaries and benefit programs, or handling the records management operations. The legal manager should have the authority to actually make these decisions and not have to clear it with someone else.

Obviously, from a political standpoint, there are certain things that you do clear through other people and there are others that you don't. The successful legal manager is the person who understands this and knows when to talk to someone and when not to.

Over the years as an administrator, I had the good fortune of reporting really to one person, and I bounced my ideas off him. He generally agreed with me, and we went about running the law firm. This is the ideal situation, of course, but it is one that you build to over a period of time, once you gain the respect of those for whom you work.

Salary Considerations

Let me now address a subject near and dear to the hearts of all of us. Fortunately or unfortunately, salaries for legal managers have risen dramatically over the past several years and are now at an all-time high. Much of it is due to the fact that administrators keep moving from firm to firm, which causes salaries to ratchet up. I hope that they don't get to the point where the profession prices itself out of the market.

Many administrators are probably not worth as much as they are paid. Firms are beginning to realize that it might be better to take on a young partner and put him or her in charge of the firm, which would cost a lot less than hiring a legal manager. While this may be a shortsighted approach, many firms around the country are trying it.

I doubt others share this opinion, but I don't believe in bonus systems. I didn't believe in bonuses for myself or for any of my immediate managers and supervisors. My reason is that a bonus represents payment for work done over and above the call of duty during a twelve-month period. It's very difficult to determine, in fact, what has been done over and above the call and what has been done because it was part of the job description. If my managers came in and said that they had worked fifty hours a week all last year, my response was that's what they were being paid for. If my word-processing supervisor came in and said she had developed a new word-processing system, my response was that's what she was being paid for. Many times people are rewarded with bonuses for work that they are being paid to do in the first place.

The question is not really whether or not you get a bonus, but if you are being paid what the job is worth for as long as it takes to perform it. Whether the firm has a good year or a bad year isn't relevant. As a matter of fact, a manager probably works harder when times are bad than when times are good, but makes less money. But because I was going to work just as hard whether I got a big bonus or no bonus, I didn't want to stand around for twelve months and worry about it.

Now this doesn't mean that if you do an extraordinary job in a particular area during a twelve-month period, you shouldn't be rewarded. For example, suppose a manager is involved in a major office move and, as a result of that move, he or she works an extraordinary amount of hours, at night and on weekends. This is over and above the call and probably justifies a bonus.

Rules of Survival

One of the interesting things about legal administrators is that the turnover rate continues to be one of the highest of any profession. Generally, most administrators last about two-and-a-half years in a firm, and the average life in the profession itself is about four to five years. I am often asked how I survived not only staying in the profession for almost sixteen years, but staying with the same firm all that time. I followed what I call my "Rules of Survival for the Legal Administrator" and tried to adhere to them. I hope that they help other administrators stay with their firms and in the profession.

1. *Reconcile yourself to the idea that most lawyers are generally smarter than you are.* I don't really mean that they are better managers or better administrators, but by and large they are generally smarter. They have a higher intelligence level than most legal managers and are able to come up with ideas and comments on various proposals submitted to them that most legal managers are really unable to ascertain. Whenever I presented a proposal to my partners, I made sure that I had my act together, because I knew that there would be questions I hadn't even thought of. Most of them dealt with political implications of proposals, which legal managers may not clearly understand or appreciate. I also believe that following this rule keeps you down to earth and allows you to put your own strengths and weaknesses in perspective.

2. *If you go to the mat, make sure the issue is worth fighting for.* Winning is not important unless the victory accomplishes something. There are many instances when lawyers and staff will do things that aren't in accordance with a firm's procedures. Some things you let go by and other things you fight for. Generally, only bring to management's attention those items you believe are significant and will adversely affect the firm After you're with a firm for a while, you understand how things get done.

   Generally, the request comes to you, and you approve or disapprove it. If you disapprove it, then, depending who the person is making the request, it may go to some committee for further review. If you feel that you are going to lose at that level for whatever reason, why not approve it in the first place? While this may not sit well with you, the fact of the matter is that, in most cases, these incidental things really don't affect the overall operation of the firm.

   You have to decide when a matter comes to your attention whether or not you can live with it. If you can't and you think that the impact on the firm as a whole will be detrimental, then you have to fight for it. However, keep in mind that if you lose, you only have two options. You either buy into the program or you get out.

3. *Don't play favorites.* Treat all lawyers, particularly partners, the same. One of the reasons why many administrators don't last in their firms is that they align themselves with particular partners, provide

them with special favors, and then get caught in a crack, because they are treating some people differently than others. By not playing favorites, I could always pass the "straight eye" test. When someone asked for a particular favor, I simply told them that I couldn't do it for them because I wouldn't do it for anybody else.

Here again, exercise judgment. There are partners in the firm, particularly the senior ones, who are going to request and, in many cases, receive special favors. When this favor is requested, tell them that they have to understand that this is against firm policy and that, by doing it for them, you have to do it for everybody else. In many cases, they will back off from their request, recognizing that the impact on other partners could be significant. I followed that procedure of covering myself on each and every instance, so that the problems didn't come back to haunt me. Remember the old saying, "All partners are equal; some are just more equal than others."

4. *Don't expect everything you propose to be accepted.* Remember that 50 percent of something is better than 100 percent of nothing. During the course of a legal manager's career, many new ideas are proposed to the partnership for adoption. You develop a certain amount of frustration when most of these ideas are not agreed to by the partnership. The administrator must keep going forward, recognizing that, while everything can't be approved, some things will pass, advancing the profitability and smoothly running operation of the law firm.

Often I'm asked how I went about selling ideas to management. First of all, rightly or wrongly, I gave my subordinate managers a great amount of autonomy. Generally, if they had an idea to present to me, they would present the problem, an alternative solution, and a recommendation. Ninety-nine times out of one hundred I accepted their recommendations, because I believed that they probably had a better feel for the problem than I did.

When I presented ideas to the executive committee, I did so in the same manner. I presented the problem, some possible solutions, and then made a recommendation. When you make the recommendation, it has to be practical, it has to work, and it has to be in the best interest of the firm and beneficially affect a large number of lawyers or the staff.

Try to stay away from those kinds of policies that deal only with the exceptions. Remember that no matter what you do, you can't please everyone. Your job is to put in rules, policies, and procedures that affect the majority of the people. The exceptions take care of themselves Unfortunately, there are many instances where knee-jerk reactions are given to one or two individual problems, which, in the end, create problems for a significant number of people.

5. *Work the same hours as the hardest-working lawyer.* This means many nights and many weekends. I tried to make it a rule to be the first person in the parking lot in the morning and the last person in the parking lot at night, and I always tried to be there at least five to six hours on Saturday and perhaps even devote some Sundays. This may seem like a serenade to the workaholic. However, I think it's important that the legal manager be perceived as someone who works as hard as the lawyers he or she works for.

6. *Treat the newest messenger with the same respect as the senior partner of the firm.* Everyone should be treated with respect, especially the support staff, who are the backbone of any law firm's operations.

    This is a policy I tried to follow religiously and also tried to get the lawyers to follow. There is nothing worse than being talked down to or treated like a second-class citizen. In order to create a hard-working, hard-charging, high-morale law firm, the feeling of professionalism must exist from the most senior partner to the newest mail clerk. People who are treated this way feel good about their jobs, about the firm, and about themselves, and they produce at a higher level.

7. *Don't believe all the good things people say about you.* Over a period of time a legal manager gets many compliments about the work he or she performs. However, once you start believing that you somehow are better than all the rest, it's the beginning of your downfall. I went to work every day thinking that my job was in jeopardy and that I had to perform as well that day as I did the day before to continue to justify my existence.

8. *Recognize that a certain percentage of the people won't like you or want you around and that the firm across the street or in the next town has the same percentage.* Only the people will be different. Regardless of how good a job you do, there is always a certain number of people who don't like you. Don't get frustrated and move to another firm. All firms have people like that and with a large group of people you simply have to do the best job you can within the limits of your abilities. You must recognize that you will never please certain people.

    This is a good time to talk about job security and how to protect yourself from a group of partners who decide you should be fired. I oppose contracts *per se*. Asking for a contract puts you in an adversarial role right off and creates a strained relationship with your new firm. As a practical matter, contract or not, once a firm decides to fire you, there's really not much you can do about it. All a contract really does is to provide some type of financial security between jobs. It may also define duties and responsibilities, but in our business, this is difficult to do through the written word.

One of the provisions in my firm's partnership agreement was that I couldn't be dismissed without the same voting restrictions as a partner. If it took 80 percent in interest and 25 percent in number to expel a partner, then firing me required the same amount of votes. In addition, I asked for an agreement that my compensation could never be reduced.

These kinds of provisions, whether in a contract or a partnership agreement, do provide a certain degree of protection and financial security. But once a groundswell against you begins, there is little you can do.

9. *Be good to new associates—one of them could eventually be your boss.* It's important that you provide the associates with all the care and feeding that you can. Some legal managers tend to look down to new associates and don't give them their due respect. This could be a problem if one of them eventually becomes the administrative partner.

I generally tried to meet with all the new associates at some time during their first year to tell them who I was, what I did, who the people were that they would be dealing with on a day-to-day basis. I tried to make them feel like they were part of the firm. I tried not to give them the impression that I was some almighty powerful person who was the key to their destiny in the firm. I stressed the fact that I was a resource to them and that I would do everything that I could to help them, recognizing that our goals were the same—to work hard, provide excellent service to clients, and make money.

10. *Never lose sight of the fact that you are a nonlawyer in a lawyer's world.* Regardless of what you may think is right, the lawyers ultimately make the decisions. You have to live with that or get out.

There's no question that being a legal administrator is a tough job. It takes a thick skin, a willingness to work hard, and a politician's personality to deal with the wide variety of people you serve. You must review your own situation and decide whether or not some of the things discussed are viable options to make your life easier and perhaps less frustrating.

I speak to administrators all the time, and there is generally not one situation that is similar to another. With all of its drawbacks, however, the profession enjoys continued growth, is still gaining credibility, and still achieving financial success. How each administrator handles his or her role will depend on the degree of success and whether or not they can survive in this atmosphere.

Other Publications Written by John Iezzi

Articles on Law Office Economics and Management

Reprints of these articles are available by writing directly to

Mr. John Iezzi
Iezzi Management Group
1906 N. Hamilton St., Suite A
P.O. Box 1711
Richmond, VA 23218-1711

Please enclose $2 per reprint by check to cover copying & postage.

1. "The Auditors Are Coming! The Auditors Are Coming!" *Newsletter, Association of Legal Administrators*
2. "How Automated Timekeeping Can Be Your Key to Higher Earnings," *Manual for Managing the Law Office*
3. "How to Analyze Your Investment in Client Services," *Manual for Managing the Law Office*
4. "Cash Flow Analysis," *Law Office Economics and Management*
5. "Are You Really Making Money from Associates?" *Law Office Economics and Management*
6. "Is Timekeeping for You?" *Virginia Bar News*

237

7. "You Can Generate More Income for the Firm You Manage," *Manual for Managing the Law Office*

8. "How to Keep Control over Firm Assets," *Manual for Managing the Law Office*

9. "How to Value a Partner's Financial Interest in His Firm," *Manual for Managing the Law Office*

10. "A Private Phone System May Give You Better Service at a Lower Cost," *Manual for Managing the Law Office*

11. "How to Develop and Use Departmental Cost Statistics in Your Firm," *Manual for Managing the Law Office*

12. "Will the Real Administrator Please Stand!" *The Legal Administrator*

13. "When Do the Dollars Stop?" *The Legal Administrator*

14. "How to Initiate a Microfilm Program in Your Law Firm," *Manual for Managing the Law Office*

15. "The Changing Role of the Legal Secretary in the 1980's," *The Witness,* Richmond Legal Secretaries Association

16. "The Effect of Volume and Price on the Sale of Legal Services," *The Legal Administrator*

17. Contributor, *Webster's Legal Secretaries Handbook,* G & C Merriam Company, 1981 (not available in reprint form)

18. "The Branch Office Syndrome," *The National Law Journal*

19. "Financial Management Review Benefits Firms," *Legal Times of Washington*

20. "McGuire, Woods & Battle Takes Unique Approach to Setting Billing Rates," *Of Counsel*

21. "Computerized Financial Modeling in the Law Firm," *Manual for Managing the Law Office* (not available in reprint form)

22. "The Administrator's Role," *The National Law Journal*

23. "New Partners: What Do They Cost?" *Law Office Management and Administration Report*

24. "Turnover: A Barometer for Law Office Profitability," *Law Office Management and Administration Report*

25. "Electronic Voice Mail: An Alternative Worth Considering," *Law Office Management and Administration Report*

26. "Cost Accounting in Law Offices: Can You Do It? Is It Worth It?" *Law Office Management and Administration Report*

27. "Partner Compensation: A Different Approach," *Legal Economics*

28. "Where to Get the Capital: A Partnership Dilemma," *Law Office Management and Administration Report*

29. "Associate Leverage: Fact or Fiction?" *Law Office Management and Administration Report*

52. "Facilities Management: A New Concept in Service," *Strategy, Management and Technology*
53. "What Many Law Firm Reports Don't Report," *Law Office Management and Administration Report*
54. "What Happens When I Grow Up?" *Strategy, Management & Technology*
55. "Understanding Cash Flow," *Legal Management*
56. "How Can You Really Judge New Partner Profitability," *Law Office Management and Administration Report*
57. "Legal Services Plan: How to Benefit Both Firms and Employees," *Legal Management*
58. "Improving Management to Realize Goals and Objectives," (unpublished)
59. "Taking the Mystique Out of Strategic Planning," *Financial Management*
60. "The Effect of Technology on Workstyle and Lifestyle," *ALA News*
61. "Why Plaintiff Firms Should Keep Time," *Legal Management*
62. "The Merger A B C's," *Capital Connection*
63. "Clearing the Air on New Associate Profitability" (unpublished)
64. "The Unproductive Partner" (unpublished)
65. "Budgeting Made Simpler," *Capital Connection*
66. "Will the Legal Secretary Finally Be Retired?" *Capital Connection*
67. "Which Comes First? The Clients or the Rates?" (unpublished)
68. "Maximizing Profitability," *The Lawyer's Handbook*, third edition (not available in reprint form)
69. *Results-Oriented Financial Management: A Guide to Successful Law Firm Financial Performance*, full-length book published by American Bar Association (not available in reprint form)
70. "Full-Time Management on a Part-Time Basis," *ALA News*
71. "Who Owns the Cases?" *Trial Talk*
72. "Compensation Plan for Owners of Professional Service Firms" (unpublished), available in reprint form
73. "Key Elements of Financial Management in the Plaintiff Law Firm," *Legal Management*
74. "Reaping the Benefits of Keeping Time," *Trial* Magazine
75. "The CEO Concept Resurfaces—and It's Still Unworkable," *Law Office Management and Administration Report*
76. "Interest in Cost Accounting Soars with Emphasis on Profitability and Alternative Billing" (unpublished), available in reprint form
77. "Put Your Mouth Where Your Money Is—What Should Your Associates Know About Law Firm Finances," *Legal Management*

78. "Is Now (Finally) the Time to Rethink Your Approach to Non-Fee Billings?" *Law Office Management and Administration Report*
79. "How Law Firms Can Use Consultants," *The Journal,* monthly publication of the Virginia Trial Lawyers Association
80. "Evaluate Your Pension Plan's Performance," *Legal Management,* monthly publication of the National Association of Legal Administrators
81. "To Profit From Your Technology, Change the Way You Bill," *Law Office Management and Administration Report*
82. "Understanding Cash Flow: The Final Frontier," *Accounting for Law Firms*
83. "How to Get the Right Information From Your Firm's Financial Management Processes," *Accounting for Law Firms*
84. "A Mid-Year Review Shows If You're On Track for Greater Year-end Profits," *Law Office Management and Administration Report*
85. "How Much Are Your Law Firm's Billable Hours Really Worth?" *Law Office Management and Administration Report*
86. "Leaders Who Tackle These 4 Issues Make Value Billable Viable," *Law Office Management and Administration Report*
87. "Why Law Firms Can't Afford to Overlook Rate Discounting," *Law Office Management and Administration Report*
88. "How to Predict What You and Your Partners Will Earn This Year," *Law Office Management and Administration Report*
89. "Is This A Better Way to Measure Practice Area Profitability?" *Law Office Management and Administration Report*
90. "Take Another Look at Your Practice Area Profitability," *Law Office Management and Administration Report*
91. "Follow This Client Service Program to Grow Revenues," *Law Office Management and Administration Report*
92. "Converting Inventory into Cash: Is Your Firm on Target?" *Law Office Management and Administration Report*
93. "Looking Ahead to the Real Next Century," *Law Office Management and Administration Report*
94. "How Profitable Are Your Associates?" *Law Office Management and Administration Report*
95. "Super Servers: The Circle Is Now Compete," *Virginia Lawyer's Weekly*
96. "Developing An Incentive Piece to the Annual Compensation Plan," *Law Office Management and Administration Report*
97. "Accumulating Equity in a Professional Services Firm," *Partner's Report*

98. "Evaluating Practice Support Costs," *Accounting for Law Firms*

99. "Don't Panic When Times Get Tough," *Law Office Management and Administration Report*

100. "Quick and Dirty Profitability Method," *Law Office Management and Administration Report*

101. "What Does All This Information Mean Anyhow?" *Accounting for Law Firms*

102. "Billable Hours Are Not All That They Seem to Be," *Law Office Management and Administration Report*

103. "Simplifying the Evaluation of Firm Operating Results," *Partner's Report*

104. "Dispelling the Originations Myth," *Partner's Report*

105. "Will Value Billing End the Need to Record Billable Hours?" *Accounting and Financial Planning for Law Firms*

106. "Is There an Alternative to the Non-Equity Partner?" *Law Office Management and Administration Report*

About the Author

John G. Iezzi, CPA, is President of Iezzi Management Group, in Richmond, Virginia. The Iezzi Management Group provides consulting and business management services to law and accounting firms and include financial management, strategic planning, technology, and matters directly involving the partners, such as compensation and firm ownership. He developed sophisticated financial reporting systems for office, client and partner profitability, which have become industry standards. During his tenure, he was instrumental in a merger that at the time was one of the biggest in the history of the profession.

Mr. Iezzi is a 1963 graduate of Duquesne University with a degree in Business Administration. He spent eight years with Price Waterhouse in Pittsburgh, Pennsylvania, and became a Certified Public Accountant in 1967. From 1972 to 1988, Mr. Iezzi managed McGuire, Woods, Battle & Boothe (now McGuire Woods), a law firm of over 300 attorneys, headquartered in Richmond, Virginia. Mr. Iezzi was a Senior Manager with the Law Firm Consulting Services Group of Price Waterhouse and was the Director of Consulting Services with Information Technologies Corporation in Richmond, Virginia.

Mr. Iezzi is a member of Virginia Society of Certified Public Accountants, and the Association of Legal Administrators. He is nationally recognized in the field of law office management and has written more than 100 articles in many of the leading law office management magazines and periodicals. He has appeared as a guest lecturer in more than 600 seminars and conferences across the country for lawyers and administrators.

In addition to his consulting services, Mr. Iezzi is an Adjunct Professor at the T. C. Williams School of Law at the University of Richmond where he teaches a course in Law Office Management as part of the Law School curriculum, and provides part-time management services to DurretteBradshaw, PC, a 20-attorney firm headquartered in Richmond, Virginia.

Index

About the CD

The accompanying CD contains the Billing Rate Formula Model (**billrateformula.xls**), the Financial Planning Model (**ABCDPC.xls**), and the file **budsimple.xls**, which creates a budget for a firm using the bottoms-up approach. The files are in Microsoft® Excel format.

For additional information about the files on the CD, please open and read the "readme.doc" file on the CD.

NOTE: The set of files on the CD may only be used on a single computer or moved to and used on another computer. Under no circumstances may the set of files be used on more than one computer at one time. If you are interested in obtaining a license to use the set of files on a local network, please contact: Director, Copyrights and Contracts, American Bar Association, 750 N. Lake Shore Drive, Chicago, IL 60611, (312) 988-6101. **Please read the license and warranty statements on the following page before using this CD.**

CD-ROM to accompany

Results-Oriented Financial Management: A Step-by-Step Guide to Law Firm Profitability, Second Edition

WARNING: Opening this package indicates your understanding and acceptance of the following Terms and Conditions.

READ THE FOLLOWING TERMS AND CONDITIONS BEFORE OPENING THIS SEALED PACKAGE. IF YOU DO NOT AGREE WITH THEM, PROMPTLY RETURN THE UNOPENED PACKAGE TO EITHER THE PARTY FROM WHOM IT WAS ACQUIRED OR TO THE AMERICAN BAR ASSOCIATION AND YOUR MONEY WILL BE RETURNED.

The document files in this package are a proprietary product of the American Bar Association and are protected by Copyright Law. The author, John G. Iezzi, retains title to and ownership of these files.

License

You may use this set of files on a single computer or move it to and use it on another computer, but under no circumstances may you use the set of files on more than one computer at the same time. You may copy the files either in support of your use of the files on a single computer or for backup purposes. If you are interested in obtaining a license to use the set of files on a local network, please contact: Manager, Publication Policies & Contracting, American Bar Association, 750 N. Lake Shore Drive, Chicago, IL 60611, (312) 988-6101.

You may permanently transfer the set of files to another party if the other party agrees to accept the terms and conditions of this License Agreement. If you transfer the set of files, you must at the same time transfer all copies of the files to the same party or destroy those not transferred. Such transfer terminates your license. You may not rent, lease, assign or otherwise transfer the files except as stated in this paragraph.

You may modify these files for your own use within the provisions of this License Agreement. You may not redistribute any modified files.

Warranty

If a CD-ROM in this package is defective, the American Bar Association will replace it at no charge if the defective diskette is returned to the American Bar Association within 60 days from the date of acquisition.

American Bar Association warrants that these files will perform in substantial compliance with the documentation supplied in this package. However, the American Bar Association does not warrant these forms as to the correctness of the legal material contained therein. If you report a significant defect in performance in writing to the American Bar Association, and the American Bar Association is not able to correct it within 60 days, you may return the CD, including all copies and documentation, to the American Bar Association and the American Bar Association will refund your money.

Any files that you modify will no longer be covered under this warranty even if they were modified in accordance with the License Agreement and product documentation.

IN NO EVENT WILL THE AMERICAN BAR ASSOCIATION, ITS OFFICERS, MEMBERS, OR EMPLOYEES BE LIABLE TO YOU FOR ANY DAMAGES, INCLUDING LOST PROFITS, LOST SAVINGS OR OTHER INCIDENTAL OR CONSEQUENTIAL DAMAGES ARISING OUT OF YOUR USE OR INABILITY TO USE THESE FILES EVEN IF THE AMERICAN BAR ASSOCIATION OR AN AUTHORIZED AMERICAN BAR ASSOCIATION REPRESENTATIVE HAS BEEN ADVISED OF THE POSSIBILITY OF SUCH DAMAGES, OR FOR ANY CLAIM BY ANY OTHER PARTY. SOME STATES DO NOT ALLOW THE LIMITATION OR EXCLUSION OF LIABILITY FOR INCIDENTAL OR CONSEQUENTIAL DAMAGES, IN WHICH CASE THIS LIMITATION MAY NOT APPLY TO YOU.

Selected Books From . . .
THE ABA LAW PRACTICE MANAGEMENT SECTION

The ABA Guide to Lawyer Trust Accounts. Details ways that lawyers should manage trust accounts to comply with ethical & statutory requirements.

Changing Jobs, 3rd Edition. A handbook designed to help lawyers make changes in their professional careers. Includes career planning advice from dozens of experts.

Collecting Your Fee: Getting Paid From Intake to Invoice. Author Ed Poll outlines the basics and the systems you need to set in place to ultimately increase your bottom line and keep your clients happy while doing it. Learn how to increase your collections, decrease your accounts receivable, and keep your clients happy. CD-ROM with sample forms, letters, and agreements is included.

Compensation Plans for Law Firms, 3rd Ed. This third edition discusses the basics for a fair and simple compensation system for partners, of counsel, associates, paralegals, and staff.

Complete Guide to Marketing Your Law Practice. Filled with dozens of fresh and innovative ideas, this book features the strategies form the country's top legal marketers.

Complete Internet Handbook for Lawyers. A thorough orientation to the Internet, including e-mail, search engines, conducting research and marketing on the Internet, publicizing a Web site, Net ethics, security, viruses, and more. Features a updated, companion Web site with forms you can download and customize.

Do-It-Yourself Public Relations. A hands-on guide (and diskette!) for lawyers with public relations ideas, sample letters, and forms.

Easy Self-Audits for the Busy Law Office. Dozens of evaluation tools help you determine what's working (and what's not) in your law office or legal department. You'll discover several opportunities for improving productivity and efficiency along the way!

Effective Yellow Pages Advertising for Lawyers: The Complete Guide to Creating Winning Ads. This new book by Kerry Randall, "the world's foremost expert on Yellow Pages advertising," shows you how to create more powerful Yellow Pages advertising—the best *lawyers* do not get the most calls; the best *ads* get the most calls.

Essential Formbook: Comprehensive Management Tools for Lawyers, Vols. I & II. Useful to legal practitioners of all specialties and sizes, the first two volumes of The Essential Formbook include more than 100 forms, checklists, and sample documents. And, with all the forms on disk, it's easy to modify them to match your needs.

Flying Solo: A Survival Guide for the Solo Lawyer, Third Edition. This book gives solos, as well as small firms, all the information needed to build a successful practice. Contains 55 chapters covering office location, billing and cash flow, computers and equipment, and much more.

Handling Personnel Issues in the Law Office. Packed with tips on "safely" and legally recruiting, hiring, training, managing, and terminating employees.

HotDocs in One Hour for Lawyers, Second Edition. Offers simple instructions, ranging from generating a document from a template to inserting conditional text and creating dialogs.

How to Build and Manage an Employment Law Practice. Provides clear guidance and valuable tips for solo or small employment law practices, including preparation, marketing, accepting cases, and managing workload and finances. Includes several time-saving "fill in the blank" forms.

How to Build and Manage a Personal Injury Practice. Features all of the tactics, technology, and tools needed for a profitable practice, including hot to: write a sound business plan, develop a financial forecast, choose office space, market your practice, and more.

How to Start and Build a Law Practice, Millennium 4th Edition. Jay Foonberg's classic guide has been completely updated and expanded! Features 128 chapters, including 30 new ones, that reveal secrets to successful planning, marketing, billing, client relations, and much more. Chock-full of forms, sample letters, and checklists, including a sample business plan, "The Foonberg Law Office Management Checklist," and more.

Law Office Policy and Procedures Manual, 4th Ed. A model for law office policies and procedures (includes diskette). Covers law office organization, management, personnel policies, financial management, technology, and communications systems.

Law Office Procedures Manual for Solos and Small Firms, Second Edition. Use this manual as is or customize it using the book's diskette. Includes general office policies on confidentiality, employee compensation, sick leave, sexual harassment, billing, and more.

The Lawyer's Guide to Extranets: Breaking Down Walls, Building Client Connections. Well-run extranets can result in significant expansion in clientele and profitability for a law firm. This book takes you step-by-step through the issues of implementing an extranet.

The Lawyer's Guide to Marketing on the Internet, Second Edition. This book provides you with countless Internet marketing possibilities and shows you how to effectively and efficiently market your law practice on the Internet.

Legal Career Guide: From Law Student to Lawyer, Fourth Edition is a step-by-step guide for planning a law career, preparing and executing a job search, and moving into the market. This book is perfect for students currently choosing a career path, or simply deciding if law school is right for them.

Making Partner: A Guide for Law Firm Associates, Second Edition. If you are serious about making partner, this book will help you formulate your step-by-step plan and be your guide for years to come for your decisions and actions within your firm.

Managing Partner 101: A Guide to Successful Law Firm Leadership, Second Edition is designed to help managing partners, lawyers, and other legal professionals understand the role and responsibilities of a law firm's managing partner.

Persuasive Computer Presentations: The Essential Guide for Lawyers explains the advantages of computer presentation resources, how to use them, what they can do, and the legal issues involved in their use. It covers how to use computer presentations in the courtroom and during meetings, pretrial, and seminars.

Running a Law Practice on a Shoestring. Offers a crash course in successful entrepreneurship. Features money-saving tips on office space, computer equipment, travel, furniture, staffing, and more.

Successful Client Newsletters. Written for lawyers, editors, writers, and marketers, this book can help you to start a newsletter from scratch, redesign an existing one, or improve your current practices in design, production, and marketing.

Telecommuting for Lawyers. Discover methods for implementing a successful telecommuting program that can lead to increased productivity, improved work product, higher revenues, lower overhead costs, and better communications. Addressing both law firms and telecommuters, this guide covers start-up, budgeting, setting policies, selecting participants, training, and technology.

Through the Client's Eyes, Second Edition. Includes an overview of client relations and sample letters, surveys, and self-assessment questions to gauge your client relations acumen.

Wills, Trusts, and Technology. Reveals why you should automate your estates practice; identifies what should be automated; explains how to select the right software; and helps you get up and running with the software you select.

Winning Alternatives to the Billable Hour: Strategies that Work, Second Edition. This book explains how it is possible to change from hourly based billing to a system that recognizes your legal expertise, as well as your efficiency, and delivery winning billing solutions—for you and your client.

Women Rainmakers' Best Marketing Tips, Second Edition. This book contains well over a hundred tips you can put to use right away that will have a positive effect on your marketing strategy. Anyone involved in marketing a firm can benefit from the down-to-earth advice in this book.

Order Form

Qty	Title	LPM Price	Reg Price	Total
_____	ABA Guide to Lawyer Trust Accounts (5110374)	69.95	79.95	$_____
_____	ABA Guide to Prof. Managers in the Law Office (5110373)	69.95	79.95	$_____
_____	Anatomy of a Law Firm Merger, Second Edition (5110434)	74.95	89.95	$_____
_____	Changing Jobs, 3rd Ed.(511-0425)	39.95	49.95	_____
_____	Compensation Plans for Lawyers, 3rd Ed. (5110452)	84.95	99.95	$_____
_____	Complete Guide to Marketing Your Law Practice (5110428)	74.95	89.95	$_____
_____	Complete Internet Handbook for Lawyers (5110413)	39.95	49.95	$_____
_____	Computerized Case Management Systems (5110409)	39.95	49.95	$_____
_____	Connecting with Your Client (5110378)	54.95	64.95	$_____
_____	Do-It-Yourself Public Relations (5110352)	69.95	79.95	$_____
_____	Easy Self Audits for the Busy Law Firm (511-0420P)	99.95	84.95	$_____
_____	Essential Formbook, Vols. I and II	*Please call for information*		
_____	Flying Solo, Third Edition (511-0463)	79.95	89.95	$_____
_____	Handling Personnel Issues in the Law Office (5110381)	59.95	69.95	$_____
_____	HotDocs in One Hour for Lawyers, Second Edition (5110464)	29.95	34.95	$_____
_____	How to Build & Manage an Employment Law Practice (5110389)	44.95	54.95	$_____
_____	How to Build & Manage a Personal Injury Practice (5110386)	44.95	54.95	$_____
_____	How to Start & Build a Law Practice, Fourth Edition (5110415)	57.95	69.95	$_____
_____	Law Firm Partnership Guide: Getting Started (5110363)	64.95	74.95	$_____
_____	Law Firm Partnership Guide: Strengthening Your Firm (5110391)	64.95	74.95	$_____
_____	Law Office Policy & Procedures Manual, 4th Ed. (5110441)	109.95	129.95	$_____
_____	Law Office Staff Manual for Solos & Small Firms (5110445)	59.95	69.95	$_____
_____	Lawyer's Guide to Marketing on the Internet, 2nd Ed. (5110484)	69.95	79.95	$_____
_____	Living with the Law (5110379)	59.95	69.95	$_____
_____	Making Partner, Second Edition (511-0482)	39.95	49.95	$_____
_____	Managing Partner 101, Second Edition (5110451)	44.95	49.95	$_____
_____	Persuasive Computer Presentations (511-0462)	69.95	79.95	$_____
_____	Practicing Law Without Clients (5110376)	49.95	59.95	$_____
_____	Running a Law Practice on a Shoestring (5110387)	39.95	49.95	$_____
_____	Successful Client Newsletters (5110396)	39.95	44.95	$_____
_____	Telecommuting for Lawyers (5110401)	39.95	49.95	$_____
_____	Through the Client's Eyes, Second Ed. (5110480)	69.95	79.95	$_____
_____	Wills, Trusts, and Technology (5430377)	74.95	84.95	$_____
_____	Winning Alternatives to the Billable Hour, Second Ed (5110483)	129.95	149.95	$_____

*Handling
$10.00-$24.99 .... $3.95
$25.00-$49.99 .... $4.95
$50.00+ $5.95   MD residents add 5%

**Tax
DC residents add 5.75%
IL residents add 8.75%

Subtotal

*Handling $_____
**Tax $_____
TOTAL $_____

PAYMENT

☐ **Check enclosed (to the ABA) ~ ☐Bill Me**
☐Visa   ☐MasterCard   ☐American Express

_____

Account Number   Exp. Date Signature

Name _____ Firm _____
Address _____
City _____ State _____ Zip _____
Phone Number _____ E-mail address _____

Mail: ABA Publication Orders, P.O. Box 10892, Chicago, Illinois 60610-0892
♦ **Phone: (800) 285-2221 ♦ FAX: (312) 988-5568**
E-Mail: service@abanet.org ♦ Internet: http://www.abanet.org/lpm/catalog

Source Code: 22AEND499

 **THE SECTION OF LAW PRACTICE MANAGEMENT**

CUSTOMER COMMENT FORM

 ABA

Title of Book:_____

We've tried to make this publication as useful, accurate, and readable as possible. Please take 5 minutes to tell us if we succeeded. Your comments and suggestions will help us improve our publications. Thank you!

1. How did you acquire this publication:

☐ by mail order   ☐ at a meeting/convention   ☐ as a gift

☐ by phone order   ☐ at a bookstore   ☐ don't know

☐ other: (describe) _____

Please rate this publication as follows:

	Excellent	Good	Fair	Poor	Not Applicable
Readability: Was the book easy to read and understand?	☐	☐	☐	☐	☐
Examples/Cases: Were they helpful, practical? Were there enough?	☐	☐	☐	☐	☐
Content: Did the book meet your expectations? Did it cover the subject adequately?	☐	☐	☐	☐	☐
Organization and clarity: Was the sequence of text logical? Was it easy to find what you wanted to know?	☐	☐	☐	☐	☐
Illustrations/forms/checklists: Were they clear and useful? Were there enough?	☐	☐	☐	☐	☐
Physical attractiveness: What did you think of the appearance of the publication (typesetting, printing, etc.)?	☐	☐	☐	☐	☐

Would you recommend this book to another attorney/administrator? ☐ Yes ☐ No

How could this publication be improved? What else would you like to see in it?

_____

_____

_____

Do you have other comments or suggestions? _____

_____

_____

Name _____

Firm/Company _____

Address _____

City/State/Zip _____

Phone _____

Firm Size: _____ Area of specialization: _____

We appreciate your time and help.

Fold

BUSINESS REPLY MAIL

FIRST CLASS   PERMIT NO. 16471   CHICAGO, ILLINOIS

. *POSTAGE WILL BE PAID BY ADDRESSEE*

AMERICAN BAR ASSOCIATION
PPM, 8th FLOOR
750 N. LAKE SHORE DRIVE
CHICAGO, ILLINOIS 60611–9851

Fold

LawPracticeManagementSection

MARKETING • MANAGEMENT • TECHNOLOGY • FINANCE

JOIN the ABA Law Practice Management Section (LPM) and receive significant discounts on future LPM book purchases! You'll also get direct access to marketing, management, technology, and finance tools that help lawyers and other professionals meet the demands of today's challenging legal environment.

Exclusive Membership Benefits Include:

- **Law Practice Magazine**
  Eight annual issues of our award-winning *Law Practice* magazine, full of insightful articles and practical tips on Marketing/Client Development, Practice Management, Legal Technology, and Finance.
- **ABA TECHSHOW®**
  Receive a $100 discount on ABA TECHSHOW, the world's largest legal technology conference!
- **LPM Book Discount**
  LPM has over eighty titles in print! Books topics cover the four core areas of law practice management – marketing, management, technology, and finance – as well as legal career issues.
- **Law Practice Today**
  LPM's unique web-based magazine in which the features change weekly! Law Practice Today covers all the hot topics in law practice management *today* – current issues, current challenges, current solutions.
- **Discounted CLE & Other Educational Opportunities**
  The Law Practice Management Section sponsors more than 100 educational sessions annually. LPM also offers other live programs, teleconferences and web cast seminars.
- **LawPractice.news**
  This monthly eUpdate brings information on Section news and activities, educational opportunities, and details on book releases and special offers.

Complete the membership application below.

Applicable Dues:
☐$40 for ABA members   ☐$5 for ABA Law Student Division members

(ABA Membership is a prerequisite to membership in the Section. To join the ABA, call the Service Center at 1-800-285-2221.)

Method of Payment:
☐Bill me   Charge to my: ☐Visa   ☐MasterCard   ☐American Express
Card number _____ Exp. Date _____
Signature _____ Date _____

Applicant's Information (please print):
Name _____ ABA I.D. number _____
Firm/Organization _____
Address _____ City/State/Zip _____
Telephone _____FAX_____ Email _____

Fax your application to 312-988-5528 or join by phone: 1-800-285-2221, TDD 312-988-5168
Join online at www.lawpractice.org.

I understand that my membership dues include $16 for a basic subscription to *Law Practice Management* magazine. This subscription charge is not deductible from the dues and additional subscriptions are not available at this rate. Membership dues in the American Bar Association and its Sections are not deductible as charitable contributions for income tax purposes but may be deductible as a business expense.